ONE
NATION
UNDER
THE
GUN

ONE NATION UNDER THE GUN

Rick Hornung

Pantheon Books
New York

All rights reserved under International and Pan-
American Copyright Conventions. Published in the
United States by Pantheon Books, a division of Random
House, Inc., New York. Originally published in Canada
by Stoddart Publishing Co. Limited, Toronto in 1991.
A portion of this work was originally published in *The
Village Voice*, May 15, 1990.

Library of Congress Cataloging in Publication Data

Hornung, Rick.
    One nation under the gun: inside the Mohawk
civil war / Rick Hornung.
    Includes index.
    1. Mohawk Indians—Politics and government. 2.
Gambling—Akwesasne Indian Reserve (Québec and
Ont.) 3. Gambling—New York (State)—Saint Regis
Mohawk Indian Reservation. I. Title.
E99.M8H67   1992   971.4'34—dc20   91–50836
ISBN 0–679–41265–4

Book design by M. Kristen Bearse

Manufactured in the United States of America
First American Edition

CONTENTS

For Peg,
the woman with jade eyes

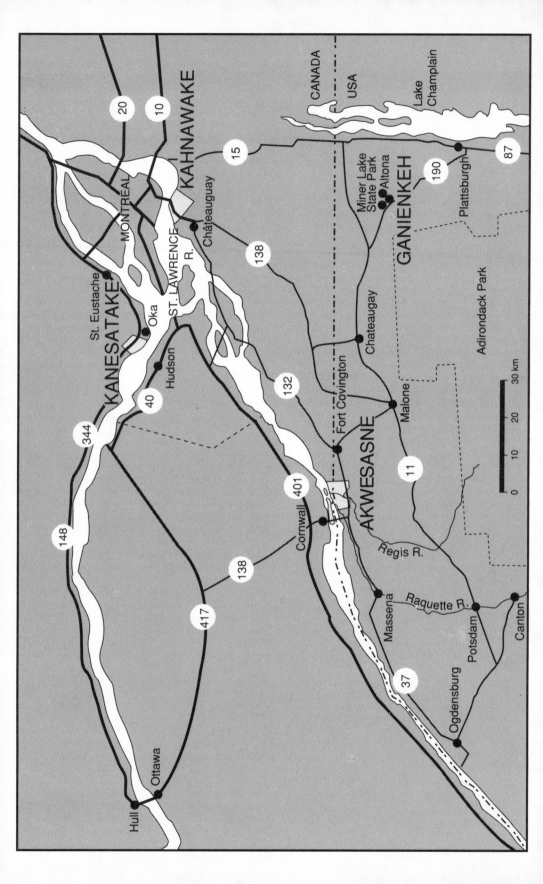

ACKNOWLEDGMENTS

This is a book of reporting on the fly, running between interviews, shootouts, car rammings, standoffs, troop deployments, and press conferences. Since September 1989, I have had the opportunity to meet dozens of Mohawks, speak with them at length and reconstruct the events that dominated their community. I am forever grateful that so many Mohawks opened their lives and told me their stories, their versions of the civil war that is so painful to them.

While the Mohawks trusted me to listen, I must also thank those who showed their trust by giving me the chance to write. Marty Gottlieb offered shelter and encouragement at *The Village Voice*, then Jonathan Larsen gave generous support and guidance. As I worked to refine my writing and reporting skills, editors Daniel Bischoff, Richard Goldstein, and Scott Malcomson were always available to help.

A very special thanks goes to former *Voice* executive editor Michael Caruso, the editor who never lost faith in my abilities. Under his guidance, "One Nation Under the Gun" first appeared as an article in *The Village Voice* of May 15, 1990. Another special thanks goes to Barry Michael Cooper, who shared so much.

Also in New York, Chris Calhoun, and John and Dava Stravinsky provided critical assistance at Bradley's and in Brooklyn. When organizing the material and thinking it through, I frequently called upon the wisdom given to me by my colleagues at the Center for Contemporary Radical Thought, Dr. James A. Miller and Mac Margolis. The insights of dear friend Robert Orsi were of great importance.

During the months it took to finish the manuscript, Ben and Ruth Hornung, and Dr. George Palmer and his wife, Dorothy, gave me the chance to write in their homes. Mark Hornung, Jacqueline Pardo, Richard Palmer, Jennifer Pettit, and Emily Cohen listened to my gripes and jokes, while Peggy Palmer, and Sarah and Gabriel Hornung always cheered me on. Michael Hertz and Amy Horowitz gave thoughtful counsel. Lauren Johnston's fifth-grade class at the Independent Day School sent cards that sparkle and delight.

At Stoddart Publishing, my Canadian publishers, Angel Guerra was the first person to recognize the possibility of a book about the Mohawks, while Maya Mavjee took the logistical steps needed to make it happen. Leslie Maunder patiently put up with all the changes.

And the last, but most important, thanks go to editors Charis Wahl and Alison Reid, who lovingly gave their sweat and labor, muscle and wit, compassion and gentility.

**ONE
NATION
UNDER
THE
GUN**

PROLOGUE

A quarter moon glimmers over the partially frozen St. Lawrence River. A small, open boat lands two Mohawk Warriors, two Mohawk women, two AK-47s, and several boxes of bullets on a shore rising a hundred feet. The iced crevices make for a stooped climb to a line of trees whose barren branches are silhouetted against the red-and-white flash of a New York State Police roadblock.

Once in the snow-covered grove, the men and women easily evade the conspicuous cops. They know the hidden danger comes a mile past the S-shaped bend, where the road is barricaded by bales of hay, tree stumps, plywood, dented cars, and a group of men in hunting jackets gathered around a kerosene heater. These bundled figures and the Warriors are fighting to determine who will be the guardians of Mohawk tradition in this irregularly shaped piece of land cutting into New York, Ontario, and Quebec. If the men on the barricade detect the Warriors, a gun battle will erupt.

The Mohawks didn't always settle their differences this way. Before the Europeans arrived, one faction would simply leave and stake out a new territory. That possibility, however, was forever eliminated by the colonial advance and the creation of the United States and Canada. For two centuries thereafter, intratribal disputes were confined to reserved lands, where they remained invisible to white society. But that changed in the early 1980s, when the United States government en-

3

couraged its aboriginal populations to buy a piece of the American dream by developing high-stakes bingo parlors and casinos designed to attract large amounts of white money. Within a few years, the Mohawk factions that had fought over religion and hunting rights were battling each other over blackjack, dice, roulette, and that unique Mohawk version of poker called "deuces, jacks, and men with the ax."

The allure of fast tax-free money inflamed and emboldened the Mohawks who entered the gambling business, even as it weakened those holding on to the old ways. A new class of bingo chiefs were beating the odds, dealing with the white economy on favorable terms. The traditionalists counterattacked, claiming that Mohawk life was being corrupted by men who profit from games of chance rather than work. White bureaucrats and politicians, police and prosecutors initially saw this dispute as a brawl over gambling; but the Mohawks believed they were fighting for the right to continue the way of life that began around 14,000 B.C., when roving bands of hunters followed the receding glaciers that scoured the basin for an enormous body of cold water known to archeologists as Lake Iroquois.

Throughout the Mohawk lands, men and women can recount that this massive lake, stretching east-west from what is now Brantford, Ontario, to Watertown, New York, and north-south from Peterborough to Ithaca, triggered geological changes that led to the creation of spruce and pine forests that provided cover for mammoths, bison, elk, moose, and caribou. In less than half an hour, Mohawks can weave an elaborate mix of fact and mythology that encapsulates more than three thousand years of pre-history in which the people of the forest hunted game and followed the fresh water to the salted gulf, where they tamed snapping turtles and sea monsters.

For the men and women running the guns and for those manning the barricade, this past lives in the present. When asked why they are fighting over this corner of the world, the Mohawks describe the period known as the Valders Ice, which froze the tundra around Lake Iroquois about 9,000 B.C. and forced the hunting bands to climb the Adirondacks to reach the shores of what became Lake Champlain. Through the telling of these tales, many Mohawks touch an era when they had the power and skill to kill mastodons and mammoth with flint-tipped tools. In these moments, it becomes clear that the battle over gambling is also a battle over who will control history.

Frequently, heavily armed Mohawk men would shrug when asked if they feared the automatic rifle in their hands. With a bitterly sarcastic demeanor that mirrored the expression of ancient ceremonial masks, many would scowl as if to say, "Why should I worry about a gun when my people killed moose with flaked stones?" Risk of death and physical injury seemingly meant little to people fighting for the honor and spirit of ancestors.

On all sides of the gambling issue, Mohawk men and women saw themselves as the direct descendants of great hunters. A discussion of dice and roulette, long odds and short payouts easily turned into an argument over who was best suited to pass on the mythic knowledge. Mohawks opposing the casinos wanted control over this mythical past because they believed that only faith could ultimately restore the power to overcome the loss of their land and wealth. Pro-gaming Mohawks staked their claim to tradition on the belief that a steady cash flow was the only weapon strong enough to keep whites out.

For several years, the gaming dispute remained a battle between preachers and hustlers, moralists and materialists, idealists and pragmatists. When the struggle appeared deadlocked, a third group emerged, taking bits and pieces from each side. Known as the Akwesasne Warriors Society, these men and women mixed the lore of the great, pre-historic civilization with the street smarts of a modern underground economy that smuggled cigarettes and fuel oil.

As the casinos radically changed the social, political, and economic landscape, the Warriors assembled their own mythology: they were the great Mohawk hunters of this generation, the men and women who battled beasts in the form of the police, bureaucrats, and politicians. To prevail, the mighty hunters needed firepower that could scare away the monsters or mow them down if they dared attack.

On the American side of the border, authorities saw the Warriors agitating for a bigger and better deal in the society that values entrepreneurial skill and self-reliance. For police and bureaucrats, the issues were the right to gamble and the right to tax commerce on Mohawk land. In Albany and Washington, politicians considered the factional strife to be painful but important stages of American democracy in action. The authorities handled the Warriors as yet another fringe group exercising their distinctly American rights to dissent and bear arms. At worst, the Warriors were seen as thugs and minor criminals, never as a political threat to the Republic.

In Canada, citizens do not have a constitutional right to bear arms, particularly against the government. Aware of the chaos that firearms have brought to their southern neighbors, the Canadian public is both afraid and outraged by an open display of weaponry. When the Warriors crossed the border, provincial and federal officials immediately saw the presence of heavily armed Mohawks as an insurrection: the police had to be supported by the mobilization of troops. What was once a fight over Mohawk identity turned into a surreal uprising that pitted soldiers in tanks against camouflaged "freedom fighters."

Though the soldiers regained control of the land, they never defeated Mohawk mythology.

What they did was ensure that history will continue to split the Mohawk nation. Men and women still run guns along the moonlit St. Lawrence, for the day that will mark the return of Mohawk independence.

DEUCES, JACKS, AND MEN WITH THE AX

PART I

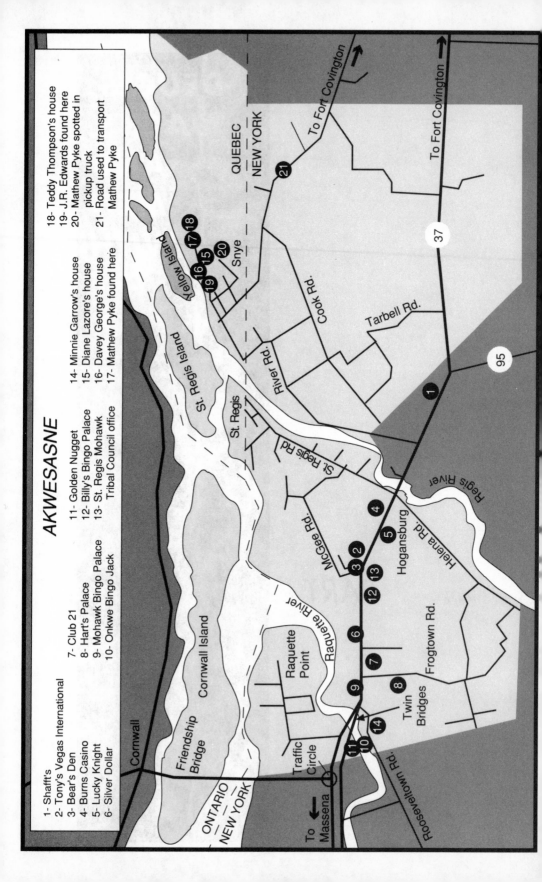

AKWESASNE

1- Shafft's
2- Tony's Vegas International
3- Bear's Den
4- Burns Casino
5- Lucky Knight
6- Silver Dollar
7- Club 21
8- Hart's Palace
9- Mohawk Bingo Palace
10- Onkwe Bingo Jack
11- Golden Nugget
12- Billy's Bingo Palace
13- St. Regis Mohawk
   Tribal Council office
14- Minnie Garrow's house
15- Diane Lazore's house
16- Davey George's house
17- Mathew Pyke found here
18- Teddy Thompson's house
19- J.R. Edwards found here
20- Mathew Pyke spotted in
   pickup truck
21- Road used to transport
   Mathew Pyke

1

THE BROTHERS SUNDAY
BLUFF, THEN FOLD

"I had this baseball bat," recalls Mike Laughing, his thick hands form-ing the grip that he used on the morning of June 6, 1989. "It was three against two. I wasn't swinging hard and I didn't want to crack heads. I just wanted to get out of there."

Laughing says the fight started after last call at Shafft's Tavern. "Frankie Roundpoint had come in with Wanda Johnson and that was the beginning. You see, Wanda had broken up with Eric Sunday and Eric was in the place. So Eric sees his old lady out with another guy at four o'clock in the morning. He was pissed off."

"Wanda and I worked together at the casino and we got off the shift and decided to have a drink," says Frankie Roundpoint. "It was a warm night. The weather was great, and all up and down the territory people were on their porches or on the streets, parked under a tree, having a good time. Wanda and I took two cars and we drove to Shafft's. It was nothing more than a drink."

A windowless, brown corrugated building, the bar sits on the edge of state Route 37, a two-lane strip of asphalt to the Akwesasne reser-vation from the Franklin County seat at Malone, New York. After dip-ping and curving through cornfields and cow pastures, the road angles into the rocky, milkweeded plain split by the St. Regis and Raquette rivers.

"We walked in," recounts Roundpoint in a slow, deliberate cadence, "and everything is all right for a little while. When Wanda gets up and leaves her seat, Eric says something. I say something back and he takes me on and I push him back, waving for Wanda to get out to the parking lot and drive off.

"That's when it really began."

As Roundpoint made it to his car, Eric and his cousins, Bobby and Tyler Sunday, who are brothers, climbed into theirs. The chase sped north on Route 37 toward Hogansburg, a four-street village perched over a concrete bridge that spans the St. Regis. Racing past the blinking yellow light that marks the middle of town, Roundpoint pulled over when he saw Mike Laughing's truck.

"Frankie told me about the Sunday boys getting mad over Wanda," says Laughing. "You could see their trucks rolling up the road. I figured we should stay here and end it. I told him I could get a bat at my uncle Tony's casino, just up the road about a mile.

"The Sundays follow us, and pull over into the parking lot in front of Tony's Vegas International. It was just getting light. They were ready to fight. I raised the bat and warned them. I told them I'd use it and I started to swing. They wouldn't listen. I yelled again and they wouldn't listen. They saw the bat and they kept coming."

The Sunday boys insist that the brawl began with Roundpoint bringing Wanda to Shafft's and insulting Eric. When the men stepped out of the bar, the Sundays claim, Roundpoint threw a punch that failed to connect, and then took off.

"He ran, looking for help. That's why he drove off," says Bobby. "He knew he couldn't take us by himself. It was in Hogansburg, right after four corners. All of a sudden Mike Laughing shows up. They go up the road. He runs into his uncle's and comes out swinging."

The bat opened a gash in Eric's scalp.

"We weren't going to let him get away with it," says Bobby, his voice shrill with anger.

"They said it wasn't going to end," Laughing adds. "They wanted to kick our asses right then and there."

Casino owner Tony Laughing knew that trouble had arrived when his nephew Mike and trusted employee Frank Roundpoint explained their predicament. Between their boasts and dares, Tony saw the possibility of a counterattack led by Tyler Sunday, a Mohawk cop who hated the gambling business that tore the reservation into opposing political factions. "I figured it was only a matter of time," Tony says. "The Sunday boys were humiliated and they were drunk. They were going to come looking for Mike and Frank. None of it had to do with gambling or the casino or local politics. It was some bar fight that spilled over."

The Sunday boys arrived before 8:00 a.m. Tony sent his chief of security, balding, barrel-chested Muzz McDonald, to meet them in the parking lot.

"We were yelling and screaming, swearing and doing all that shit," says McDonald. "Tyler kept pointing to Eric's bloody face, saying, 'We're not leaving until this is taken care of.'"

"We wanted the Sundays to leave us alone so we could get on with our business," explains Tony. "They were whupped, but they couldn't face it. So they had to get people on their side by telling them that I was using my gambling business to beat up others. That's when it got out of hand."

During the next hour, as the morning haze broke into clear, hot sunshine, the Sundays gathered recruits. "They were parked just outside of Hogansburg," says Rowena General, who passed the Sunday brothers on her way to work at the local radio station. "They told me that they were going over to Tony's to get his nephew because he had hit Eric with a bat. I figured it was no big deal. Either they'd get him or they wouldn't."

The Sundays led their column of 20 supporters to the glass door of Tony's Vegas International and renewed their demand for Tony and Mike. On the concrete steps, the bat-wielding McDonald and Roundpoint vowed to crack skulls if anyone took a step closer.

"It looked like something got out of hand," says General, "but later I realized that it turned into much more. At the radio station, we share space with *Indian Time*. Its editor, Doug George, is one of the leaders of the anti-gambling faction. When he hears that this is going on at the casino, he decides to cover the story.

"He thinks it's a political confrontation, that Tony and his nephew bashed Eric's head to intimidate the people who are opposed to casinos. So Doug writes a news bulletin to be read over the air. He got it to the deejay before I could see it. When I heard it over the speaker, I asked him what the hell he was doing. He wanted people to get down to Tony's and close the casino. I told him the radio station couldn't be used like that. He just laughed."

Shortly after 9:00 a.m. on June 6, 1989, the call came to the New York State Police outpost at Massena on Route 37 about 11 miles from the casino. "We took it seriously, but it came from the anti-gambling faction and we knew the call was steeped in tribal politics," says police spokesman Sgt. Michael Downs. "We didn't want to barge in there and make matters worse."

For months, troopers had watched factions on the reservation battle over the rapid rise of casino gambling. On the anti-gaming side were the tribal councils, whose leaders were elected by reservation residents, and the traditional council, whose chiefs were appointed according to ancestral rites thousands of years old. On the other side were the casino owners and the Warriors Society, a loosely organized band of men and women who reject the elected councils and challenge the appointed chiefs' interpretation of traditional law.

"Throughout late 1988 and early 1989, the elected leaders of these councils contacted us, the FBI, the governor's office, the White House, the Justice Department—just about everyone—in their attempt to shut down the casinos," notes Downs. "The Warriors Society didn't want the police. They felt that the reservation was a sovereign nation that did not fall under the jurisdiction of the white man's law."

That morning, Downs said, a second and third call from elected tribal officials well known for their anti-gambling views warned of thugs from the gaming houses ready to crack heads.

"At that time, we had no idea how it started," says Downs. "We were told that it was a pro-gambling faction ready to tee off at the anti-gambling faction. We had to go in because the request came from members of the councils that we recognize as the legitimate authority."

Police records show that it took less than an hour to dispatch a squad of troopers. With red Mars lights flashing and sirens blaring, a half dozen blue-and-yellow Fords streaked along the highway. "Before the police came, both sides were screaming and shouting," says Cindy Terrance, the reporter, editor, and publisher of the pro-gambling newspaper, *The People's Voice.* "The Sundays were whipping up the crowd. So were Doug and Brian Cole, a man who worked for the St. Regis Mohawk Tribal Council. They were threatening to go into the casino and drag out Tony and Mike. The cops pulled up and ran out between the crowd and the casino entrance. They formed a little wall and it worked."

At first, the confrontation centered on claims, which proved to be erroneous, that Tony ordered the beating given to Eric Sunday. A jagged line of 40 anti-gamblers pressed for Tony and Mike Laughing to face the consequences. "We didn't think that was such a good idea," says Downs, "especially when we started asking questions. It became clear that Eric Sunday got hit for something that had nothing to do with the casino. But the crowd thought we were protecting Tony and they got louder. We radioed for help."

While the cops kept an uneasy peace, a delegation from the Warriors Society directly challenged their authority to do so. "That morning, the Warriors didn't take a position on gambling," adds Downs. "They just wanted us off the land and that made things a whole lot worse. The anti-gamblers went nuts as soon as the Warriors appeared. First, they wanted our cops to protect them from the casinos, then they wanted us to protect them from the casinos and the Warriors."

"To us, the Warriors are thugs," charges Jake Swamp, an appointed chief of the traditional Akwesasne National Council. "They are not sanctioned by any legitimate council. They tried to intimidate us."

Replies Warrior Art Montour: "Anyone who welcomes the police on our land we consider a traitor, and we told that to Jake Swamp. He wants the police because he wants to use their power for his purposes."

By 11:00 a.m., the cops were worried. "The anti-gamblers had the blessings of the elected and traditional chiefs and they were getting louder and bolder," explains Downs. "Tony Laughing and the people in the casino just wanted everyone to go away so gambling could continue. And the Warriors said we shouldn't be there."

"The troopers said they were called to our land by tribal officials who complained about a situation at Tony's casino," says Montour. "I told them the Warriors would not interfere as long as they stuck to Tony's. We didn't want this to become an invasion."

With the crowd swelling to several hundred, Downs relates, the cops and the casino owner talked for an hour, looking for a deal that would prompt the crowd to disperse.

"The police were getting nervous and jittery," says Tony Laughing, "and that's when they're dangerous. All I wanted to do was keep the business open. They said to me, 'If we get you out of here, then we can use the troopers to clear the parking lot.' They said they couldn't make it look like they were protecting me. It would have to look like I was being taken away. They said, 'We'll have to arrest you. We'll just take a slot and get you on the misdemeanor of promoting gambling.'

"That was no problem. I called my lawyer and talked it over. The cops said I'd get bail right away. So I said, 'Sure, I'll take the deal.' It was a nothing charge. I wanted to open that night. This is a business. Every night I stay closed can cost me tens of thousands in cash flow."

Downs acknowledges that the police negotiated the deal. Shortly after 12:30 p.m., an unmarked police car pulled up to the glass doors. Flanked by two troopers, Tony Laughing climbed into the back, while officers placed a slot machine in the front. The gray Ford wheeled toward the parking-lot exit and the anti-gamblers cheered.

"We figured that our job was done and the police had kept their word," says Warrior Art Montour. "We left."

A few minutes later, anti-gamblers stormed the casino, pulling out slot machines and smashing gaming tables. "That was the real riot," says Cindy Terrance, whose newspaper published pictures of tribal officials walking in and out of the casino while it was being ransacked. "There were 45, maybe 50 people hitting slots and tables with crowbars and ripping down the chandeliers."

Within an hour the mob caused more than $400,000 damage. The police returned at 2:00 p.m., bringing 100 troopers and two U-Haul trailers, which officers filled with 150 slots from Tony's and 50 from the nearby Bear's Den Trading Post. Though a handful of Warriors tried to block the trailers, the cops easily cleared the road.

"If we didn't come in and remove the slot machines," says state police Major Ronald Brooks, which covers the reservation, "there would have been bloodshed."

"That's always the police excuse," says Montour.

On the bright Wednesday morning of June 7, about 18 hours after the mob trashed his casino, Tony Laughing examined a cracked blackjack table. "It was planned," Laughing says. "The crowd didn't come until after the police left, and I think there was a connection. The cops said they would stay and protect the building. They didn't. They got me off the reservation and the crowd bust in. We'll be open this afternoon— a busload of tourists from Ottawa. I made some calls and the new slots should be coming soon, maybe by the weekend."

Asked if he feared more violence, Laughing shrugged. "It's not going to stop me. Nor are the police. I believe we are a sovereign nation and we should be able to do what we damn well please on this reservation."

A few minutes later, dozens of state police cruisers pulled to a halt along Route 37. Divided into teams, more than 150 troopers sealed off

Burns Casino, the Silver Dollar, the Golden Nugget, Club 21 and Hart's Palace.

"It went like clockwork," says Sergeant Downs. "On the second day, we knew exactly what we wanted to do, how we wanted to do it, and we had enough people."

With hand trucks and dollies, the gray-suited troopers carted out dozens of slots, loaded them into rented trucks, and drove them off the reservation. "We wanted to strike quickly and cleanly," adds Downs. "The day before we got into tribal politics and the fights between factions. This time, we wanted to achieve our objective of removing what we believed to be illegal gambling machines and getting out. It was designed as a straightforward search and seizure. In New York, the law prohibits the use of electronic gambling devices.

"Of course, there was arguing and shouting, but we just let them express themselves. It's America and everyone has a right to an opinion."

2

AKWESASNE: ALL JOKERS ARE WILD

Welcome to the northeast's last frontier: to the United States government it's known as the St. Regis Indian Reservation, to the Canadian, the St. Regis Indian Reserve. To the Mohawks, the land straddling New York State, Ontario, and Quebec is Akwesasne, "Land Where the Partridge Drums." A 28,000-acre configuration of islands, coves, and peninsulas, the territory sits directly north of the Adirondack Mountains, at the edge of a plain that carries two swirling rivers—the St. Regis on the east, and the Raquette on the west—into the choppy current of the St. Lawrence.

Since the events of June 6, 1989, the 8,500 Mohawks who live here have been fighting one another, the New York State Police, the Ontario Provincial Police, the Sûreté du Québec, the Royal Canadian Mounted Police, and the FBI. Roving bands of gun-toting Mohawks, shotgun-wielding cops, barricades and blockades, outbursts of gunfire, and widespread arson have created an ongoing state of siege in this community of weather-beaten clapboard houses. School officials have refused to send in buses to pick up students, businesses have been shut down, cars have been torched, dozens of families have fled to dormitory-style shelters in Ontario, and Mohawks have beaten each other with baseball bats and fists. On May 1, 1990, after 11 months of conflict, Mohawks killed two of their own, the climax to a wild, all-night shooting spree that is commonly called the firefight.

"This is a struggle that could become as bloody and violent as Wounded Knee," says Art Montour, who prefers to be known by his Mohawk name, Kakwirakeron, pronounced Gah-gwee-la-geh-loo, which means "Many Branches Lying about on the Ground." To him, the events of June 6 triggered a vicious civil war. On one side are the men and women of the tribal or band councils, Mohawks willing to accept American- or Canadian-style elections to select chiefs who then negotiate with bureaucrats for economic development and social-welfare grants. The other side consists of self-styled traditionalists or the men and women of the Longhouse, the ancestral religion, Mohawks who openly reject the white-sanctioned elections and seek a government in accord with the Great Law, the constitution of the Iroquois Confederacy that dates to the seventeenth century.

Though this division has plagued Akwesasne Mohawks for nearly two centuries, the rise of lucrative casinos in the 1980s inflamed the tensions. Among the Mohawks who vote for tribal and band council chiefs, bitter rivalries grew between anti- and pro-gambling groups. Roughly patterned on American politics, these disputes took the shape of Republicans versus Democrats, a pro-gambling slate of candidates versus an anti-gambling slate. In 1983, the pro-gaming Mohawks controlled the elected council on the New York side and attracted white financial support to build a high-stakes bingo parlor that would enjoy the tax exemption extended to all businesses located on reservations in the U.S.

The venture was an immediate success until 1987, when the traditionalist council cast aside centuries of rejecting white authority and took the unprecedented step of asking the New York State Police and the FBI to launch anti-gambling raids. Shocked by this appeal for white power to settle a Mohawk dispute, many Longhouse men and women openly accused the traditional chiefs of betrayal and demanded their removal.

"You never call the police or the FBI, the representatives of a foreign power, to handle our problems," says Kakwirakeron. "To us that is like calling the master to deal with his slaves, the king to deal with his subjects."

Two years later, the factions had hardened into three armed camps, each with its own ideology to justify a violent competition for money and power. First, the traditional leaders formed an alliance with antigambling elected chiefs. Led by Jake Swamp and Tom Porter, appointed to the Akwesasne National Council in accordance with matrilineal custom, Head Chief Harold Tarbell, elected to the St. Regis Mohawk Tribal Council on the American side, and Grand Chief Mike Mitchell, elected to the Mohawk Council of Akwesasne on the Canadian, these men eagerly sought money and authority for their councils through the elaborate bureaucracies of Ottawa, Washington, Quebec City, and Albany. Despite the overtly political nature of this campaign, Swamp and Porter cast themselves as men of the spirit, while Tarbell and Mitchell made themselves out to be agents of reform. A second group clustered around the entrepreneurial Mohawks such as Tony Laughing, Eli Tarbell, Billy Sears, and Guilford White— the men who built bingo halls and casinos, then sponsored candidates in the local elections. These were the men and women of commerce and pragmatism, voices of the future. The third group called itself the Warriors Society, drawing its strength from Kakwirakeron, Francis Boots, his brother John, Minnie Garrow, and Diane Lazore—Longhouse men and women who vigorously object to any form of white authority over Mohawk land. They claim to be the genuine heirs to the Great Law of the Iroquois Confederacy, and operate according to its loose rule of consensus. Positioning themselves as descendants of ancestral braves and the fierce protectors of Mohawk sovereignty, they make decisions as a group, presenting issues to whoever is at hand, discussing the merits, and coming to an agreement. They chose to defend gambling as part of their defiance of elected chiefs like Tarbell and Mitchell, traditionalists like Swamp and Porter, bureaucrats, or police officers. The Warriors see themselves as nationalists, but other Mohawks see them as opportunists.

"We have to figure out who we are," says Kakwirakeron, a strapping 48-year-old, originally from Kahnawake reserve in Quebec, who stands six foot four, with long black braids falling over his shoulders. "Are we a nation? If we are a nation, do we rule ourselves? Are we sovereign? This is the real issue behind gambling. When one group of Mohawks began to express a desire for sovereignty and nationhood by establishing an economy, another group of Mohawks asked the police to come in. It is the troopers' job to exploit the division among us. The police are not the source of the problem. It is how we work among ourselves. The casinos are only the surface—look beyond them and see what we are as a community.

"Though the anti-gamblers say they want to protect our heritage, they use the tools of white politicians. We don't accept these councils and we don't participate in their elections or their decision-making.

Before the police invasion of June 6, some of the anti-gamblers were talking about a state and federal taxation plan. That's treason. We do not pay taxes to a foreign government for any business on our homeland. That is recognized by treaty."

"It looked like the wild, wild West to people who saw it on television," says state police Capt. Kenneth Cook. "Ride into town, knock a few down at the saloon, play a few hands of poker, then shoot up the joint. But there's a history behind all of this. Behind the chaos is a tightly organized society threatened with extinction. Many Mohawks feel that they are fighting for their life and the casinos are just the front for this battle."

The ongoing threat of another police raid and the increasing tensions within the native community prompted Mohawks to fight on a new battleground—the media, which came in droves after hundreds of troopers seized the slots. Reaching out to reporters, Mohawks on all sides of the gambling and sovereignty issues explained how the casinos exacerbated disagreements among tribal factions that date to the colonial wars. For weeks, reporters heard expositions on treaties, land claims, and ancestral customs—along with tips on the latest beating or firebombing—all in the name of protecting tradition.

Disagreements over casinos became a smoke screen for deep-seated divisions about the course of Mohawk history. Within weeks of the June 6 brawl, it became impossible to discuss casinos without an examination of the coming of Christianity, the fur trade, the differences between the Catholic French and the Protestant British, the Mohawk alliance with King George III against the revolting colonies, the Continental Congress, United States and British treaties made in the 1790s, state legislation of the early 1800s. Individuals from all three factions presented themselves as the true guardians of Mohawk heritage, supporting their arguments by picking and choosing among tales and anecdotes, laws and edicts, customs and rituals that track the 15,000-year evolution of nomadic clans into villages, and then into nations with their own polities.

"In the earliest days of the white man, you honored our existence as a nation by negotiating treaties from our leaders to your kings or your Congress or Parliament," says Kakwirakeron. "This was our land and you had to respect our knowledge. Then you used the gun and the Church to change the rules. We have been consistent for hundreds of years. We want to deal with you as nation to nation."

Dozens of anecdotes describe the transition from a hunting and gathering, clan-based society to a fragmented world of highly skilled migrant workers. Before the Europeans, a tightly organized, rigid but pantheistic system of dividing labor allowed villages to utilize the bounty of forests and streams, fertile plains and marshes. In the colonial era, Christianity and transatlantic commerce undercut the religious power of the clan, leaving women to run the villages and communal life, while men trapped bear and beaver for the whites. After the fur trade was exhausted in the early nineteenth century, Mohawk men turned to the lumber trade on the St. Lawrence. For decades, they used their agility to raft oak and maple to the mills. When the railroad came north in the 1880s, so did the need for steel bridges over the rushing water. As employees of the Dominion Bridge Company, Mohawks showed their extraordinary skill at working heights, earning the reputation as fearless ironworkers. By the early years of the twentieth century, Mohawk crews began walking the high steel in big cities across the continent. "We built large portions of your country," says Kakwirakeron, "and you took our land and divided it with an invisible line that says America over here and Canada over there."

For Mohawks, the borders are potent symbols of humiliation and colonization; they are an administrative nightmare to the Americans and Canadians who spend more than $30 million each year on two local governments—the three-member St. Regis Mohawk Tribal Council in New York and the 12-member Mohawk Council of Akwesasne in Quebec and Ontario. A third panel, the traditional council—also known as the Akwesasne National Council—is not recognized by white law, and receives no government funds, but it wields considerable influence as the only body claiming jurisdiction on both sides of the border, because council members are appointed by the clan mothers according to the tenets of the Great Law of the Iroquois Confederacy.

"We are the real government of the people," says Akwesasne National Council member Jake Swamp. "We are the men who carry on the traditions of our ancestors, who were given all of this land and learned how to live in peace." This council draws its legitimacy from the Iroquois Confederacy, formed by the seventeenth century as a loose alliance of the Seneca, the Cayuga, the Onondaga, the Oneida, the Mohawks, and eventually the Tuscarora after 1723. By the colonial era, the association had developed a sophisticated network of interlocking councils, overseen by the Grand Council of Chiefs, that governed vast stretches of territory from the Gulf of St. Lawrence to the Great Lakes.

"You can't get around the traditionalists if you are to initiate any kind of program," says Dr. Henrik Dullea, director of State Operations in New York, "especially on the levels of the local councils, because the New York council does not have any power in Quebec or Ontario and vice versa. In many ways, it's easier to get something done for millions in New York City."

Dullea and his Canadian counterparts proudly point to the millions funneled into the elected councils, which finance platoons of secretaries, social workers, teachers, health-care officials, public-health workers, public-works crews, and even a Mohawk police force, on the Canadian side. But in the private sector casinos appear to be the only success stories. The construction of the St. Lawrence Seaway and the Robert Moses hydroelectric dam and power plant has choked the river with ore-filled flatboats for the furnaces and smokestacks of massive foundries and factories built by ALCOA, Reynolds Metals, and General Motors near Massena, New York, about 11 miles away. What was once the domain of proud fishermen has turned into a poisoned, mucus-colored current. For decades, the industries have dumped toxic waste near the mouth of the Raquette and St. Lawrence rivers. Nearby, environmental officials discovered a snapping turtle with 3,000 parts per million of carcinogenic PCBs—more than 1,000 times the acceptable limit. Mullet, pike, and bass are routinely pulled out of the rivers with open sores and deformed fins and tails. In nearby pastures, cattle have lost their teeth because of the pollution.

"There is no way to live off our land," declares Kakwirakeron, noting that hundreds of millions of dollars and many years would be needed for a cleanup. "Many of our people are out of work." Other than casinos, the territory's private sector comprises a handful of merchants, two truck stops, several car mechanics, two convenience stores, two bars, a pizza parlor, an appliance-repair shop, and videocassette rentals. According to the U.S. government, the average income is less than $13,000.

"Our constituents are very, very poor," says L. David Jacobs, a New York–based Mohawk who left the reservation to earn a doctorate in psychology and teach at universities across the country. After an absence of two decades, he returned in the late 1980s and entered tribal politics on a pro-gambling platform. "Poverty is our biggest problem, and we have to figure out a way to enrich ourselves in accordance with the law, with the rights that we have as American citizens," he continues. "On this side of the border, the law gives us a chance to start our bingo and gambling businesses and we should. The gamblers brought money here. They've brought jobs here. In Canada, the government won't allow gambling. That's their problem. Let Ottawa or Quebec keep dishing out grants and subsidies. Washington and Albany want us to go on our own. And it's hard, but it can work if we do it right. The Americans and the Canadians have two separate approaches to our problems. And I'm choosing to stay with the Americans."

In New York State, tribal membership and the right to vote in reservation elections are subject to a residency requirement. To participate in the government-backed tribal council, a man or woman has to prove that his or her Mohawk heritage comes from the U.S. portion of the territory. Similarly, an individual's political and economic rights are tied to the reservation and the grants it receives. "If your house falls on a certain patch of land that is in New York and not Canada, then you can vote for the St. Regis Mohawk Tribal Council," says lawyer Vaughn Aldrich, who has worked for the local government. "It's a matter of geography, not race or ethnic origin."

Canadian law emphasizes ethnicity or race rather than residence and territory. According to the provincial and federal statutes, Mohawks are classified as a government-protected band of aboriginal peoples. Therefore, they are entitled to set their own membership criteria and create their own membership list. Once the provincial and federal authorities approve of that list, each band member receives a government-issued identity card that allows him or her to vote for the Mohawk Council of Akwesasne and one grand chief.

"In Canada, the law is set up to protect the culture and traditions of native people," says Mohawk Council of Akwesasne Grand Chief Mike Mitchell, a leader of the anti-gambling faction. "We are given the chance to determine who we are, who is a member, and who belongs. Then we can organize and use government grants and subsidies to help us preserve these traditions, which are the center of our lives as Mohawks."

For many other Mohawks, the border presents an opportunity in the lucrative cigarette trade, commonly referred to as "buttlegging," an elaborate scheme that shuttles money and tobacco, credit and cash between Akwesasne and the Kahnawake reserve that overlooks the St. Lawrence southeast of Montreal. During the past 20 years, this free-floating enterprise has come under the protection of the Warriors, who came together at Kahnawake. In 1971, a group of young Mohawk men received the support of traditionalists in openly opposing the Canadian-backed council, which supported the rights of non-natives to settle on Mohawk land. For two years, the Warriors wrangled with the elected chiefs in confrontations that verged on violence. By 1973, the elected chiefs ordered the Kahnawake Mohawk constabulary to disband the Warriors, but the 10-member force quit rather than attack their own people. Desperately trying to keep control, the Canadian chiefs called in the Quebec provincial police, the Sûreté du Québec, but the Warriors drove them out.

Emboldened by their success in Canada, the militant Mohawks prepared to establish a new settlement at Moss Lake, New York, a 612-acre tract purchased by the state for a wilderness reserve. On the morning of May 13, 1974, the Warriors and a caravan of Mohawks occupied the land, nailing up a sign that read: "This area is part of the land under the legal and aboriginal title of the Mohawk Nation. We Mohawks have returned to our homeland."

The state police arrived and the armed standoff began: Mohawks brazenly displaying their guns patrolled the perimeter of the land. "One of the rules for taking part in that land repossession was that each participant shall be armed—men, women and children," notes Louis Hall, a former member of the traditional council at Kahnawake, who acted as an elder and guide to the Warriors. "The state police shot first. When someone shoots at you, you have a right to shoot back. They couldn't break us."

But Warrior bullets struck two white girls. "I was urged by government officials to use all-out violence," recalls Robert Charland, the former state police major in charge. Instead, Charland offered to negotiate. The Warriors sent out a team led by Kakwirakeron, then 32 years old. "It was only through his arrival that explosive violence did not erupt," insists Charland.

After close to three years, Kakwirakeron negotiated a deal with then secretary of state of New York, Mario Cuomo. A trust of 5,000 acres of state-owned land was created for the Mohawks to hunt, fish, and grow crops. Located 60 miles west of Akwesasne, near Altona, New York, the tract was dubbed Ganienkeh, "Land of the Flint." "It's an equitable settlement," Cuomo said at the time. "The state demonstrated that it could be trusted to address Mohawks' concerns."

The new territory greatly strengthened the influence of the militants from Kahnawake. As part of their rejection of white authority and its symbols, many Mohawks established what they call "international free trade" in heating oil, building supplies, and cigarettes. Since the late 1970s, Mohawk traders have used their tax-free status in

Canada to buy truckloads of cigarettes. They are then sold to whites in one of the many smoke shops in Kahnawake or shipped south for sale to Americans. If the cigarettes stay in Canada, the Kahnawake Mohawks are responsible for the money; but running the cigarettes to America presents complications. It requires credit, a transportation network, and a means of returning the cash. To handle the American end of this business, the Kahnawake Mohawks get help from their counterparts in Akwesasne.

"There is money around, and you might want to ask where it is," says Francis Boots, a Cornwall Island resident once employed as a drug and rehabilitation counselor. Selected by clan mothers, he now serves as war chief of the Akwesasne Warriors Society—that person, according to the Great Law, responsible for organizing the society into a defensive force. "Well, a lot of it ends up underground in our own economy that operates between our communities. Through a Mohawk at Kahnawake, I can place an order for, let's say, 500 cartons. The person at Kahnawake lays out the money and I arrange for a pickup and promise to pay him back within 30 days. We have people coming from Buffalo, Watertown, Syracuse, Plattsburgh, Massena, Malone, buying cigarettes without taxes. But most of the money doesn't stay down here. It goes back to Kahnawake to pay the people who initially bought the cigarettes."

In Akwesasne, buttlegging operations range from informal, spur-of-the-moment cigarette runs to well-organized computerized enterprises. In the mid 1980s, the territory's Canadian-elected chiefs, led by Mike Mitchell, and the appointed chiefs of the traditional council, led by Jake Swamp and Tom Porter, sought to regulate the business by issuing licenses to cigarette dealers and requiring them to pay a surcharge for every carton brought into Akwesasne. This led to a buttleggers' uprising in November 1986, when Swamp, Porter, and Mitchell ordered armed Mohawk constables to seize a truckload of cigarettes belonging to Ellias H. Attea, Jr., a non-native Buffalo wholesaler who frequently dealt with Mohawks on both sides of the border. According to Canadian and tribal council records, Attea paid $88,000 for cigarettes that could be resold at a 75 percent profit.

After taking the cargo, Mitchell, Swamp, Porter, and others agreed to hide the stash in the St. Regis Mohawk Akwesasne Police station on the Canadian side of the territory. Within weeks of the seizure, the elected and appointed chiefs sold the cigarettes without a public accounting of the proceeds. When the New York State Police and the state Department of Taxation and Finance learned of the incident, Swamp and others agreed to meet with the authorities to discuss taxing earnings from bingo, buttlegging, gambling, and the sale of heating oil and construction supplies.

When buttleggers heard of the meeting, they were outraged and refused to cooperate. "It was a shakedown and a front for letting the state come in here and impose taxes," says Francis Boots. "Our business is our business. It has nothing to do with state or federal authorities."

The bingo bonanza arrived in the persons of two Mohawk businessmen, Basil "Buddy" Cook and Guilford White. "I owned the truck stop and the parcel right around it," Cook says. "Our plan was to get an outside investor and work with the tribal council. The investor would finance construction and get part of the profits. The Mohawks would build it, work there, and own the majority share.

"There weren't any secrets. We got the idea from the tribes out west. They were beginning to make money from bingo. We went straight to our tribal council and laid it out."

Cook and White saw their bingo hall as part of a larger plan to develop the territory into a tourist attraction with a shopping center and hotel, a self-sufficient trade zone that generated its own capital and labor. "Bingo is everywhere, in church, in schools, in hospitals," notes Cook, "why can't it be here?" "There wasn't any business up here that could hold our community together," said White.

Like any other Indian bingo operators, the new entrepreneurs counted on the feds to support the game, while a statutory loophole prevented the state from enforcing its law that capped church bingo jackpots at $1,000. "This is our land and we have the right to play for whatever stakes we want," claims Cook.

Though state officials did not concede it was legal to play for higher stakes, they looked the other way as the tribal council, under Chief Lawrence Pyke, aggressively backed plans for construction of a warehouse-like building that would hold up to 1,500 patrons. In late 1983, the estimates came in at $1.3 million, including the use of Mohawk Construction Management Enterprises, a company subsidized by the tribal council. "But we didn't have the cash," White said. "We had to get help. The most logical people to call were the Bureau of Indian Affairs. They were controlling gaming and they knew the business."

"At that time, there were 40 to 50 games in the whole country," says Charles Shaw, the BIA assistant director for Public Information. "They were starting to generate millions of dollars, and we actually encouraged communities to look into bingo as a way of raising money. The federal government can't bankroll everything. So we encouraged native people to get involved in their own businesses that generated cash. We felt bingo was a step in the right direction."

After discussions with Cook and White, the regional officials of the BIA, a subcabinet division of the U.S. Department of the Interior, forwarded a list of potential investors.

According to the initial contract, the tribe was to receive $10,000 a month or 51 percent of the annual profits, whichever was higher. Mohawks from Akwesasne would have first call on virtually all jobs except managerial posts, which would be controlled by the outside white investors recommended by the BIA. After the contract was signed, White and Cook claim, the leading investor, Emmet Mumley of Las Vegas, spoke of having made payoffs to a BIA official who helped put the deal together. "Mumley told me that it cost him 10 to 11 grand to get the BIA approval," White alleges. "Emmett says the guy wanted more."

A few days before the 1985 grand opening and the first $100,000 jackpot, Cook says, a BIA official stood in the parking lot and solicited a bribe. "We were right in front," Cook claims, "and he says, 'I should have a couple thousand more coming. You guys are going to buy me a ranch up here. I'm going to retire up here.'"

The BIA investigated, but could not find enough evidence to support an arrest.

The Mohawk Bingo Palace became an overnight success, and within 18 months six new bingo parlors were being planned or built. By the beginning of 1987, the strip on Route 37 was drawing busloads of players from Montreal, Ottawa, Syracuse, Plattsburgh, and Watertown. The tribal council, however, declined to enter into revenue-sharing agreements with any of the new casinos. "It's hard to believe, but the tribal council only got money from one of the bingo palaces," says Larry Thompson, a former ironworker who parlayed the savings from his wages and buttlegging profits to open the Onkwe Bingo Jack with his wife, Dana Leigh Bush. "There were folks from Massena or Syracuse who were willing to invest with a Mohawk. They figured it was best worked out directly between the owners and the governments, not the councils."

The unregulated, frontier-town atmosphere eventually attracted the attention of the state police, which launched a 4:00 a.m. raid on the morning of December 16, 1987. More than 200 cops raided six locations, taking 293 slots, 30 other mechanized gaming devices, and a large quantity of pull-tab tickets. The cops charged six people with the misdemeanor of promoting gambling. The defendants easily posted bail and resumed their gaming operations within days. Though many Mohawks openly resented the police and denounced the raid, it was clear that this was going to be business as usual for the casinos.

During the next two years, the casinos generated millions in cash, and overturned the old political, economic, and social orders: high-rolling bingo chieftains were the new elite. Power and status were measured by money, not by the traditional alignments of clans, hunting, and schooling in native culture. A fast car and a boat meant more than knowing how to track deer and shoot a bow; a regular job shuffling cards off Route 37 brought more money and far less travel than the itinerant days of walking the high steel. Instead of facing this change and addressing its implications, the traditional and elected chiefs panicked. They asked the police to restore the old order to solve Mohawk problems.

"The whole bingo business was corrupt to begin with, and it corrupted our entire way of life," says Jake Swamp, proudly pointing out that he repeatedly called for the police to make arrests. "We see it as an abomination, another trick of the white man who wants to weaken us and divide us. Gambling will ruin what we still have a chance to hold on to: knowledge of our past and respect for our ancestors. Money, neon lights, cars—there is no good that can come out of it. It will only bring further tragedy. This is not who we are. We are the men and women who have been here forever."

3

THE FEUDING TARBELLS
UP THE ANTE

The Bear's Den Trading Post is a sprawling complex of three red-brick buildings opening into a maze of angled corridors. They connect a restaurant, gift shop, banquet room, video store, leather-crafts concession, jewelry outlet, cellular-phone dealer, citizens' band radio shop, home-audio store, showers, a video-game arcade, and the hall for the slots that were removed by the cops and replaced. Owned and operated by Eli Tarbell and his brother Ricky, the Bear's Den sits directly across Route 37 from the tribal offices and is the area's unofficial gathering spot. As president of the Mohawk Chamber of Commerce, Eli Tarbell has definite opinions on the gambling dispute. "Our so-called chiefs were asking for the occupation of our land," he says. "That's how the Warriors found support among the businessmen. They want Mohawks to solve their own problems."

According to Eli Tarbell, the open hostility toward gambling began in the summer of 1988, when two anti-gaming candidates won three of the New York–chartered tribal council seats. The voters installed as head chief Harold Tarbell (no relation to Eli), who openly campaigned to close the casinos. "Less than three months after Harold takes office, my truck stop gets hit," Eli Tarbell says, referring to the September 16, 1988, raid that took slots from the Bear's Den. "I wasn't going to be intimidated."

Eli Tarbell contacted Gov. Mario Cuomo's office directly in the hope of luring the governor into overriding the tribal council's author- ity. "The American law says that the tribe can enter into a gaming compact with the state. So I figured let's do that." When he failed to get the governor's attention, Eli Tarbell announced that he would con- tinue with slots. He sent a telegram to Cuomo, purporting to speak on behalf of the elected council, advising that the tribal council "in- tends to enter into a tribal-state compact concerning Indian gaming on Indian reservations within New York State."

"It was a scam and a ploy," says Head Chief Harold Tarbell. "All of the slot machine businesses on the St. Regis reservation are owned by individuals. They are not tribally owned or tribally licensed."

"The anti-gambling members of the tribal council thought that Eli Tarbell wanted to bypass the local chiefs and come right to us," says Jeff Cohen, a gubernatorial aide who handles Indian affairs. "Well, they were right. Eli Tarbell tried to pull a fast one. But we have to deal with the council, and the elected officials did not intend to enter into any agreement concerning gambling. There was no reason for us to talk to Eli Tarbell."

To show the casino owners that he intended to take control of the territory, Harold Tarbell ordered the closure of all gaming halls except the Mohawk Bingo Palace, which was partially owned by the tribal council.

"It was a betrayal," counters Eli Tarbell. "The elected Mohawk chiefs were telling me that I could not operate my business on my land. I didn't think we did that to our own people."

Over the next four months, the casino owners defied Harold Tar- bell's edict and counterattacked in the local papers, accusing his ad- ministration of mismanagement of funds or outright theft. In February 1989, the Warriors weighed in, branding elected councils of New York and Canada "puppets" who were too busy enforcing white law to accommodate the needs and desires of Mohawks. Harold Tar- bell was a traitor, they said. His threat to close the gaming halls was the same as turning his back on his own people.

In April, the anti-gaming faction mounted a protest rally along Route 37. For four hours, 30 Akwesasne residents handed out flyers and carried placards that denounced the "criminal" activities of gam- bling and smuggling. A few days later, Harold Tarbell and elected chief Brenda LaFrance led two dozen Mohawks to the St. Lawrence County seat of Canton 30 miles southwest of Akwesasne, where U.S. Presi- dent George Bush's brother, Jonathan, was attending a Republican

Party fundraiser. The April demonstrations and the increasing calls for closure of the casinos ran up to the tribal council's annual elections. Harold Tarbell, LaFrance, and Rosemary Bonaparte headed up the anti-gaming slate; L. David Jacobs and Lincoln White ran on a pro-gaming platform. As the campaign began, Tarbell tried another tactic—shutting off the water to Tony's Vegas International and Hart's Palace.

"That was it," says Eli Tarbell, who used water from his three wells at the Bear's Den to keep the other casinos open. "When Harold cut off the water, we knew that he would do anything to close us down."

Six days later, Harold Tarbell turned on the water. He also wrote a three-paragraph letter to Washington and Albany, requesting that the state and federal governments send in the police and FBI to close down the casinos. Two weeks later, on June 3, the voters returned Tarbell, and elected Jacobs and White. The pro-gaming faction now had the majority on the tribal council.

"That's when the riot happened, three days after the election," says Eli Tarbell. "Harold couldn't control the council. A fight broke out, and the cops invaded. Harold's a dumb-ass sore loser."

On June 7, an hour before the police carted away the last slot machine, the Warriors began to gather in a cramped office in the back of the Bear's Den. Viewing the police raid as an attack on Mohawk land, the Warriors believed that they had to challenge both the anti-gaming Mohawks and the police. "We could not let the so-called leaders hand over our land to invaders," says War Chief Francis Boots, and the Warriors called a press conference for that afternoon—their first statement to the white media. "We are citizens of the Mohawk Nation," John Boots began his rebuttal of anti-gaming claims that the Warriors were violent vigilantes hired by the casino owners. "We are peacekeepers, whose only purpose is to protect ourselves from outsiders and traitors. We have no intent to provoke violence, nor do we want to hurt any one of our brothers and sisters in the Mohawk Nation."

Kakwirakeron then pointed out that the Warriors see the elected tribal councils as mere adjuncts to the U.S. and Canadian governments. Denouncing these councils for inviting the police onto the territory, Kakwirakeron vowed, "We will patrol our own land as the Mohawk Sovereign Security Patrol, and we will persist like the people of Vietnam and Afghanistan until the outside intervention is stopped. Just as Afghanistan was to the Soviet Union and Vietnam to the United States, Akwesasne will be to New York State and the United States. Our patrol is just the beginning. Suffice it to say that every time New York State comes in here, they will have to come in again and again."

As the Warriors organized their patrols, Harold Tarbell tried to craft a legal strategy that would force state authorities to close the casinos. According to invoices sent by the law firm of Pirtle, Morisett, Schlosser & Ayer, Harold Tarbell and Brenda LaFrance spent dozens of hours discussing ways to deputize themselves and make arrests while avoiding prosecution for their role in the June 6 destruction at Tony's Vegas International.

Though Harold Tarbell acknowledges the incongruity of dodging the cops while asking for their assistance, he says, "The casinos and gamblers made a mockery of our authority. The law was being violated and someone had to stand up and say 'No more.' I did. I wanted the police, the governor, the FBI, the federal bureaucracy, the BIA—anyone—to come in and restore order. If they didn't want to come in, then I said give us the power, deputize us. Get the casinos out, reestablish our authority and then make significant reforms like a constitution, a judicial system. If we were going to be a nation, then we had to behave like one. We couldn't have gamblers walking around proclaiming sovereignty. We had to have the rule of law."

"Tarbell wanted us to know that he was in control," says state police Maj. Ronald Brooks, "and to understand that the law says his council is the proper authority."

With police officials publicly criticizing the riot that trashed Tony's Vegas International, Tarbell knew he had to defend himself and others from investigation. As the casinos were unlawful operations, the council lawyers reasoned, the anti-gaming faction could argue that they were destroying property used to further illegal activity. Harold Tarbell relayed this explanation to police brass, who decided they would not press charges.

"If Harold Tarbell could guarantee us peaceful activity, then we were happy to let the Mohawks argue about gambling among themselves," says Sgt. Michael Downs. By June 9, Tarbell was encouraging anti-gaming activists to form Determined Residents United for Mohawk Sovereignty (DRUMS), which scheduled a protest march for the next day. Tarbell also continued to consult with the tribal council lawyers and the police in an effort to win the power to deputize Mohawks.

On the rainy morning of June 10, Harold Tarbell and DRUMS organizers distributed black armbands to about 100 demonstrators, to symbolize the loss of rights due to the continued presence of gambling. The marchers sloshed down the road to the casinos, where they tried to discourage patrons with placards reading "Hey, Gamblers Turn Around Go Home We All Win" and "Ayatollah Lives in Eli Tarbell."

The next day, in bright sunshine, pro-gaming Akwesasne residents formed a mile-long column that included a motorcade of race cars, old convertibles, and makeshift floats on the backs of pickup trucks. With balloons and flags, placards and banners, the festive crowd paraded up and down Route 37, wearing white ribbons on their arms. "We wanted to use white ribbons because the antis used black," Eli Tarbell said. "The white was for peace, purity, rights, everything that is opposite of black, which stands for evil and communism. We had people counting and there was a little over 600 adults. Our goal was 300 to 400. This shows you how democracy is supposed to work."

The day after the pro-gaming march, a special team of FBI and IRS agents were assigned to wide-ranging criminal investigation of the casino owners. Picking up tidbits from the newspapers, Harold Tarbell, Swamp, Tom Porter, and other anti-gaming activists, reviewing BIA files and sending undercover agents into the casinos to check out the action, the feds figured they could step in where the state left off.

"There's only so much the state can do," says John Brunetti, the assistant U.S. Attorney who oversaw the investigation. "Cases were pending, but the casinos were still open. The federal government has laws that concern the payment of taxes, the flow of currency, the interstate transportation of gaming devices. In most places around the country, we investigate these kinds of crimes, so why not on the reservation?"

Harold Tarbell and traditional chiefs Jake Swamp and Tom Porter encouraged the feds, notes Brunetti. "You could go up and down the halls of Congress and virtually everyone had received a letter or a telegram or something. There were allegations of money laundering, organized-crime activity, illegal gambling, drug smuggling, and weapons violations. Many of the people who made these allegations were elected chiefs or traditional chiefs and they were describing the situation among their own constituents. It was a rare situation. We couldn't just turn our backs. We had to investigate."

As if to fuel the federal probe, the casino owners posed for pictures with their new slot machines. "Tony Laughing gets busted and two days later his picture is on the front page. He's inviting everyone to come back and gamble. He shows off the new slots. He says that there are six square miles of Mohawk land where people do not have to live in compliance with the law. So what did you think we were going to do?" asks Brunetti. "Sit back and let it go on?"

State and federal authorities planned an elaborate attack. While the cops and FBI agents scouted positions for a decisive show of force, Brunetti familiarized himself with the case law that regulates gaming on Indian land. In 1987, the U.S. Supreme Court rendered a six-to-three decision upholding the rights of Indians to use their land for bingo and gambling enterprises provided that they are approved by the elected chiefs and state authorities. "It's a double-edged sword. The highest court in the land says Indians can gamble on their land, but that doesn't mean they can just open up casinos, tell the state to stuff it, and violate other laws concerning currency and taxes," says Brunetti. "Nor does it mean that they can go against federal legislation that requires gaming halls to be registered with the proper tribal authorities. The investigation was not questioning the right to have bingo or whatever. The question was whether they could have casinos without the approval of the tribal council and the state. So we targeted the owners.

"According to the Supreme Court ruling, the state and federal governments require that elected tribal authorities and the casinos strike their own deal. At the St. Regis reservation, you had six casinos going without any formal sanction. That was a clear violation and it became the legal cornerstone of our probe.

"If the casino owners had gone to the elected chiefs, made a proposal, or won some kind of approval to operate, then we might not have come in," muses Brunetti. "If the council wants to do it or negotiates a deal to have gambling, then the Justice Department usually leaves everybody alone. But the situation was just a bunch of Mohawks saying their birthright allows them to do what they want. No, the law doesn't work that way."

4

THE FEDS DEAL
FROM THE BOTTOM

The assignment seemed simple to FBI agent Donald Greene: weed out the identified criminal element, and get out of the territory, leaving the Mohawks to solve their own problems. Greene knew that the surprise strike was to paralyze the reservation temporarily, to allow teams of state police officers and FBI agents to enter and secure the six casinos on the territory. As the search teams seized evidence of illegal gaming, the arrest teams were to locate the targets—virtually all casino owners and managers—take them into custody, and drive them to Syracuse for arraignment in federal court.

But what might have been a relatively simple anti-gambling, law enforcement patrol elsewhere was an international military operation at Akwesasne. To prevent the accused from fleeing north, the FBI and the state police had to win the cooperation of the Sûreté du Québec, the Ontario Provincial Police and the Royal Canadian Mounted Police, which would seal off the Canadian side of the reserve while the raid took place.

More than 400 FBI agents and state troopers assembled on the evening of July 19,1989, from the wooden barracks in Massena to the redbrick Troop B headquarters in Raybrook. Around 10:00 p.m., state police brass dispatched several pairs of undercover officers to serve as scouts in the casinos. "Our assignment was to advise our command of any unusual activity prior to the arrival of the search-and-arrest teams," recounts trooper Norman Gibbons, who spent the night of July 19 and the early morning hours of July 20 at Tony's Vegas International with his partner, Peter Arcadi.

Shortly after midnight, the brass deployed the search-and-arrest teams, bringing hundreds of cops within striking distance of the reservation. "At 1:30, I departed the staging area at Raybrook, leading a search team of 11 New York State Police representatives and six agents of the FBI," Greene says. "I was traveling in a New York State Police car driven by Lt. Alfred Crary, my police-commissioned counterpart." Greene's search team "C" was to secure the Club 21 casino on Route 37, about a half mile west of Tony's.

By 4:00 a.m., the FBI and police teams rolled toward their final positions. "It became clear," Gibbons recalled, "that the operators were alerted to the impending raid. Some of them began moving slot machines out of their establishments."

"Everybody knew the police were coming back," says War Chief Francis Boots. The Warriors had spent most of June and July organizing their patrol of two dozen men who drove the territory from Snye, Quebec, to Raquette Point, New York, to Cornwall Island, Ontario. Using citizen's-band radios and walkie-talkies, these men reported car accidents, ambulance runs, harassment, fistfights, and most important, the presence of the state police.

Around 4:30 am., Gibbons says he noticed Mohawks' cars pulling up near the casino entrance on Route 37. Ten minutes later, Greene and Crary were radioed that 30 Warriors had been observed in the parking lot outside Tony's and the Bear's Den. At 4:45 a.m., Arcadi observed Mohawks loading "four or five high-powered rifles" into cars.

A few minutes later, state police investigators John Welch and Stephen Maher left their undercover post beside the Mohawk Bingo Palace and drove east along Route 37. Near the Bear's Den, Welch says, "We were confronted by a roadblock of approximately six cars parked across the roadway. At this roadblock were seven Indians with semi-automatic weapons along with rifles and shotguns. My partner asked one of the Indians next to our car what the weapons were for. The Indian took his finger off the trigger, pointed to the rifle with his left hand, and made the gesture of squeezing his right index finger numerous times, like shooting the rifle." When Welch and Maher turned around and started west, they spotted another group of Mohawks with "rifles and scopes and assault-type weapons."

As the Warriors took their positions, gambling continued uninter-
rupted. Inside Tony's, Gibbons says, people remained at the tables
even though they could see the flashing red lights of a police cruiser
pull up to the roadblock. About 5:00 a.m., he saw the cruiser "turn
and reverse its direction, along with others that were in line with it."
When Arcadi reached a telephone, the command post at the Massena
barracks told him "that the original plan had been altered," says Gibbons. "The detail had been stopped by the roadblock and had been
told not to assault the roadblocks because of the possibility of weapons being used against them."

Around 5:20 a.m., state police Capt. Gregory Sitler and Sgt. Claude
Bennett steered their unmarked Plymouth Fury onto Route 37, heading east from the Raquette River toward Hogansburg. "As we were
passing by the Bear's Den," Bennett says, "a group of Indians ran at our
car. One of the Indians had a shotgun slung over his shoulder." Adds
Sitler, "Indians ran into the road in an attempt to block the roadway.
An unidentified Indian threw a rock at the vehicle, striking and breaking the windshield."

After Sitler and Bennett sped from the roadblock, Lieutenant Crary,
FBI agent Greene, and state police Lt. Kenneth Cook received an order
to execute the warrants. "Immediately east of Tony's Vegas International," Greene says, "we were confronted by a roadblock consisting
of three to four vehicles parked perpendicularly across the road with
approximately 15 to 20 individuals manning the roadblock. Lieutenant Crary stopped his vehicle 50 to 70 yards away from the roadblock.
Members of my team, as well as members of a second search team,
which arrived shortly after us, exited their vehicles. Lieutenants
Crary and Cook went forward.

"I then advanced to join in the conversation. As I reached the midpoint between the position of the roadblock and the bulk of law-
enforcement personnel with their cars—approximately 30 to 35 yards
from the roadblock—an unidentified male gestured and announced,
'Don't come any farther or someone's going to get hurt.' Not knowing
what was said [between the Mohawks and Crary or Cook] and how my
actions would affect any negotiations between the police and the
people at the roadblock, I decided not to advance any farther."

Walking toward the roadblock, identifying themselves, Crary and
Cook spotted Kakwirakeron. "I saw him gesticulating to the others to
join the group I was confronted with," Crary recalls. "The others appeared to be guided by his gestures. When I was confronted, several
persons made threatening remarks, and I called for the road to be

opened. Claims of sovereignty were made, accompanied by such threats as 'If you don't get those guys out of the reservation, we are going to kick all of your asses.'"

Despite the tough talk and the previous sighting of guns by undercover cops, the Mohawks did not display any firearms. "Although I never observed anyone at the roadblock or in the vicinity of the roadblock with weapons," says Greene, "I was operating tactically with the assumption that an armed confrontation could occur at any time."

For most of the morning, Maj. Ronald Brooks stood in the cramped communications room of the Massena barracks, tracking the search-and-arrest teams as they approached the reservation, took up positions, and awaited the order to enter the territory. At 4:35 a.m., Brooks says, he received a radio dispatch about a gathering of Warriors in the parking lot in front of the Bear's Den. Five minutes later, undercover cops observed Mohawks "loading long guns" into trucks parked in front of Tony's. At 4:40, after receiving another report mentioning guns, Brooks called state police Capt. Fenton Thompson, the senior officer at the scene.

"The latest information was that there were approximately 30 armed Indians outside of Tony's," Brooks says of his conversation with Thompson. "They appeared to be members of the Warriors Society. He told me that he believed there were more Warriors at the Bear's Den. I requested that Captain Thompson place a call to the Bear's Den, asking to speak to Art Montour. I wanted to establish contact between Montour and myself."

Shortly before 5:00 a.m., he issued a dispatch advising all search-and-arrest teams "to stand by and await further instructions." At 5:25 a.m., Brooks was told he could speak with Kakwirakeron on a cellular phone in the parking lot of Tony's. Making the call, Brooks told Kakwirakeron "that the detail en route to the reservation was not a state police operation, but was an FBI operation with the intention of executing search warrants." According to Brooks, Kakwirakeron replied that the Warriors considered the presence of federal agents "a violation of all treaties."

FBI agent Michael Sputo, who stood beside Brooks in the communications room, tells a slightly different story: "Major Brooks explained that unlike previous search warrants which had been executed in the past by state police, these were federal search warrants. According to Major Brooks, Mr. Montour responded, 'If these are federal warrants, this means war, and we are declaring war back.' The line then went dead."

At 5:50 a.m., Brooks reached Kakwirakeron again. "Art stated that he planned to maintain his barricades," Sputo says. "Major Brooks explained that there was no need for anyone to get hurt and that the search warrants would be executed in the normal manner. Montour responded that the road would stay blocked."

While police and FBI brass ordered the arrest teams to hold their positions outside the strip, undercover cops Gibbons and Arcadi remained inside Tony's Vegas International, where gambling continued despite word of the raid. Between 6:00 and 7:00 a.m., the two cops observed that Tony's employees were given electric cattle prods, which give a shock when touched. "I believe these were to be used against detail members," Gibbons claims.

Gibbons and Arcadi also saw casino employees take money out of slots and remove the machines' inner workings to the second-floor office and storage area. "When it became apparent that state police would not cross the roadblock," Gibbons says, "the employees removed slot machines outside to personally owned vehicles." Around 7:00 a.m., Gibbons stepped into the parking lot, where he overheard employees talking among themselves. "I learned that the slot machines were being dumped in a field off the McGee Road and the employees were afraid that a spotter plane had observed them dumping the machines, and that they would have to be moved."

For the next 45 minutes, Gibbons roamed the parking lot. "There were several Indians standing in a group near the vehicles, and all of them armed with rifles," he explains. "One of the vehicles faced east and the back door was open. I could hear what I believed to be a person loading rounds into a magazine and observed a short, stocky Indian male with a beard who was holding what I believe to be an AK–47 assault rifle with a 30-round clip."

At the roadblock, Gibbons notes, two Mohawks were lying on top of cars, pointing high-powered rifles with scopes at the police positions on Route 37. Another eight Mohawks stood within the roadblock, Gibbons adds, "each holding a rifle in anticipation of a police assault."

By 7:45 a.m., the Mohawks led the gamblers out of the area through a Warrior-controlled checkpoint west of Tony's. Gibbons and Arcadi fell into line and followed the gamblers through a second checkpoint of several cars and six Mohawks with rifles. Though the Warriors believed they had repelled police, Brooks and FBI brass had ordered their troopers and agents to circle back to Helena. They reassembled into their search-and-arrest teams and sped north on Helena Road to Frogtown Road. There one column turned west and curved behind the Warriors roadblock to the back of Club 21 and Hart's Palace. The second column headed north into Hogansburg along Route 37 to a left-hand turn that brought them to the entrance of Burns Casino, a quarter mile east of the Warriors' barricade.

Without resistance, troopers and agents entered the Golden Nugget, Hart's, Club 21, and Billy's Bingo Palace. They took bags of cash, slot machines, payroll records, bank statements, personnel files, business records, playing cards, dice, and other gaming equipment. By 9:30 a.m., the police had nine people in custody—Bill Sears, the 40-year-old owner of Billy's Bingo Palace, Paul and Tarek Tatlock of the Golden Nugget, Hattie and Renee Hart of Hart's, David Mainville and Roderick Cook of Club 21, and Tony Laughing's brother Gerald. At the Burns Casino, the cops and FBI agents were held at bay by 60-year-old Peter Burns in his wheelchair brandishing a .12 gauge pump-action shotgun.

"He was surrounded by uniformed cops and FBI agents wearing windbreakers that had the big orange letters 'FBI,'" recalls Joe Gray, then a reporter for the Massena daily *Courier Observer* and now director of public information for the tribal council. "Pete had his shotgun pointing up in the air and he was yelling, 'Don't take a step closer. This is my land.' You could tell that the cops and the agents thought that Pete could snap at any moment and blow someone's head off. They thought he was a wild old geezer.

"So an FBI guy held up his hands to show that there weren't any guns and he started to walk toward him. 'Mr. Burns, cool down,' he says. 'No one needs to get hurt. Just let us do our jobs.' Pete looked at him and yelled back, 'Don't do it.' But Pete never pointed the shotgun at him and the FBI agent just kept walking one step at a time. 'Be calm; take it easy,' he was telling Pete. Pete's talking about how this is his land and no one is going to take it away from him. The FBI guy says that's not going to happen. They just have to do their job. He keeps coming, you know, one slow careful step at a time. The FBI guy would look at Pete, then his eyes would dart to the gun. And gets close enough to put his hands on Pete. That's when the second guy rushes forward and they get the gun away.

"As they're carting him out of there, Pete starts laughing and yelling. 'It wasn't loaded anyway, guys! It wasn't loaded!'"

Executing their search warrants, the agents used a torch to burn a

12-inch hole in the safe holding the casino's records, cash, and chips. Watching the authorities cart out boxes of ledgers and bags of cash, Alex Burns shook his head. "They're taking it all," he says. "Who knows if we'll ever be back in business."

By the afternoon of July 20, 1989, state police barricades had sealed off the reservation along Helena Road, Frogtown Road, Rooseveltown Road, and two points on Route 37—the four corners in Hogansburg and the traffic circle that guided cars and trucks to Massena or the Friendship Bridge over the St. Lawrence River into Canada. Inside the territory, the Warriors posted their own roadblocks on Route 37— the first a few yards away from the parking lot that connects Tony's and the Bear's Den, the second on the twin bridges that span the Raquette River.

"The police shut everything down," says L. David Jacobs, the newly elected pro-gaming chief on the New York–chartered St. Regis Mohawk Tribal Council. "The cops put us under siege."

Outraged by the massive show of force and the police-FBI claim that anti-gaming Chief Harold Tarbell requested it, Jacobs and the other newly elected tribal council chief, Lincoln White, faxed an angry letter to Gov. Mario Cuomo. "The sovereign Mohawk territory at Akwesasne has been invaded and is currently occupied by the United States via the FBI, the New York State Police and possibly other federal authorities. This invasion is an act of war." The letter criticized Tarbell's cooperation with the police and FBI agents. "Because you and a Mohawk informant are an integral part of the decision-making group that authorized this act of war against the Mohawk Nation, the St. Regis Mohawk Tribal Council is holding you two individuals responsible for any abuse or acts of racism that may occur to any of our people."

The harsh tone won widespread support for Jacobs and White and drew the attention of the police and FBI. In phone conversations with Major Brooks and FBI agent John McEligot, Jacobs announced he would convene a tribal council meeting the next morning and introduce a resolution to dismantle the roadblocks. "If we were going to get the police out of here," Jacobs says, "we had to show them we were willing to establish our own authority. I wanted to show the police we can govern ourselves."

According to McEligot, the confrontation offered Jacobs his first chance to deal with Kakwirakeron and the Warriors. When the search was completed, McEligot says, "Dave went to Art Montour, told him the police were gone, and asked him to take the roadblocks down. Montour refused, saying he represented the people and was there to protect Mohawk sovereignty. Jacobs then asked Montour under what authority he was acting, and Montour responded in a rambling manner, referring to God and giving Jacobs no definite origin of authority."

During the evening of July 20 and the following morning, Jacobs says he demanded several times that Kakwirakeron and the Warriors remove the roadblocks. "I didn't want to negotiate or lead him to believe that we were negotiating," says Jacobs. "I wanted him to know that I did not recognize his authority or the legitimacy of the Warriors Society."

On the morning of July 21, Brooks called Kakwirakeron, hoping to persuade him to ask the Warriors to remove their barricades. When Brooks mentioned Jacobs and the tribal council's refusal to recognize the Warriors Society, Kakwirakeron grew defiant. "He stated that roadblocks were there only to protect against an invasion force, like the New York State Police or federal law-enforcement agencies. He further stated that if I removed the state police blockades, his society would set up blockades at the end of Akwesasne," Brooks recalls. "Montour said no state police would be allowed on the reservation by his society. That's how we left it."

During the early hours of what they were calling the occupation, the Warriors scrambled to close ranks and organize lines of communication and a chain of command. Kakwirakeron marshaled two dozen men in and out of roadblocks that included logs and an overturned tractor trailer. Larry Thompson, his wife, Dana Leigh Bush, and his brother Loran offered War Chief Francis Boots and the Warriors the Onkwe Bingo Jack as an operations base complete with maps, food, radio, phones, and walkie-talkie consoles. To ferry food or messages too sensitive to broadcast, Francis Boots and his brother John coordinated a fleet of trucks and cars to run between the roadblocks. They also chartered state police positions and sent out teams of women to scout the territory.

While Kakwirakeron and Boots were consolidating their power base, a third force emerged in the person of Mark Maracle, a former U.S. Marine and itinerant ironworker who settled at the Six Nations Reserve near Brantford, Ontario. A six-foot-six chain-smoker with long black hair falling over shoulders wider than a door, Maracle came to Akwesasne after the June 6 and 7 police raids to support the Warriors. Known throughout the territories as a hard-core militant, he quickly won over younger men convinced that confrontation, not negotiation, was the only way to sovereignty. Arguing that the police invasion forced Mohawks to take up the gun to defend their land and honor, Maracle embodied the myth of the defiant Mohawk and concentrated on the procurement and inspection of weapons. "We have to show our power and determination. We have to make the people who want to crush us think about the price they have to pay," he says.

Though friendly, Kakwirakeron and Maracle offered a different set of tactics. Citing his experience at Moss Lake in the 1970s, Kakwirakeron argued that Mohawks had to first stabilize their position on Route 37, then force a standoff and open negotiations. He counseled a non-violent war of attrition aimed at neutralizing the police and forcing politicians to bargain. Maracle favored hit-and-run guerrilla moves against the police. Since the cops were unwilling to test the Warriors' roadblocks, Maracle figured the Mohawks had a military advantage. Under the cover of darkness, Warriors could sneak through the woods around the troopers' barricades and slash tires at their outposts in nearby Helena or Massena. Maracle also suggested that Mohawks use their radio scramblers to jam the cops' communications system.

As the Warriors wrestled with these differences, the authorities agreed on a long-term strategy. First, top-level FBI, U.S. Justice Department, and New York State officials asked Canadian federal and provincial authorities to monitor their side of the border and prevent Warriors from fleeing. Then FBI agent Michael Sputo and Assistant U.S. Attorney John Brunetti drafted a three-page affidavit to support an arrest warrant charging Kakwirakeron with using a deadly weapon to interfere with a federally authorized search. "While no one actually saw him physically touch a weapon," says Sputo in his affidavit, "he admitted responsibility for arranging, organizing, and persisting in the establishment of armed roadblocks."

Finally, the state police set up a perimeter around the reservation from Massena to the west, to Bombay to the south, and Fort Covington to the east. Deploying more than 150 officers, the police stopped every car that came within several miles of Akwesasne's borders. "We cannot offer any sort of police service to any member of the public or any member of the reservation in the event of an incident," said Maj. Ronald Brooks, explaining his order to choke all roads leading into Mohawk territory.

"We wanted to go right at the Warriors," says Brunetti. "We had arrested 10 of the 12 Mohawks we wanted on gambling charges. The eleventh, Eli Tarbell, contacted our office to surrender, and the twelfth, Tony Laughing, was going to be a fugitive, keeping his casino open behind the Warriors' roadblock. So we thought it made sense to go after the Warriors' leader, who was preventing law enforcement from doing its job. We wanted to tell Mohawks that gambling was fine as long as it followed the federal law. The Warriors clearly did not want us to get that message across."

As the police sealed off the territory, tribal chiefs L. David Jacobs and Lincoln White circulated a call for a reservation-wide referendum on casino gambling, to isolate the anti-gambling head chief, Harold Tarbell, their rival on the New York–chartered tribal council. "We wanted to show once and for all that the people of Akwesasne had an opinion on gaming and we could abide by their wishes," says Jacobs.

Jacobs presented himself to state and federal authorities as a moderate who could facilitate negotiations to legalize gaming. He denounced the Warriors, but refused to accept the legitimacy of the police presence. "I wanted to make it clear to everyone that there was a choice between the police and the Warriors. If the residents wanted gambling and jobs," says Jacobs, "then we would hold the referendum, vote for gambling, and follow the law by drafting gaming regulations which would be enforced by the tribal council." Jacobs's ballot would give voters four options: 1) full rejection of gambling; 2) acceptance of traditional forms of Indian gaming, such as peach stone; 3) acceptance of lotto, bingo, and similar games; 4) acceptance of card games like poker, blackjack, and other casino games including slot machines.

"The referendum was a politician's move," says Kakwirakeron. "It had more to do with the politics of the tribal council and the business climate than the real issue of sovereignty."

The casino owners endorsed the referendum. "Win, lose, or draw," says Tony Laughing, "I'll respect the people's wishes. If people don't want my slot machines here, I'll take them elsewhere. But obviously I don't think we're going to lose."

As the police tightened their grip on the reservation, Kakwirakeron, Boots, and Maracle knew the Warriors needed to recapture the initiative and present sovereignty, not gambling, as the key issue. With Maracle pushing for a confrontation, Kakwirakeron had to project militancy but stop short of any display of force or armament. He saw that the Warriors were caught in a vicious power play: to openly battle the police raised the possibility of massive retaliation; to denounce Jacobs and the gaming ballot was to help white authority further divide the Mohawks; and to remain at the roadblock was to allow the police, Jacobs, and the anti-gaming faction greater control.

The police blockade prevented the Warriors from talking to Akwesasne residents, reporters, and the clergy, doctors, and lawyers who offered their services. This was particularly frustrating because Kak-wirakeron and Boots persuaded Maracle that the first step was to appeal to the public and rally Warrior sympathizers. "We needed to show the world who we were and speak freely about our point of view," says Kakwirakeron.

On Sunday evening, July 23, the Warriors agreed to hold a press conference at 12:30 p.m. the following day. Reporters would be escorted onto the territory, where Kakwirakeron would detail the Warriors' position and answer questions about the occupation.

When the reporters arrived at the traffic circle, they were cordoned off by a squad of gray-shirted troopers with riot sticks. "We can't guarantee your safety," Brooks told them, adding that police had blocked traffic on all the other roads as well. "No one was allowed to enter or leave," says *The People's Voice* editor Cindy Terrance. "Mohawks were being held hostage in their own land."

With reporters unable to move, the Warriors decided to bring Kak-wirakeron to them. A rag-tag column of 40 men, women, and children walked the mile to the traffic circle. There they encountered a dozen troopers, their nightsticks drawn. The police allowed Kakwirakeron to recite the traditional blessings before he approached.

"After observing a couple of minutes of silence," says Terrance, "he asked troopers why they were denying Mohawk people their rights. He asked why no outside press was being allowed in. Suddenly, an FBI agent with state troopers broke through the crowd and announced that they had a warrant for Montour." As seven or eight troopers wrestled with Kakwirakeron, a wedge of 100 troopers, including two dozen from the elite Mobile Response Riot Squad, stormed over a nearby ridge.

"They came at us with guns drawn and swinging their nightsticks," recalls Kakwirakeron's wife, Verna Montour. "I was clubbed on my arms and legs, and one of them punched me in the face as I was trying to reach my husband."

The melee left 11 Mohawks with cuts and bruises, including three-year-old Carla General, who was struck by a wooden club in the mouth.

State police Sgt. Michael Downs denies that troopers overreacted. "We did what we had to do with minimum force necessary. I can't explain why they would bring two- or three-year-old children in a situation like that. Certainly the fact that children got injured is unfortunate. I think you understand that we weren't clubbing children."

As Kakwirakeron was sped to a holding cell in the Syracuse federal courthouse, the Warriors turned to Maracle for leadership. "We had to show the police that we would not crumble," says Maracle. "By the time we got back from the traffic circle, there were hundreds of troopers in the area. And many of our people were busy wondering if their brother or cousin, husband or wife or daughter got hit by a billy club."

Maracle went to fortify Warrior positions. Dragging logs across Route 37, arranging cars in zig-zagging formations, the Warriors created several lines of defense at each location. Behind the first barricade stood masked teenagers and young men with walkie-talkies, making sure the cops did not move forward. Less than 20 yards behind them were pickup trucks, rifle-wielding men in the beds aiming over the cabs. A third set of barricades consisted of old rusted and dented sedans pulled into a V-formation, which shielded several masked men and their AK-47s.

The next morning, Saranac Lake lawyer Seth Shapiro received a phone call from William Kunstler, the famed New York City defense lawyer who represented the Sioux indicted for the 1973 shooting of FBI agents at Wounded Knee. "I used to live in New York City and I followed Kunstler's career, but I didn't know him," says Shapiro. "About six weeks before Kakwirakeron's arrest, I got a case up here and I wanted some advice, so I called Kunstler and he was very helpful. I told him if he ever heard of anything up here, he should keep me in mind. I didn't expect Kakwirakeron to be my first shot. After all, I had never conducted a major criminal case in federal court before, and all I knew about the Mohawks was what I read in the newspaper."

When Kunstler offered him the opportunity to represent Kakwirakeron at the bail hearing, Shapiro immediately drove to Syracuse, where Kakwirakeron was being held. "He was isolated and treated as the highest possible security risk," says Shapiro. "Now, I had never met him and he never met me. I walked into the room, a guard posted at the door, but it was all right. Kakwirakeron looks right into my eyes and offers his hand and we start to work.

"I'm all nervous and he is calm and straight to the point. He expected the FBI to seek to deny him bail and keep him out of Akwesasne. He expected the government to produce Mohawks who would give statements against him. Our point was to cast him as a natural leader who stood up for his people but shunned violence. We had to make sure the magistrate knew the difference between violence and confrontation. That was very important.

"I am an observant Jew and I stood in court, ready to begin, when I thought, the Warriors are like the Hasidim. They cannot see the present without looking to the past. Their point of view is filtered through a tradition and a history that is beyond our experience. So I figured the way to present my client was in this framework, a man who truly believes in himself and his people. The magistrate might think of him as someone who is out of touch, but there is nothing dangerous about a person like this. What the prosecution called dangerous, I called passion and personal conviction. The real Kakwirakeron and the real Warriors—they're true believers."

As Shapiro prepared his arguments, Maracle surveyed the battle lines. "The police don't understand how serious we are about our history and our claims to the land," he says. "They think we are just a bunch of funny colored men with long hair who talk about weird dances and hunting or fishing when we drink too much. This is our history and we were raised with it as you were raised with the pilgrims and the *Mayflower*.

"We look at all of the northeast and see our people. Fishing on the coast of Labrador and Newfoundland, or running the rapids of the St. Lawrence, or hunting bear and moose, even buffalo in the woods that stretch across New York and into Canada. The police look at us and see six square miles and a bunch of crazies talking shit. They don't understand that we are a lost nation trying to restore the dignity of our past."

"I want to bring my tribe into the twentieth century," proclaims tribal Chief L. David Jacobs, who saw the Warriors' claims of sovereignty as a dangerous sideshow threatening the casino business. "This is about economic development, government, and money. The past is the past and it can't be changed. Let's make the money we are entitled to make and improve the condition of our people. Guns and speeches and roadblocks will not help."

Jacobs knew that rebellious Warriors could upset his carefully constructed plan to hold a referendum that would encourage the state police and FBI to leave the territory and allow casinos to re-open. He decided to support the FBI's request to deny Kakwirakeron bail, and thereby prevent him from returning to the reservation. Like the feds and the state cops, Jacobs mistakenly thought the Warriors could be neutralized by removing their most eloquent spokesman.

But that decision merely added credibility to the Warriors' claim that the New York–chartered council and its chiefs were puppets who betray Mohawk patriots. With Jacobs, Lincoln White, and Harold Tarbell divided over gaming but united in their cooperation with the FBI and the state police, the Warriors easily cast themselves as the voice of Mohawk nationalism. The towering presence of Maracle presented the most visible alternative to a police force vilified as an occupying army. Whenever Jacobs or Tarbell tried to deal with the authorities, Maracle decried the elected chiefs as traitors.

"If the police just beat up on your women and children who are marching down the road, you don't turn around and negotiate the next day," says Maracle. "What is there to negotiate about? The police were wrong. But the tribal council still wanted to cut a deal. Instead, they were cutting their own throats."

Though they desperately wanted Jacobs's referendum, the casino owners saw the need to distance themselves from the unpopular tribal council by praising the Warriors for their courage. "They're standing up for us all," says Tony Laughing, "not gamblers or slot machines."

While Laughing's comments appropriated the language of politics and sovereignty, he and other owners focused on the bottom line. "We've lost close to a half million dollars already," Guilford White said on the seventh day of the blockade. "With police controlling the roads, we're not doing any business. This puts 130 people out of work, just with this one legitimate business. Unemployment around here runs close to 30 percent and we have been providing jobs for our people."

Having surrendered on gambling charges and posted $5,000 bail, Eli Tarbell returned to Akwesasne to run the restaurant in the Bear's Den. "It would be cheaper for me to close up right now," he says. "But I'm not going to give in. I'll still run my business."

Even businesses off the reservation were suffering. To the east, just outside Fort Covington, Rajesh Patel, owner of the Mary-Jo Motel, says the police blockade cost him 30 to 40 customers a night. To the west, on the outskirts of Massena, the Jayne Lisa Restaurant revenues dropped $300 to $400 a night as few customers were willing to be frisked by shotgun-wielding troopers before dinner. Frank Alguire, the executive director of the Massena Economic Development Council said, "Let's face it, people come here to play blackjack or win the real big jackpots."

For anti-gaming advocates Doug George, Harold Tarbell, and Jake Swamp, the riot and the referendum spelled political disaster. Each day of the occupation helped the Warriors and casino owners. "When the state police are on our land, blocking access and stopping traffic,"

begins *Indian Time* Editor George, "we knew the people would be focused on them, not the casinos, and the original issue gets lost in the
shuffle.

"The Warriors, the gamblers, they don't want order. They say they
want sovereignty, but what they really want is anarchy. How would
they unite Akwesasne? What kind of relations would they set up with
New York State? Ontario? Quebec? They never discuss these matters.
All they talk about is sovereignty, which really means their right to
make a buck by crap games or tobacco smuggling."

Yet George, too, admits to some inconsistencies in his political
thinking. "A year ago, I would never have seen the police as a necessary and stabilizing force, and I still don't really want to," he says,
"but, our situation is changing too fast. There is no leadership. We are
divided in ways that can become hopeless.

"The occupation can be seen as an opportunity. We have to work
with each other and show our strength. It's hard for me to hear it out
of my own mouth, but I think the police had to come. We have no
other way to stop the Warriors and the casinos from destroying our
community."

George argues that a job as a card dealer or casino security guard
does not produce a proud, well-educated Mohawk who knows history
and honors the traditions of clans and family. Pumping gas or waiting
on tables is a far cry from learning a skill, opening a business, working
a trade. For him, Mohawk life must be more than a casino economy
and fragmented government. The Warrior alternative to the status quo
was not acceptable. "We, the people, know that the Warriors are violent outlaws. We want the police to leave so we can call our community meetings and organize into a political force and government
structure that will cover all of Akwesasne. Most Mohawks are fed up
with split jurisdiction between Canada and the United States. We
want to make one council, one government. The Warriors stand in the
way of that. We have to get them to lay down their weapons and go
away so we can get the police out of here and build a government ourselves."

Behind the scenes, New York Head Chief Harold Tarbell and his
Canadian counterpart, Grand Chief Mike Mitchell, bad-mouthed the
casinos, pro-gaming Chief Jacobs, and the Warriors to high-ranking
state, provincial, and federal officials. While Mitchell remained in
close contact with Harold Tarbell and the anti-gaming faction on the
New York side of Akwesasne, the Canadian governments did their

best to avoid any visible presence. Instead, the provincial police forces, and the offices of then Ontario premier David Peterson and Quebec Premier Robert Bourassa kept in contact with each other and with New York police officials. "Gambling is not allowed on native lands or any place else in our country," said Sylvie Goldin, a spokeswoman for Bourassa. "It is an American problem and, though we are watching and interested, using the provincial and federal ministries of Indian Affairs to stay in touch with Chief Mitchell, it is not for us to take action."

On the New York side of the border, Head Chief Harold Tarbell was in constant touch with the FBI, the state police, and representatives of Gov. Mario Cuomo, hoping to temper their enthusiasm for Jacobs's referendum. "Gambling is only going to corrupt our people," he says. "We are poor and unemployment is high, so men and women will jump at jobs. Casino owners are treating our territory as an underdeveloped area that should be grateful for any business. We can do better than this, better than tour buses of bingo players and all-night dice games. We are people who understand nature, not a three-to-two payoff."

Throughout the first week of the occupation, Cuomo repeatedly refused to meet with Tarbell. "We considered this an internal dispute among the Mohawk community," says Robert Batson, the governor's aide who served as one of Cuomo's liaisons to the cops and Mohawks during July and early August. "The governor is always willing to hear various points of view. However, he does not want to involve himself in a situation that requires the community to reach its own consensus first."

Batson saw two separate problems in need of solution: "First, the police have to have jurisdiction for all criminal offenses and they can go in and out of Mohawk territory as they see fit. To put it mildly, the Warriors disagreed.

"But in our minds, that disagreement could be taken away from the second problem about gambling and the referendum. We said federal law allows Mohawks to have poker, blackjack, roulette, dice, anything permitted under state law, whether Harold Tarbell or anybody else likes it. The Mohawks could have most forms of casino gambling except slots, because the state has a very clear law banning the use of these gaming machines, no matter what the vote in the referendum. So you see, we had two areas of dispute—the Warriors and the state clashed over the jurisdiction of the state police, and the casino owners raised the question of slots."

According to Batson and other state officials, the governor felt that he could not let the Warriors box him into any compromise concerning the jurisdiction of the state police, but he could and would support a move for gambling without slot machines. "In practice, that meant Harold Tarbell was having less influence, while Dave Jacobs was getting more," says Dr. Henrik Dullea, Cuomo's director of State Operations.

Doug George and Harold Tarbell tempered their rhetoric for the media, the bureaucrats, and politicians, but traditional Chief Jake Swamp took on the task of viciously attacking the Warriors. "They are our worst enemies," he declares. "To them, sovereignty is measured by a gun, not by reason or compromise, fruitful discussions."

Swamp tried to undermine the sympathy for the Warriors that followed the traffic circle riot. Branding Kakwirakeron an outsider provoking confrontation and furthering his own political standing, Swamp fumed, "Look at the man who calls himself Kakwirakeron. He will tell you that he is doing this for our nation. Nothing is further from the truth.

"He will tell you about Moss Lake and how he fought for the Mohawk Nation. Well, what happened? They won the territory at Ganienkeh, and he went there with his family. Within a few years, he left for California. He did not go back to his people at Kahnawake. He wandered and earned money as an ironworker until 1984, when he had a chance to rent a house in Bombay, off the reservation, on disputed land.

"He did not come onto Mohawk land and join the community and participate in our life. But as soon as there is talk of the state police, he shows up with his long braids and big shoulders. A good picture for the newspaper and the television, but this is not his land, not his territory."

But Swamp's adversaries immediately discredited him by raising his participation in the 1986 seizure and sale of cigarettes. They also pointed out that this self-styled guardian of Mohawk land was considering renting or selling part of his parcel near the St. Regis River for use as a dump for construction debris tainted by hazardous chemicals.

To show their support for Kakwirakeron, dozens of Mohawks drove to Syracuse on July 26 and packed the courtroom for the first part of his bail hearing. "The police and prosecutors are only trying to do their jobs by trying to put Kakwirakeron away," says Mark Maracle. "That's the system—whites dividing and conquering nonwhites. But when Jake Swamp attacks Kakwirakeron, everybody knows that Jake is only helping the cause of the FBI. So we had to have Mohawks show the world and our community that we will stand up for our own."

The next day, the anti-gaming faction suffered another setback. The Syracuse *Herald-American* published a story under the headline "Mohawks Denied Medical Care During Conflict, Doctor Claims." The article cited the records of the Mohawk Volunteer Ambulance Council and Dr. David Gorman, a Malone physician married to Mohawk activist Lorraine Montour. The newspaper detailed how cops refused to let the reservation's ambulance corps bring a 75-year-old diabetic to the hospital. The article also claimed the police did not let ambulances bring bleeding women and children off the reservation to the emergency room in Massena. Doug George blamed the Warriors for the injuries in that they allowed women and children to march. "If you're a leader, you're taught—at least the population of Akwesasne is taught—think of women and children first," George told the newspaper.

"That was it," says Rowena General, mother of the three-year-old who was struck by a police nightstick. "I had worked with Doug. I could understand that we had differences of opinion and that politics sometimes gets in the way. But it was becoming clearer and clearer that the anti-gaming faction wanted the police here and wanted the police to use force against us. How could anyone listen to him after he tried to excuse the police for hitting children?"

6

JACKS OR BETTER TO VOTE

Fletcher Graves flashed his U.S. Justice Department credentials and drove through the state police barricades on the bright morning of Friday, July 28. His last visit to Akwesasne had been 10 years earlier, when the territory's residents and the police squared off at Raquette Point after the Franklin County district attorney pressed criminal charges against two dozen Mohawks who allegedly turned a political dispute into a riot. "It took over a year to get things straightened out," says Graves, a federal mediator who specializes in Indian conflicts from the northeast to the plains. "The issues in 1979 turned on the type of government the community wanted and the rights of the state to call in the police. Now it's the same, but the territory seems more divided."

In the late 1970s, militant Loran Thompson and traditionalist Jake Swamp worked with Doug George and Mike Mitchell. "Ten years ago, we were all on the same side," Thompson says. "When it came to the presence of the police, Jake and Doug worked hard to keep our community united against the police. Today, we can barely speak to one another."

Thompson admits that the underground economy, bingo, and growing Canadian government grants changed their relationship. As Thompson and his brother, Larry, participated in the cigarette trade, Mitchell gained control of tens of millions in grants and subsidies and

Swamp consolidated his power on the traditional council. By 1987, the men became locked in a bitter feud over leasing space to *Indian Time*. Thompson, the landlord, wanted to evict George and his anti-gambling newspaper, which received support from Mitchell and his council. The disagreement escalated into property damage and shots being fired. It climaxed with Swamp's supporting Thompson's removal from the traditional council.

"That's why we need Fletcher," says Thompson, who considers himself a member of the Warriors but not a leader. "He had direct contact with us 10 years ago and he knows all about us. I went to the other Warriors and the casino owners and suggested that they request he come here. Fletcher is smart enough to see through gambling and see that the state police barricades and the Warrior roadblocks are the central part of what's going on here."

When he arrived, Graves received a warm reception and an escort from the Warriors. "We wanted him here," says Francis Boots, "because we believed in a resolution." Adds Mark Maracle, "The Warriors are always interested in serious dialogue. If the state is ready to talk, so are we."

For the troopers, too, Graves was a welcome sight. "One of our biggest problems was reaching the right people," says Sgt. Michael Downs. "Harold Tarbell couldn't speak for the tribal council, nor could David Jacobs. Francis Boots wasn't the only person making decisions for the Warriors. Jake Swamp and the traditional council did not speak for the entire anti-gambling faction. Fletcher Graves knew how to get people in the same vicinity, so negotiations could begin to take shape."

By Friday afternoon, Graves was holding discussions in the Bear's Den. Just a few hours later he saw a sign of progress, as Jacobs and White agreed to postpone the referendum for one week to defuse some of the emotion between anti- and pro-gaming factions. Graves also won a commitment from the Warriors to meet with state officials and the tribal council to consider drafting rules that would allow troopers access to Route 37 and give the Mohawk Sovereign Security Force the right to patrol Indian land. Finally, he assured the casino owners that the authorities would uphold their right to have casino gambling as defined by federal law.

"It was really the first time that all the parties were in contact with each other and exchanged the full extent of demands," says Downs.

All parties accepted the need for flexibility regarding casinos and the referendum. By agreeing to delay the referendum, Jacobs and the casino owners turned the tables on their arch rival, Harold Tarbell, and demonstrated that the pro-gaming faction was not associated with the Warriors. When Jacobs pushed for a meeting with Gov. Mario Cuomo, state officials proved reluctant, but willing to allow casino gaming if Mohawks followed the law. "After the first day of talks, I didn't think gambling was a very big matter," says Cuomo's aide, Robert Batson. "If he could run his casino and not get prosecuted for it, Tony Laughing didn't care if the state police rolled up and down Route 37.

"However, the police were openly frustrated by the Warriors' insistence that the troopers did not have the right to enter Akwesasne and conduct criminal investigations."

"The Warriors' initial position was bizarre," adds Downs. "If we wanted a suspect, then we should approach the Warriors and request that they take him into custody and hand him over—that is, if they agreed the person should be arrested. Then if we wanted to ride through on Route 37 or go on patrol or even answer a call for help because of an accident, we should contact the Warriors before going onto their territory."

While negotiations were under way, the police hauled concrete highway dividers in front of their cruisers and pitched striped tents to shade troopers from the scorching midday sun. "We felt that we really had to dig in and prepare for any kind of possible attack," continues Downs. "The Warriors were not showing any signs of movement."

Replies Maracle, "We wanted the police to understand that we are a sovereign nation, not a subdivision of New York State. We cited the treaties made between the first United States administration and our people. We deal nation to nation, not nation to state. Of course the police didn't agree. They cited acts of Congress, the state assembly, this law, that rule. But we told them, 'Look, this is our land and we have a right to patrol it. Just like the citizens in the United States have the right to bear arms on their land, so do we.' All we asked for was to have what is ours—the right to keep peace on our own land."

To isolate the Warriors and solidify support for legalized gaming, Jacobs scheduled a community meeting at the Mohawk Bingo Palace for Saturday afternoon, July 29. His strategy was to show the community that the Warriors' intransigence was the last obstacle to the removal of police barricades. But Jacobs was totally upstaged by a spontaneous demonstration against the police stranglehold organized by Akwesasne resident Cindy Herne. Herne directed her column down the same route that led to the traffic circle riot on July 24. "I support the march as all Warriors support anything peaceful," said Warrior John Boots. "If this march can help the so-called elected leadership understand that they have neglected us and our needs as Mohawks, then it will be a real success."

The police did nothing to interfere with the demonstrators. "These were men, women, and children who wanted to be heard," says Downs. "We understood that."

An hour later, at the Bingo Palace meeting, Eli Tarbell immediately won the crowd's attention by ferociously attacking the anti-gaming faction as traitors seeking to deny employment and prosperity to the people of Akwesasne. In a blistering speech sprinkled with profanity, Eli Tarbell urged the crowd to resist the police and accept the Warriors as Mohawk patriots. The response was overwhelming, a major setback for Jacobs and a clear message to Graves.

"We wanted the mediator to see that we could not, would not sit back and let the tribal council take away the gains we made," says Minnie Garrow, a college educated 44-year-old grandmother from a long line of Mohawk militants. "We wanted him to know that our voice had to be heard. That we had to be included or there would be no solution."

That afternoon, Graves suggested to the state police and the tribal council that all the roadblocks could be removed if the Warriors could have an unarmed patrol on Mohawk land. "We could live with that," says Downs. "You could say it was like a neighborhood or community group deciding to drive around their own neighborhood and see what was happening. From our point of view, it was a breakthrough."

A few hours later, Cuomo agreed to chair a negotiating session on Monday with the tribal council, representatives of the federal government, and the state police. But the meeting was anti-climactic as the governor quickly cut to three negotiating points: 1) the police agree to contact an elected chief or the Warriors Society before sending troopers onto the territory to conduct a criminal investigation; in exchange for this prior notice, the police have the unrestricted right to patrol Route 37 and enforce state law; 2) casino gambling would be permitted if the residents supported it at the polls and the casino owners, the state, the federal government, and the tribal council worked out a "gaming compact" that spells out regulations, to be enforced by Mohawks, in compliance with state and federal laws; and 3) if there were an agreement on the first two points, Cuomo would immediately order the police to remove the roadblocks but maintain a high profile near the reservation.

Though Harold Tarbell was clearly shaken by the governor's seeming support of gambling and reluctance to have troopers directly confront the Warriors, Jacobs and White jumped at Cuomo's opening for casinos. Said Jacobs, "The governor clearly told the tribal council to pull together, hold a referendum, and work toward the legalization of gambling. He wants us to develop an economy. He wants us to work out our differences without the police on our land."

For the state, the meeting was relatively easy. The governor's top aide, Dr. Henrik Dullea, says that Cuomo's objectives were making the Mohawk chiefs understand that they had to figure out their own position on gaming as a council, while accepting the state police right to patrol Route 37. According to Dullea, Cuomo knew he could not attack the casinos. "We knew they were there to stay," he says. "Once the buildings were up, you couldn't tear them down. These are not people from Queens or Binghamton or an upstate town coming to us with a complaint. These are people of a distinct culture, a nation that lives within our state, not an ethnic group to be absorbed or assimilated. Gambling is their decision, providing they follow the law."

The Mohawks left the governor's chambers by 4:00 p.m. Three hours later, the state police withdrew their barricades. The next morning, Harold Tarbell reluctantly announced that the gaming referendum would be held in five days, on the weekend of August 7 and 8. Then he revealed that the tribal council, the state police, and representatives of the Warriors would begin three-way discussions "to determine the specific protocol and jurisdiction of the state police on the reservation."

"Fletcher Graves did his work," says Loran Thompson. "With his help, the state officials heard our voice."

The morning after the police withdrew, dozens of Mohawks drove up and down Route 37, waving, honking horns, spinning U-turns and stopping to socialize on the gravel shoulder. At the Bear's Den, business picked up by breakfast; at the post office off four corners in Hogansburg, Postmaster Margie Beaubien stood on the loading dock with a broad smile as the Massena run arrived for the first time in 11 days. "During the occupation, the police wouldn't let the truck from Massena come to Akwesasne, but that's how we get our mail. So I asked them if I could drive to Massena and pick it up. They said no.

Now, what can I do? I'm a federal employee and the state is saying 'No mail.' Well, we struck a deal. They let me drive to Massena with outgoing mail and then I could come back. But nothing came in for 11 days.

"You should have seen that truck when it arrived after the occupation. It was stuffed and stuffed with all kinds of letters, packages, junk mail, and who knows what else. People were in here at seven o'clock in the morning, just waiting for the mail."

The territory erupted into a fury of activity once the police pulled back. "I don't know how many families lived on rice or canned soup or a sandwich or a bag of chips and cans of soda, whatever they could get or swap or share," said Cindy Terrance of *The People's Voice*. "People couldn't go to work. They couldn't go to the store, to the bank. Anywhere. The police wanted us to turn against the Warriors, but it wasn't going to happen. The troopers themselves weren't the problem—they were just doing their jobs—but we couldn't understand all the politics within our own community. Why did our lives have to be so complicated that Mohawks called the police to punish other Mohawks?

"And when the troopers finally left, the tribal council was still divided, the casinos wanted to open, and the Warriors were stronger than ever. So we figured it was time to stock up before something happened again."

As Akwesasne residents filled their depleted shelves, the leaders of various factions began formulating proposals and counterproposals, striking deals and seeking consensus. Elected Chiefs Harold Tarbell, Dave Jacobs, and Lincoln White tried to set aside their differences over gaming. Despite Tarbell's opposition to the ballot, the chiefs agreed on the need for face-to-face negotiations with the state police to establish guidelines for routine patrols on Route 37 and criminal investigations on Mohawk land.

Having learned from his mistakes, Tarbell ensured his participation in the discussions by phoning the state police, the governor's office, and mediator Fletcher Graves to tell them of the tribal council's willingness to meet all parties. By noon, Graves had devised a plan that called on the tribal council to meet first with the Warriors, then with the police. "There are differences to be resolved within the Mohawk community before the police or an outside government gets involved," says Graves.

Tarbell, Jacobs, and White were hesitant to appear to be legitimizing the Warriors, but figured it was best to follow Graves's suggestion.

They told him to schedule a session for that afternoon. To control the agenda and set boundaries for the discussion, the chiefs asked local lawyer Vaughn Aldrich to draft a proposed settlement that would recognize the interests of the state police, the tribal council, and the Warriors. The proposal asked the police to agree to regular patrols on Route 37 for the purpose of enforcing motor vehicle laws and traffic safety; to limit travel on secondary roads unless troopers were specifically requested by an Akwesasne resident; to notify the Mohawk chiefs if they were asked to go onto a secondary road; to refuse to raid the casinos providing they remain closed until the tribal council held its referendum and began certified compliance with federal gaming laws; and, finally, to guarantee that no criminal charges would arise from the traffic circle riot.

Thereafter, the proposal called on the Warriors to remove all weapons from public view; to work with the tribal council to set up an unarmed Community Services Security Patrol to escort and monitor the cops when asked to come onto the reservation for purposes other than patrol of Route 37; to allow the police to make arrests without interference, providing troopers properly notified the Community Services Security Patrol; and to keep the casinos closed until the federal government ruled that the tribal council had complied with relevant gaming laws.

Though the elected chiefs were not satisfied with Aldrich's proposal, they saw it as the beginning for serious negotiations with the Warriors. By setting up the unarmed Community Services Security Patrol, the chiefs reasoned, they would be allowing Warriors to monitor police and protect Mohawk territory from hostile invasion. From 2:30 to 4:30 p.m. on August 2, the chiefs sat in their office, awaiting a call from the Warriors. "We didn't hear from them," says Tarbell.

"They're crazy," replies Warrior Mark Maracle. "The tribal council wants us to work for them. They work for the white man's government and we work for our own people."

The Warriors insist they told the council and Graves that negotiations would not start until the society held an 8:00 p.m. strategy session at the Onkwe Bingo Jack. "We were not going to be rushed," explains Francis Boots. "We knew that our roadblocks and our presence forced the police to pull back. We had shown the state police that we were serious about this being our land and they are visitors."

Boots and Maracle believe that the Warriors were expected to see the withdrawal of state police as a concession that would lead to recognizing the authority of the tribal council. "That's totally foolish,"

says Maracle. "Our position was and still is that the police didn't belong here in the first place." At the strategy session, more than 40 men
and women overwhelmingly supported this refusal to place the Warriors beneath the tribal council. Intending to press their advantage
over the elected chiefs, the Warriors insisted the state police be present during all negotiations with Harold Tarbell or Dave Jacobs. "The
tribal council chiefs are puppets," says Maracle. "If we are going to
talk to them, then the puppeteer should be present."

Maracle and Boots told the crowd that the Warriors should support
the right of any Mohawk to run the business of his or her choice, but
they did not want to participate in any ballot that would comply with
federal regulations and urged the Warriors to decline a formal position
concerning the upcoming referendum. Others argued that a lukewarm
attitude toward the referendum could jeopardize the support of casino
owners, who had gone out of their way to help the Warriors during the
occupation. As a compromise, Larry Thompson, owner of the Onkwe
Bingo Jack, convinced the rank and file to agree that the casinos
should remain closed until the tribal council ballot. "Though we had
differences of opinions with the casino owners, we wanted to show
them that we could work together," recounts Maracle. "So we called
them one by one and told them our position. Except Tony's had already re-opened. A few of us got into a car and drove over there. We
told him that the Warriors could not allow gambling unless the people
voted for it. Tony wanted us to honor the referendum and the wishes
of his employees. He wasn't angry, he just wanted to know if we
were all on the same team. So we talked about it and Tony thought
about it."

Later that morning, Laughing and the Warriors came to an agreement. The casino would close at 9:00 p.m. on Thursday, August 3, and
wait for the results of the referendum. If the voters supported gaming,
Laughing would re-open and refuse to deal with the tribal council unless the elected chiefs agreed to Maracle's demand that the police not
be allowed in Akwesasne without permission from the Warriors' leadership.

After being stood up by the Warriors, the elected chiefs moved
quickly, scheduling negotiating sessions for the next two days, August
3 and 4. The chiefs met with Brooks and his two top assistants, Capt.
Fenton C. Thompson and Capt. Robert B. Leu. "We wanted the tribal
council to know exactly how their land fits into our duties," recounts
Brooks. "We have an enormous amount of territory to cover. I wanted
the council to see the people to whom I delegate authority, and I

wanted the captains to help work out whatever agreement we could make."

Knowing that the tribal council recognized the troopers' right to patrol Route 37, the major and his captains saw the real threat was gun-toting Warriors who rejected the authority of the tribal council. Brooks repeatedly pressed the tribal council to include the Warriors in all negotiations, but Tarbell and Jacobs claimed that would be an insult to their authority. At the end of the first day of negotiations, it became clear to Brooks that the tribal chiefs looked to the police as the last means to keep the Warriors away from the territory's political apparatus.

"It was too late," says Brooks. "The chiefs had a political problem. I had a public-safety problem."

On the second day of negotiations, the Warriors heard of Brooks's desire for their participation in negotiations. "When we heard that the police wanted discussions with us," says Maracle, "we knew that the police understood that the elected chiefs could only go so far."

By Saturday morning, August 5, Brooks had prevailed on the chiefs to sign a protocol effective from signature to September 15. The police won the right to patrol Route 37 for traffic violations and motor vehicle safety, but troopers "shall not enforce the vehicle and traffic laws off Route 37 unless acting in response to a specific complaint." The police would respond to any request for their presence on Mohawk land, but "telephonically advise a chief or subchief any time it becomes necessary for a state police member to leave Route 37." In exchange, the tribal council, however reluctantly, "recognizes that peaceful implementation may necessitate direct contact between the state police and the Warriors Society, also known as the Mohawk Sovereign Security Force, to develop procedures for the purpose of implementing this temporary agreement."

"Harold Tarbell and Dave Jacobs had to know that they were signing away a good part of their power," says Francis Boots. "And they did it so the police could talk with us, not arrest us, not criminalize us, but negotiate with us. This was a very big step forward." Though Maracle and Boots knew that militancy and determination had carried the Warriors this far, they also understood that the group had to prepare for lengthy discussions with the police and constant sniping from the tribal council. "Nobody gives us power," says Maracle. "We have to take it and make sure it stays with us. Harold Tarbell and Dave Jacobs were not going to roll over."

Recognizing that the agreement meant that they could no longer prevent the Warriors from strengthening their foothold in Akwesasne, Tarbell and Jacobs lost their common ground and parted ways over the referendum and gaming. On Monday morning, August 7, when the tribal council offices opened for voting, Tarbell led a small demonstration to denounce the referendum. He claimed the vote was illegal because the council had failed to post a legal notice 30 days prior to the date and hold two public hearings. With two dozen supporters walking a circle in the parking lot, Tarbell vowed to refuse to heed the outcome of the vote. Jacobs asked the police to send troopers because he was unsure the demonstration would remain peaceful.

"We sent a couple of cars," says Downs. "Harold Tarbell explained that he had no intent to do anything violent. He just wanted to express his opinion as did the people with him. There was no problem for us."

Mediator Fletcher Graves kept the ballot box in his bedroom over Monday night. Voting resumed Tuesday morning at the same slow trickle. That afternoon Jacobs sensed he was on the verge of victory when Brooks joined him at a press conference. The major announced that his troopers would abide by a pro-gaming vote and decline to make gambling arrests as long as the tribal council worked to comply with federal laws.

In another conciliatory message sent to the pro-gaming faction, Brooks said that arresting fugitive Tony Laughing "is not a priority at this time." When asked about police relations with the Warriors he replied: "We hope to reach an agreement with the Warriors about the presence and role of the state police on the reservation. We know the possibility of confrontation exists, but we hope to implement a plan that will avoid any uncomfortable situations."

The major's friendly demeanor and his plea for cooperation gave Jacobs the chance to cast himself as the only elected chief who could reach out to the police without betraying his fellow Mohawks. "Both sides had to have a victory," explains Jacobs. "The police needed the road, which was fine if we could have the casinos." A few hours later, at 5:00 p.m., the polling place closed. The pro-gaming faction won by a landslide—480 yes, 57 against, and nine abstentions. Though the small number of ballots indicate that many voters heeded the Warriors and boycotted the referendum, Jacobs claimed victory. "This shows the will of the people," says Jacobs. "There can be no doubt as to what we want and our intention of following the federal gaming laws to get it. Let's move forward."

As the casinos re-opened, the Warriors found themselves in an unfamiliar position. "We spent most of our time creating the patrols and making sure we had enough people to drive around the territory," says Maracle. "Drafting proposals and figuring out who was calling the shots and how do we deal with politicians and bureaucrats—it was a change, a big change."

"We had to have a program," says Boots. "We had to identify ourselves as the Warriors Society that wants specific changes and specific goals. Oh shit, it's hard to do it at any time, but we really had to hurry and deal with our own divisions."

Three groups had come together to provide the skills and materials needed by the Warriors. Most prominent were the young men who manned the roadblock. "I have lived here all my life," says 24-year-old Bobby. "I've gone to school and I have held a job here and there, wherever I can, but all I have is this land. I don't mind digging a ditch, driving a bulldozer, building a house, whatever I have to do, fixing a car or pumping gas, as long as this land remains Mohawk land."

The second group were men who defined themselves as "more practical"—Larry and his brother Loran Thompson. These men in their 40s see militancy as a means to keep the police at bay so the underground economy can run its course. Throughout June, July, and August, they worked on the logistics of patrol, obtaining radios and walkie-talkies.

The third element consisted of those who had a long-term commitment to the creation of a far-reaching political program aimed at re-establishing a Mohawk nation. As Maracle and Boots skillfully guided the Warriors through the standoff with police, Minnie Garrow, Diane Lazore, and Rowena General began to shape the group's ideological agenda.

"The men were focused on the police and protecting our community from outsiders. These are very real problems that require enormous concentration; but we also have to see beyond this role," says Garrow. "The Warriors had to begin to think about how we relate to other Mohawks. In June and then [during] the occupation in July, the police were the most important issue until they pulled back and announced their decision to deal with us. That was a big moment and we weren't prepared—we didn't think that they would ever listen to us. How do we go from a group always fighting the police to a group that is willing to stand on our own?"

Politics is a natural calling for Garrow, whose father was a former war chief, and whose mother served prison time for resisting white authorities. During the Vietnam War, Garrow organized student marches in Syracuse, where she studied medical technology and met her husband, a Mohawk ironworker. "To see our fight in terms of gambling or the police is to be shortsighted," she continues. "We will always lose if we define ourselves according to white institutions and white rules."

When Brooks requested a meeting with the Warriors, Garrow and Lazore worked with Maracle and Boots to develop a negotiating strategy: the Warriors would patrol the territory and set up a central dispatcher. If the police wished to enter Akwesasne, troopers would contact the dispatcher to request permission, which would be granted for purposes of enforcing motor vehicle laws and traffic safety. For criminal investigations or other complaints, the police would be escorted by Warriors.

"We had to go to the police with a firm position," says Lazore, a 43-year-old woman who participated in the Raquette Point uprising and earned her living by occasional forays into the cigarette trade. "We had to show the police and our own people that the tribal council was not needed to protect the safety of Mohawks. We had to show the police that the Warriors protect the nation, that we protect our sovereignty and our land. After showing our force, we had to show our intelligence, and that meant a clearly defined, simply stated proposal telling the state police how to behave when they are on our land. The troopers are guests and they will get treated courteously if they show respect. If I come to your house, I knock on the door or call first. We want the same treatment.

"The people trusted us for protection. Now we had to win their trust for leadership, so they could look to us and think independently as a people who have their own identity."

While Garrow and Lazore refined the Warriors' political thinking, Rowena General concentrated on the legal proceedings against Kakwirakeron. "We were worried that no one would pay attention to the possibility of a widening offensive in federal court," explains the 36-year-old General. "The state police said they were willing to work with us, but we considered the FBI arrests, especially the kidnapping of Kakwirakeron, a brutal attempt to divide and weaken us.

"We had not gone through FBI SWAT teams, bail hearings, and the kind of assault that went down at the traffic circle before. Someone had to follow the court proceedings, keep track of the dates, the information that was needed for a defense, the issues, the media. I took that job because it was my daughter who got clubbed.

"After Kakwirakeron's arrest and when the bail hearings were starting, we had to contact lawyers for ourselves, or just know which courthouse to go to and why Kakwirakeron was in Syracuse or why other cases went to the local courts."

Garrow, Lazore, and General refused to be intimidated by the cops or Warrior machismo. "The men just wanted to go out there and kick ass," General says. "Down the road, the state police were ready to kill us and we were in here shouting like kids, getting mad and insulting each other. The men would talk about their guns and Minnie would yell back, 'What will that do when everyone is dead?' The women knew that we had to have guns, but we also knew that there had to be some brains, some real hard thought. And the men—" General smiles "—they got the message."

For three days after the referendum, the Warriors and the state police pushed and pulled over the negotiating table. "The Warriors knew that Albany or Washington would always send somebody to protect the government and enforce the laws," says Downs. "And by talking to them, we got to see that this wasn't personal. They were willing to establish and continue a dialogue if there was a degree of respect maintained.

"We got to see them as individuals, and there was a chance to have a real insight into their belief. It's rooted in their view of history. They believe that the Mohawks were given this land by God or the creator of the universe. You don't have to agree, but you have to see that the Warriors believe this. There was a way to work with this position, and I think that they saw that we were willing to work with them. Both sides knew that we wouldn't be best friends or allies, but it's possible to live side by side, do our jobs and not hurt each other."

According to Maracle and Boots, Brooks and the brass were reluctant to commit to seeking Warrior approval every time a trooper entered Mohawk territory: but the major said Troop B officers would contact the group if police were called for a criminal investigation. He also offered a guarantee that troopers would not stray from Route 37 during routine traffic patrols and a pledge to have supervisors meet with Warriors should they have a complaint about police conduct.

"For the first time," says Garrow, "the police saw that we were not being aggressive, only honest in our desire to protect our land. We made them understand that."

7

A HOT HAND AT THE
LUCKY KNIGHT

A week after the referendum, when the state police and the Warriors had established an uneasy but functioning truce, key members of Gov. Mario Cuomo's staff approached pro-gaming Chief L. David Jacobs to discuss gambling and taxation. "It was the stick-and-carrot approach," says Jacobs. "The governor said he'd help us get legalized casinos if we helped him stop the smuggling and considered some taxation of the tobacco and gas sales."

In 1988, state tax officials and the Seneca elected council agreed to allow the tribe to impose their own tax. New York Tax Commissioner James Wetzler said the new levy would provide the Seneca with millions of dollars in extra funds. But more than 6,000 Seneca strongly objected, forcing the elected Seneca chiefs to cancel the agreement.

"The Seneca showed the governor and he didn't learn," says Jacobs. "We gave up the land. In exchange, the government waived its right to tax us. It's very simple and plain. The governor should know better."

Instead of backing off, Cuomo dashed off a letter to the St. Regis Mohawk Tribal Council in which he presented himself as familiar with aboriginal struggles and referred to his role as the state's top negotiator at Moss Lake in the 1970s. First, he plunged into the question of political authority, reviewing the federal laws and constitutional issues on the basis of which Congress granted New York State criminal jurisdiction over Mohawk land. Provoking the Warriors and backing Jacobs, Cuomo firmly stated his support for the tribal council and the process of electing chiefs. Only within this framework, he wrote, could the state, the federal government, and the Mohawk people reach an agreement in the "sensitive areas" of gambling and taxation. With regard to casinos, Cuomo said his office was "obligated" to approve them once Mohawks met the requirements of state and federal law.

But the second part of the letter—"on the long-standing issue of tax-free sales of cigarettes and motor-fuel by Indian vendors to non-Indians"—sent a different message. With an Indian-imposed tax boosting the sale price, Cuomo reasoned, fewer people would travel to the reservation to buy cheap gas and cigarettes. "This would effectively stop widespread bootlegging," Cuomo wrote.

Anti-gaming Head Chief Harold Tarbell tried to discredit Jacobs as the leader who was willing to bring the taxman onto the territory in exchange for casinos. "The governor wanted to get his taxing powers in our community and he was using Dave Jacobs as his messenger," says Tarbell.

It was an effective attack, and Jacobs had no choice but to distance himself from the governor. "There was no way I could support any proposal about taxes," he says. "This is a long-standing position recognized by everyone. We gave up the land and the government cannot tax us."

Many of the Warriors involved in the cigarette trade saw Cuomo's comments as a direct attack. "There's no question that he wants to come after us," says Francis Boots. "Government officials will use any excuse to cut in on our business." The Warriors also feared that any state tax would be followed by a federal levy. "If we open the door to taxes of any kind, then we are saying welcome to taxes from the government of New York or the officials in Washington. The state always seems to be the first one to get here and try to push its will down our throats. Then comes the federal government, which is bigger, more resourceful, and probably a little bit more crafty."

With Cuomo's letter refueling the rivalry between elected Chiefs Tarbell and Jacobs, the Warriors denounced any deal that might bring taxes to Akwesasne; then they opted for a low profile, figuring that they gained the most when Tarbell and Jacobs weakened the tribal council. The Warrior leadership questioned the casino owners about an agreement that would exchange Cuomo's support for gambling with the tribal council's support for taxes. "I told the tribal council and the Warriors and anybody else that taxes and gambling are two separate issues," says Eli Tarbell, whose Bear's Den truck stop sells gas at prices far lower than stations off the territory. "And I think the other casino owners and businessmen agreed completely. We can't win sovereignty by allowing casinos and then working out a tax deal with the state."

Adds Tony Laughing, "I don't see how taxes had to come into this. You can't trade our rights away. I told Dave Jacobs the same thing."

In his bid for credibility, traditionalist Jake Swamp called for a meeting with the Grand Council of Chiefs, which represents the Six Nations of the Iroquois Confederacy. Saying Cuomo's attempts to tax the Mohawks posed a threat to their communities, Swamp claimed that the governor's effort to link gambling to taxation was the result of Warriors and casino owners being eager to strike any deal that would legalize gaming.

"I wanted to go to the Grand Council to get a clear statement telling our people that the Warriors were dangerous and doing everything they could to undermine our traditional authority," says Swamp. As the Grand Council session began, Swamp and his allies from Akwesasne, Tom Porter and Ron LaFrance, were taken by surprise when three Mohawk women seized the floor. Led by John Boots's wife, Harriet, the women produced a sheaf of documents and receipts allegedly showing that Swamp joined with Canadian council Grand Chief Mike Mitchell in the November 1986 confiscation of $88,000 worth of cigarettes. Other documents confirmed that Swamp joined a 1987 meeting of Mohawks and high-ranking state tax officials interested in imposing levies throughout Akwesasne. When the Confederacy's chair, Leon Shenandoah, tried to rule the Mohawk women out of order, a contingent of Mohawk men stood behind Harriet Boots, arms folded in a show of defiance as she continued her verbal barrage.

"Everything broke down," says Minnie Garrow, one of the Akwesasne Warriors Society leaders who crafted the strategy. "And that's what we wanted. We were not going to let Jake Swamp and others go in front of the Confederacy chiefs and discredit us." By the time Swamp returned to Akwesasne on the evening of August 26, news of the confrontation had flashed across the territory. Calling up members of the anti-gaming faction the next day, Swamp spread word of an 8:00 p.m. meeting on the Quebec side of Akwesasne, where the Canadian council has offices. More than 300 people gathered to hear speeches about the need to shut down the casinos and run the Warriors Society off the territory.

"The speeches stirred things up, and about 75 people got in their cars," says Doug George, the editor of *Indian Time,* the territory's anti-gaming newspaper. "You couldn't shut the casinos until you disbanded the Warriors. So these people—and the number might have grown to more than 150—started chanting 'Disband, disband!' right in front of the Warriors' headquarters. The Warriors came out and the arguments led to fistfights. Mark Maracle was dragged across the Onkwe Bingo Jack parking lot by his long hair. The crowd was kicking him and punching him.

"People tried to separate the factions. I think people realized that beating up the Warriors wasn't going to solve anything, that the real issue was gambling. The crowd asked the Warriors if they would join a move to shut down Tony's.

"Not surprisingly, the Warriors refused and everybody piled into their trucks and cars. When folks got to Tony's, there were close to 300. Some of the security guards showed their rifles—no shit, they had rifles—and people realized this was serious. At one point, someone pulled up in a bulldozer and threatened to ram the casino, but he was talked out of it because the guards said they would shoot.

"Some people pounded the gamblers' cars and threw rocks at the buses. Others gave the word to disperse and go up the road to where the Lucky Knight casino was being built. The crowd burst into the building and scattered throughout the construction site, destroying everything they could see. This was a full-scale riot. People just watched it burn."

The Hogansburg Volunteer Fire Department showed up within minutes, but the anti-gaming mob blocked the road until the flames had totally engulfed the building.

Less than half an hour after the fire at the Lucky Knight, the state police blocked the roads leading to Akwesasne. "We had no choice," recalls state police spokesman Sgt. Michael Downs. "The situation had exploded into a riot. This was intolerable. The state police could not sit back and inadvertently get caught in the crossfire of what was becoming a civil war. This was no longer a political debate or a raucous argument over gambling. The anti-gambling faction went on a rampage. The arson jeopardized the safety of people who don't live on the reservation, but drive through. That's why we put up the barricades again. We were willing to let Mohawks settle their affairs, but others didn't have to be at risk."

As firemen doused the casino's burning joists and plywood siding, police investigators took statements from owner Veronica Adams and one of the men she employs as a security guard. "I cooperated with the police and gave them an extensive list of names of people I saw smashing chairs and tables," says Adams. "The members of that crowd brought the broken wood into a big pile, then poured gas on it, lighting the fire and watching it spread."

According to the police, investigators could not get direct eyewitness statements that incriminated specific individuals in setting the blaze. The cops told Adams they were unable to make an arrest because they needed a witness or a member of the anti-gaming faction to explain how the fire was set and by whom. "We needed someone on the inside," says Downs, "but no one would help us. The same people who wanted to come in and shut down the casinos were now stonewalling us to protect their hides."

While the Warriors were not under any suspicion, cops feared that the group might launch a counterattack against the anti-gaming faction. "We wanted to keep the two groups apart and we really didn't want the Warriors to feel that they were being punished or accused of participating in the arson," continues Downs. "So we had to let them know we clearly suspected the anti-gaming faction."

Notes Warrior leader Mark Maracle, "We got a couple of phone calls, and the police tried to calm us down. You know, the not-to-worry speech, that the barricades are there for public safety." While the police presence annoyed the Warriors, most saved their outrage for the anti-gamblers who had tried to attack the Onkwe Bingo Jack.

"We knew that the antis wanted to kick our ass," says Minnie Garrow, "but we couldn't do anything about it. If we went after the antis right away, then we felt we would be letting the government succeed at their long-term plan of having Mohawks fight Mohawks."

The Warriors realized they could enjoy a political advantage by taking the moral high road and refusing to inflict physical harm on other Mohawks. They also recognized that this could enhance their standing with the state police. "First, we are not going to be like the antis and shed our people's blood," says Diane Lazore. "Second, we could show the police our determination without showing our force or resorting to violence."

By daybreak, Garrow and Lazore had drafted a statement and convinced the men that issuing it to the press would serve as a warning to both the troopers and the anti-gaming faction. A few hours later, the Warrior leadership had called the state police and a handful of local reporters to read them the text. "The Mohawk Nation at Akwesasne is preparing for the third time in less than three months for an armed invasion. The New York State Police have set up roadblocks at the entrances to Mohawk territory, again denying non-Indians access to the territory," the statement began, in a brief but clear signal that the Warriors would resist any additional movement by the troopers.

Then the Warriors used the statement to trumpet their intention to hold anti-gaming leaders accountable for the attack on the Onkwe Bingo Jack and the Lucky Knight. Though the Warriors did not have any direct evidence pointing to particular suspects, they released a list of prominent anti-gamblers who they say were spotted at the scene. A few days later, both the anti-gaming *Indian Time* and pro-gaming *People's Voice* published the list, which claimed that Mike Mitchell, his brother Richard, traditionalists Jake Swamp, Tom Porter, Richard Cook, Jr., and Irene Thompson were part of the crowd that came to the Bingo Jack. As the anti-gamblers gathered in front of the entrance and chanted slogans, the Warriors also spotted off-duty St. Regis Akwesasne Mohawk Police officers Louis Mitchell, Ernie King, Tyler Sunday, and Peter Francis. When the Warriors confronted the crowd, fistfights broke out. The anti-gambling faction demanded that the Warriors disband, prompting a tense standoff. Eventually, the antis moved up the road.

According to the Warriors, the crowd tried to enter Tony's Vegas International but were discouraged by armed security guards. Then the Warriors saw a group of anti-gamblers converge on the yet-to-open Lucky Knight casino. Within minutes, fire engulfed the newly constructed building. The Warriors claimed that Barbara Barnes, director of the Native American Travelling College; Roger Thomas, a leader of the anti-gaming group; Louis Mitchell, St. Regis constable; Joanne Jackson, sister of traditional Subchief Tom Porter; Lorena David, daughter of traditional Chief Ross David; and Richard Mitchell, brother of Mike Mitchell, were spotted at the scene of the blaze.

Several pictures taken by photographers for both newspapers show many of the people on the list, watching the fire.

When police contacted several of these people, they claimed to have no knowledge of the arson. "It was one of those things that just happened," says a police investigator. "One group of people saw a lot and another group saw nothing at all."

Unable to pursue the leads, the troopers withdrew their barricades within two days. The reservation and its casinos opened for the Labor Day weekend, less than a week after the arson and only three weeks after the referendum. Despite the widespread publicity concerning violence and intense political strife, buses brought thousands of patrons from Montreal, Ottawa, Syracuse, and Plattsburgh. "We weren't going to be intimidated," says Tony Laughing. "The antis have to know that people want to come to Akwesasne and bet or play bingo. No matter what the antis do, people will keep coming here."

The Labor Day success frustrated many antis, who believed that Laughing and other casino owners relied on the Warriors to supply weapons and security guards. "When the Warriors started talking to the police and making deals, it became clear that they were interested in political power and protecting the casinos," says Jake Swamp. "From the troopers they were getting what they wanted. The police recognized them as a legitimate group, but we wouldn't. We knew they were trying to oust us and take over."

On Sunday morning, September 2, more than 50 antis gathered on the territory's Quebec side. Armed with baseball bats, a couple of shotguns and rifles, they drove into Hogansburg and followed Route 37 to Rooseveltown Road, where they split into two formations—one group mounted a roadblock of trucks and cars near the Twin Bridges. Less than a mile down Rooseveltown Road, Jake Swamp and Brian Cole pulled into the parking lot of the Onkwe Bingo Jack with an estimated 30 antis.

"I got a phone call and heard they were coming," says Minnie Garrow, who was home across the road from the Onkwe Bingo Jack. "They just started racing down the road," says her husband, Alec Garrow. "You know Minnie—she's always excited. She bolted right out of here and went right after them. So I stood right behind her in case anybody wanted to start a fight.

"We got to the parking lot and I saw the antis just getting out of their truck. Harriet Boots was there too, and we figured we three had to slow this down and get help. So Minnie starts yelling at them—you know how she can yell—and Harriet and I go inside and start making a barricade against the door. Then Harriet starts calling people up, telling them about the anti roadblock and to come through the woods."

Outside, Minnie Garrow stepped up to the crowd's self-appointed leader, Brian David Cole, a former teacher who worked for the New York tribal council, which had been arranged by anti-gaming Head

Chief Harold Tarbell. Gripping an aluminum baseball bat in his right hand, Cole squared off with Garrow. "I walked right up to him," she explains, "and said, 'Who the fuck are you to do this? Big man, huh? I'm not afraid of you and your bats. Go ahead, hit me.' He didn't believe it. His face turned red and he started to yell and say, 'Fuck you, fuck you.' Then he looked at his watch and said, 'You and the Warriors got 10 minutes to disband.'

"I just laughed and told him to fuck himself. I could see other people on both sides starting to arrive. I figured if there was going to be a fight, there was going to be one hell of a fight. But I really didn't want that to happen. Even if we beat the shit out of them, they would have a victory if there was violence.

"So I kept razzing him, but I told him that only a sissy and a coward would fight his own or hit another man's wife. I started asking the other antis there, 'Why are you fighting against your own people? No one wants to get hurt. Why are you believing everything Jake Swamp or Harold Tarbell or Mike Mitchell is telling you?' I told them the Warriors didn't want to let the casinos run the reservation. We wanted the government and police out of our lives.

"Some of them heard me and you could see that they were thinking about it for a few seconds. But every time that seemed to happen, Brian Cole would look at his watch and say, 'You got eight minutes to disband.' And that got the crowd riled up."

As Minnie Garrow eyeballed the antis, several Warriors appeared from the woods. "The women went outside, while the men worked on a defense inside," says Diane Swamp—who joined her husband, Herman, in supporting the Warriors against his brother Jake. "We knew that the men would immediately get in a fight, so we wanted to draw a line. If the anti-gamblers didn't attack, there wouldn't be a riot. It was in their hands. Brian Cole kept getting impatient and yelling. At one point, Minnie said to him, 'All right, if you think you're such a big man, hit us right now. Hit the women. We aren't scared of you.'"

Continues Garrow, "He kept counting everything down and then 10 minutes passed. He yelled, 'Time's up!' So I said, 'Now what, asshole?' He was really getting frustrated. So he steps past me, right up to the glass door and he takes his bat and starts pounding the glass door and it shatters. Inside there were a couple of men, but the women signaled to them to back off. We figured let Brian embarrass himself. He was acting like a four-year-old child."

"We were ready to beat anybody's head in," says Alec Garrow, "but we weren't going to start it. You could tell Brian Cole was confused and angry. Minnie was getting the better of him. She was humiliating him. He was not man enough to walk away and say, 'I don't fight with a woman.' Not man enough to say, 'I don't fight my own.' So he just knocked the glass out of the door."

"Brian pointed to the door and said, 'See what I did to that door?'" Minnie Garrow continues. "But he let the bat hang in one hand, and that's when I made a grab for it and spun it real quick. He was real surprised. I held it up right in his face and said, 'You fuckin' asshole. Get the hell out of here.' And then I threw the bat off to the side.

"For a moment, I thought it would be over. Then I realized that I just embarrassed the living shit out of him. He was really red and really angry. And that's when I could see that across the road there were a couple of guys with guns. I said to myself, Oh shit, they are really going to kill us."

Without his bat, Cole led a handful of anti-gamblers to his truck. He got in and drove around to the double metal door on the side of the Onkwe Bingo Jack. "He gunned the motor and yelled that he was going to ram the building and then the crowd was going to kick the shit out of us," says Minnie Garrow. "If the antis came in here, that really would have been trouble because I knew the Warrior men would have gone crazy and people would have really been hurt.

"It had to be stopped. So I stood right in front of the double doors as he rolled his truck. I told him, 'You'll have to kill me first. You're not getting in here unless you run over a woman.' I could see Jake Swamp and Doug George and a whole bunch of other people doing nothing, just waiting to see if we would go crazy and give them a reason to call the police or to see if Brian was cold enough to kill.

"I wasn't going to move and Brian stopped and got out of the truck. Some of the Warrior men inside opened the door and some of the antis picked up stones and threw them inside. One of Doug's brothers, Dean, ran inside and got knocked down. A Warrior grabbed an ashtray and threw it at him, hitting him right in the middle of the forehead. Pow! You could see the blood all over his face. Another anti poked in his head. Tommy Square ran right up with a bat and swung, deliberately missing, but hitting the metal real loud. That's when the antis realized we would kick every one of their asses. They knew it and they ran away."

8

A NEW PLAYER COMES
TO THE TABLE

Stanley Cohen drove 400 miles north from his New Rochelle apartment to the Bombay Township country home of his law partner, Lynne Stewart, and her husband, Ralph Poynter. As part of a Labor Day weekend of long walks through nearby fields and forests, Cohen and his friend Anne Erpino thought to spend part of Saturday in Canada. "I got up that morning and it was beautiful," recalls the 38-year-old Cohen. "Sunny, clear, and hot. So I asked Anne if she wanted to go to Canada. And she said sure. Lynne and Ralph gave me directions— follow Route 95 north to the intersection of 37, turn left, go through the reservation and the bridge to Canada is just outside of Mohawk territory. We started toward Route 37, figuring we'd find breakfast in Canada. After a few miles, we ran right into a state police barricade.

"We tried a couple of other ways to get past the police line. It didn't work. We kept hitting a checkpoint. At one point, we made a series of turns, and I can't remember how we did it, but we got onto Frogtown Road, which winds its way right to Route 37. At that point, Anne and I had decided to look for a place to eat and see what we could find out."

Shortly before noon, they pulled into a packed Bear's Den, where news of the Bingo Jack showdown between Minnie Gartow and Brian Cole dominated the conversation. "At first, I thought the people with guns were ready to face the police," Cohen recounts, "and they thought I was a tourist who wanted to gamble. I asked if they were afraid that the cops might arrest them for weapons charges or threatening an officer, and they looked at me like I didn't know what I was talking about. Someone explained that the businesses had to be protected from other Mohawks. For a few minutes, I was stunned. This was one of the most unusual situations I had ever seen. I just wanted to know more. So we kept asking questions."

During the next two hours, several old-timers sitting in the back of the Bear's Den gave Cohen the broad outlines of the dispute that had rocked the territory since June. Presenting himself as a New York City lawyer, Cohen asked the men if they could arrange for him to meet the Warriors. The men made a couple of phone calls and shepherded Cohen into an old brown Chevy sedan, driving east toward the unmarked border with Quebec. In the village of St. Regis, Cohen was taken to a small motorboat that powered up the St. Regis River to the St. Lawrence and west to the opening of the Raquette River.

The boat hugged the southern bank of the Raquette. At a craggy configuration of gray boulders forming a cliff of approximately 100 feet, the engine stopped. "There was something like a path in the rocks," says Cohen, "but it just went up and up. We were taking it very, very slowly. At the top, we followed the boatman's instructions to walk through a thin line of trees and we would see the blue siding of the building.

"Right behind the building—that's when I first heard the crowd. Then one or two pointed to something that was off to my left. I saw five or six men, a couple with rifles and a couple with baseball bats. This big guy with shoulder-length black hair steps out of the building and starts to run right at me. He grabs me and that's how I get into the Warriors' base."

"I saved his goddamned life," says Mark Maracle, chuckling. "He had no idea what he was coming to. And that's why we wanted him. We figured that an outsider could help us tell the world about the conditions up here."

Maracle led Cohen to the office area, where the Warrior leadership had gathered. After placing a number of phone calls as a security check, the Mohawks immediately learned that Cohen had been instrumental in devising a legal strategy for Larry Davis, the Bronx hood who singlehandedly held off a platoon of New York City cops and won acquittal on many of the major felony counts.

"At first, they wanted me to get their message out," explains Cohen, "but then they heard about Larry Davis and they wondered if

I had the credentials to help the Mohawks the way I helped Larry. So they started to ask me questions about everything—legal tactics, political tactics, the cops, friends in Brooklyn, where I went to school, what I did, what other cases I'd handled.

"I explained to the Warriors that I was a Bronx legal aid lawyer who joined with Lynne Stewart and Bill Kunstler to work on the Davis case. And through them I decided to leave legal aid and join Lynne in private practice. Then the Warriors told me a little bit about themselves and their feeling that they were about to embark on a long, difficult struggle with other Mohawks, who would seek the aid of the police. They said they were thinking about hiring a lawyer and wondered if I would be interested. I told them, sure, and I gave them my phone number in the city, saying I would come back and we could discuss details.

"The whole scene was kind of surreal. I started the day on vacation and ended up in the middle of a civil war. In the early evening, the Warriors took us through the woods to a waiting car and drove us back to the Bear's Den. It was a mixture of a dream and a nightmare."

Though the Warriors considered hiring a lawyer to be an important long-range goal, the fight with other Mohawks required immediate attention. Knowing their adversaries could draw on the Akwesasne constabulary recognized by the Ontario Provincial Police and the dozens of troopers dispatched by the New York State Police, the Warriors needed to solidify their patrols. First, they needed enough manpower to ensure 24-hour patrols and staffing of the communications base at the Onkwe Bingo Jack; second, the patrols had to have cars, radios, gas, and access to weapons in case of attacks; third, the Warriors needed money to pay for the patrols, telephone, office expenses, travel, food, and ammunition if needed.

"Manpower was not a real problem," says Francis Boots. "The Mohawk people wanted their own patrols and they came to us, offering their own cars and citizens' band radios.

"When the antis surrounded us on Labor Day and threatened to run down Minnie Garrow, we had to make a choice—either respond like a military group or like a political group. If we attacked the antis, then all we would have was a rumble. Our goal was not to seize power of the existing system. Our goal was to change the existing system and let the people decide on new leaders. We could not get sucked into fighting the antis on their terms. We had to continue shaping the agenda, which was and still is political, not military."

The Labor Day attack marked the re-emergence of Kakwirakeron, who had been released on bail providing he did not enter Akwesasne. He remained at his Bombay home and worked the phone to counter pressure brought by elected tribal chiefs. "Kakwirakeron knows he is the best at dealing with the police and the authorities," says Lazore. "Our biggest worry was that the antis would provoke us into a big fight and then call the police, who would come and occupy our land. We told Kakwirakeron that his biggest contribution was to handle the police and establish a clear line of communication with the major, the lieutenant—whoever he knew."

"A lot of the anti-gaming faction got angry because they saw us making Kakwirakeron into a newspaper Mohawk, who stood there with long braids and big shoulders," says Garrow. "I think the antis saw his skills and they were jealous. They wanted to be in the papers, in the magazines, but it didn't work that way."

As the Warriors concentrated on their political goals, the territory's flirtation with violence continued: on September 4, a group of anti-gaming Mohawks destroyed Warrior Dennis LaFrance's car; and on September 9, gunmen attempted to cut off power to the casinos by shooting out the transformers at the Niagara Mohawk Power Corporation electrical substation in Hogansburg. To minimize the possibility of retaliation, the Warriors met with the casino owners to get assurances that their security guards would not be provoked into a fight that would give police the opportunity to come again.

"The Warriors only asked for restraint and common sense," says Tony Laughing. "The Warriors did not want one of my guys getting into a dumb fight. I understood that. I think we all did."

At the meeting, the Warriors urged the casino owners to consider the political agenda. "We won a major victory by getting the state police to stop coming in here every time we have a fight about gambling," said Warrior John Boots. "By not coming in, the police have admitted that we have the power to determine our economy, our government."

The casino owners were convinced and instructed their security guards to ignore the anti-gaming harassment, which started to fade when it failed to ignite a reaction. For most of September, gambling continued without incident. Then a trooper spotted Tony Laughing and his girlfriend, Brenda Jock, driving the back road from Akwesasne to Fort Covington. As Laughing veered off Mohawk territory, the trooper was given the order to enforce the outstanding federal arrest warrant from the July 20 raid. Within minutes, state police cars streaked along the winding roads that wrapped around the sleepy village.

"It was like the movies," says state police spokesman Sgt. Michael Downs. "Tony floored it—and I mean floored it. We had troopers going up to 100 miles an hour on roads that were barely wide enough for a slow-moving tractor."

The chase wound through the towns of Bombay and Brasher Falls, along cornfields and cow pastures. Eventually, the cops blocked Laughing's car and he tried to escape through a cornfield. "It was a simple tackle," says Downs. "We subdued Tony and cuffed him, then notified the feds. They told us to drive him to Syracuse, and we did."

"Tony's arrest showed us that we might not be safe as soon as we step off our land," says Francis Boots. "It was time to seriously talk to a lawyer."

The possibility of retaining a lawyer underscored the group's precarious financial condition. Besides paying for the patrols and supplies, the Warriors also faced hefty legal bills arising out of Kakwirakeron's arrest. "There were lots of obligations and very little money," says Diane Lazore. "But we had to face a simple fact: if we are serious about putting forth a political program, then we have to have an economic arm."

Though some of the Warriors considered reversing their policy and asking casino owners to subsidize the patrols, the leadership quickly dismissed that idea. "We don't want that kind of alliance," says Lazore. "That would only taint our position and give credit to the people who say we are the hired thugs of gamblers." Across the territory and in other Mohawk communities, particularly Kahnawake outside Montreal, significant amounts of cash were available through the network of buttleggers. "But that brought up the same problem as taking money from the casino owners," says Lazore. "If we took from the gamblers or the smugglers, then we could easily be identified as paid guards for these interests. It was a big question that we had to resolve because we couldn't keep up this kind of sustained political fight without a small but steady amount of cash."

"At first, we just thought of the equipment and the gas, the telephone bill, the electric bill at the Onkwe Bingo Jack, and things like that," Minnie Garrow says. "Then we started thinking about our goals and what it would take. To make political changes meant we had to have money for people to travel to Albany or even Washington, Quebec City, and Ottawa. To stand up for our own members also meant money for lawyers. Kakwirakeron's defense was going to cost at least $60,000." Because the charges against him involved blocking the FBI from searching Tony's Vegas International, the Warriors sent a delegation to Tony Laughing's house and requested money. "His girlfriend answered the door, but Tony wouldn't come down," says Garrow. "We didn't get anything." (Unbeknownst to the Warriors at that time, Laughing considered buying out one of the bingo halls and giving Kakwirakeron's relatives an ownership share. The take would subsidize his defense. The plan did not materialize.)

Though unable to solve their financial problem, the Warriors moved ahead with their plan to retain a lawyer. They were introduced to Owen Young, a practitioner from Brantford, Ontario, who came recommended by militant Mohawks at the Six Nations Reserve. A softspoken, deliberate man, Young told a gathering in Akwesasne that he was familiar with sovereignty issues as they relate to Canada. "If you got the land, you sit on it, you defend it and you hold it," he told a gathering of Warriors, "because the courts will always figure out some way to take it from you. The whole point is to avoid going to court, and to settle these matters through the political, not the legal, process."

Young offered to help the Warriors with problems on the Canadian side of the border and Cohen offered advice pertaining to New York State statutes or United States federal law. "At this point in time, the Warriors had two overriding concerns—keeping themselves afloat financially and continuing to press for political change. My job was to interpret what they would call the white man's law," Cohen recalls, "and explain how the state or federal government could or would respond to the Warriors' plans."

Cohen says that Warriors spoke with him about possible sources of financial support for patrols and other activities. With disarming irreverence, Cohen admits, "There were a number of possibilities, including a declaration of independence for something you could call the Sovereign Mohawk Nation at Akwesasne. Working as this entity, the Warriors could run their own bingo hall or a high-stakes raffle, maybe a lottery. We also talked about making a new approach to the cigarette traders, helping them deliver or sell their cartons or opening a smoke shop. Some of the leaders also asked about fundraising in the liberal circles of New York City.

"I agreed to look at all of these ideas and figure out what legal mechanisms—if any—were required to undertake these initiatives. But I also told the Warriors not to expect very much because they threatened a lot of people, and that meant no one was going to come to their aid. They had to strengthen their position by living with this political and economic isolation."

9

THE PEOPLE'S VOICE
PLAYS A HUNCH

Convinced that the Warriors were outlaws flush with money from ca-sino owners, the anti-gaming faction pressed state and federal officials for police action. In discussions with representatives of Gov. Mario Cuomo's office, the state Assembly and officials from the Canadian provincial and federal agencies, New York Head Chief Harold Tarbell and Canadian Grand Chief Mike Mitchell proposed that the Ontario-sanctioned Mohawk constabulary be given power to police the New York side of Akwesasne, "especially" Mitchell said, "if the New York State Police were not going to fulfill their duty."

To bolster the image of the Akwesasne police under his control, Mitchell contacted the Canadian ministries of Employment and Im-migration and Indian and Northern Affairs, seeking grants to provide additional training for the local constabulary. "The idea was to teach Mohawk constables to be policemen in our community or other parts of Canada or the United States," Mitchell explains.

While these moves attracted the interest of bureaucrats, they drew the scorn of the Warriors and many other residents. After all, Mohawk constables had helped the anti-gaming mobs storm Tony's Vegas In-ternational and burn the Lucky Knight casino.

The push for additional police training coincided with a Lake Placid meeting between pro-gaming chiefs L. David Jacobs, Lincoln White, three officials from the governor's office, a lawyer on the staff of state Attorney General Robert Abrams, and two officials from the state Racing and Wagering Board. "It was a 'let's get together and get to know each other' session," recalls Jacobs, "and Harold Tarbell is already out there with Mike Mitchell calling for more police. So all these folks from the state see that we are openly divided and fighting with each other."

Four days later, on Sunday morning, October 15, Mitchell and Tarbell supported simultaneous anti-gaming protests—one on the Canadian side of the bridge connecting Cornwall, Ontario, to Route 37 and the other at Raquette Point Road and Route 37, the western door to Akwesasne. At each location, more than 30 demonstrators stood for more than an hour and a half handing out leaflets urging gamblers "to stay away until such time as the residents of Akwesasne can resolve the gambling problems internally."

At 11:30, four carloads of Warriors drove to the corner of Raquette Point Road and Route 37, demanded that the demonstrators allow traffic to pass without interruption, and left. By noon, the crowd had swelled to more than 70 people, as some Mohawk Bingo Palace employees argued with anti-gaming protesters. A handful of Warriors returned and routed the cars and buses around the crowd, in effect neutralizing the demonstration.

"They were outfoxed," White says of the anti-gaming faction, "but they never, never quit. By mid-week, Tarbell and Mitchell arranged to go to Albany, where they continued to push for more cops."

But the police brass ignored their plea. After three and a half months of raids and barricades, roadblocks and riots, uneasy truces and fractured negotiations, the troopers had settled into a routine of surrounding Mohawk territory without becoming directly involved. "We had finally got to the point where we could maintain some level of trust with the Warriors," says Downs. "And that was very important. We were willing to deal with them on a day-to-day basis, one step at a time."

Mohawk factionalism presented the serious possibility of a cop becoming caught in the crossfire. "These were people looking to solve a political matter and they couldn't talk it out," adds Downs. "The fuses were so short. We were worried about a barroom brawl or a fight exploding over a woman. A distressed man, who had a few too many pops, could have easily grabbed a gun and gone on a rampage."

The police reticence angered Head Chief Harold Tarbell. "I wanted a cruiser in the parking lot of every casino," he says. "I wanted the police to ticket or arrest everybody who came here and tried to gamble. I wanted them to arrest everyone who worked in the casinos. You had the Warriors running around with guns, the gamblers and smugglers with pockets full of money. This is not the way to build a stable community."

Tarbell knew that state officials were politely handling his complaints without intending to offer any satisfaction. "I made a conscious decision to raise the stakes," Tarbell says, "to get more people involved and have them take a look." Tarbell began writing letters.

"It was a way for other people to come in and make a decision for us," says his pro-gaming rival, elected Chief L. David Jacobs, who deplored Tarbell's letters to the U.S. Bureau of Indian Affairs and congressional committees. "Harold would tell these people that our land was completely under the gun, that confusion and madness reigned. It wasn't true. Whenever Harold would paint this dire picture, I would be forced to give my view, which was very different. I didn't want the police here. I didn't want the Warriors roaming around. I wanted what was guaranteed us by law, plain and simple.

"The cops were willing to let us keep the casinos open while we negotiated with the state and federal governments. I was ready, Tony Laughing and the casino owners were ready, but Harold Tarbell, Mike Mitchell, and the anti-gaming faction saw that casinos would give us a new configuration of politics. They didn't want that change."

The political debate over an increased police presence exploded into a confrontation on the evening of October 30, just after dusk, when a dark brown Cadillac turned onto Route 37, heading for the circle that sent traffic to the international bridge. Driven by Kakwirakeron's son, Art Montour, Jr., or "Sugar," the dented 1978 sedan slowed at the toll booth. Montour told of his residence in Akwesasne and passed through without paying the two-dollar toll charged to non-Mohawks. He kept a steady speed, heading for the blue steel-and-glass booth housing Canadian Customs and Immigration officials. Canadian authorities say that he rolled right through this checkpoint, failing to stop and identify himself—a procedure that would usually allow any Mohawk to pass without hassle. Within 30 seconds, the Royal Canadian Mounted police gave chase.

"I slowed down and went through Customs, telling them I live in Akwesasne," says Montour, disputing the official Canadian account.

"The security guards knew that I had done nothing wrong, but they said I had to stop, pull over, and get out. I said forget it, and they called the RCMP."

Montour raced onto Cornwall Island, heading for the eastern edge. The RCMP radio dispatches alerted the St. Regis Mohawk Akwesasne Police and the Warriors, and each group sent members to check out the incident. As Montour led cars down the island's narrow roads, two more RCMP vehicles joined the pursuit; Akwesasne Police Chief Ernie King sent six of his officers in three cruisers.

The Cadillac veered toward the wood-frame, two-story home of Dwayne Jocko, one of Montour's friends and a Warrior supporter. As the cops narrowed the chase, the Warriors charged onto the island, where they tracked the RCMP and Akwesasne police cruisers to a stretch of road that swerves past Jocko's driveway. By the time the Warriors arrived, Montour had skidded into a ditch. The police had surrounded him, their weapons drawn.

According to the police, Jocko and other residents of the island ran past the officers and circled Montour's car in an effort to prevent them from making an arrest. The newly arrived Warriors aimed their headlights directly into the eyes of the officers, hindering their vision as Akwesasne police Chief Ernie King claimed jurisdiction and stepped forward to handle the discussions with Minnie Garrow.

"I saw cigarettes stuffed in the back seat of the car and it was clear to me that Art Montour, Jr., was trying to smuggle tobacco," says King.

"They really wanted to make this into a big deal," retorts Garrow. "Ernie King wanted his cops to pull away Sugar so the antis could say that the son of the great Warrior, Kakwirakeron, was involved in smuggling. We stood at the property line and said the police had to leave. We told the RCMP that this was a dispute within our community and nothing more. Well, they agreed to lay back and let this big Mohawk crime buster come forward. And that's what Ernie did, yelling and screaming that Sugar was running tobacco and that the Akwesasne police force would not tolerate this kind of activity."

King and other Akwesasne police officers say the Warriors carried bats, and a few threw stones. "We just wanted to do our job and let people go on their way," King says, "but the Warriors were trying to intimidate us. They were calling us names, threatening to fight, and saying we had no right to do this to another Mohawk."

For more than four hours, King insisted that the police had to seize the car and arrest Montour, while Garrow objected.

"Perhaps the crowd got a little bit loud," says Garrow. "But our position was clear. Ernie King wouldn't back down. So we had to figure out a way to end this or we would still be out there yapping. While this was going on, Sugar had walked away and we knew that goal was accomplished. Ernie kept insisting on getting the car and finding evidence that Sugar was smuggling. Hour after hour. It was endless. The RCMP got back into it, saying the car had to be turned over. So we finally gave them the car."

When the police searched the vehicle, they could not find any sign of contraband or tobacco smuggling.

Three days later, shots were fired into the parking lot of the Akwesasne police station at 4:45 a.m. When the two officers on duty stepped outside, they saw that two bullets had shattered the back windshield of their cruiser, while another two had gone through the trunk.

"It certainly looks like an attack in response to the chase of Art Montour, Jr.," says Ernie King, insisting that the Warriors were determined to seek vengeance. "That's how they think."

"That's absurd," shoots back Kakwirakeron. "We do not fire on our own, no matter what we think of their politics or their job. We do not perform drive-by shootings."

Around noon the next day, November 3, the Warriors overheard radio transmissions revealing that King and another Akwesasne police officer used one of the constabulary's cruisers to drive across the border, onto Route 37. Fearing that King and the officer were trying to start another confrontation at the Onkwe Bingo Jack, the Warriors dispatched a patrol to monitor the situation.

"We say that King started to chase him," says Garrow, "and Ernie says that we began the chase. One thing is clear. Ernie King and his marked cruisers do not have any jurisdiction on Route 37. But he took a police car there and said he was doing his job."

King says the Warriors maneuvered their white GMC Blazer to the rear of the cruiser, which he hit three times. The police pulled to the side of the road and let the Blazer pass. "We chased them to the Bear's Den parking lot," King says, "but they spun their Blazer around and then rammed right into us, head on, smashing the headlights and the hood, caving in the bumper. We pulled away, but they rammed us once more from behind. This time, the trailer hitch got caught and they started pulling us backward."

About 12 hours later, Akwesasne resident Eddie Mitchell stood at his post as a security guard for Canada Customs. His wife, Joanne, sat in the living room of their ranch-style house. Her back was turned when part of the glass shattered in the picture window. Akwesasne police officers found a three-inch hole.

"In my mind, it was a bullet," says Ernie King, though his police could not find a projectile. "Eddie Mitchell works where the Art Montour, Jr., incident began. The Warriors were looking for vengeance. That's how it always is."

"Look, there's no doubt that the cruiser got hit and rammed," says Francis Boots, "but if all this happened as an unprovoked attack, do you think Ernie King would have just taken it without firing a shot? I don't think so. How come he never arrested us for ramming a police cruiser? The answer's simple. It didn't happen the way Ernie says it did. He didn't want to arrest us.

"What about the bullet in Eddie Mitchell's house? Where is it? Ernie King says it was a shot coming in? Okay, then there should be a slug, right? But there isn't. You know why? If it was a shot, it was a shot going out." Boots went on to speculate it was all a provocation by the antis to start a fight so the state police or the RCMP could come in. "We weren't gonna let them do it. They wanted a military war, a police war. We wanted a political war."

Working on the November 10 edition of *The People's Voice*, editor, reporter, photographer, and publisher Cindy Terrance wondered if she could put together the whole story from the showdown over Art Montour, Jr., to the ramming of police cars, to the shot at Eddie Mitchell's house. "It seems to me that a lot of people are lying," Terrance says. "None of this made any sense whatsoever. Sugar Montour and dozens of Akwesasne residents go over the bridge day after day without incident. People know he's a Mohawk. People at the Customs building know to let him go by. There was nothing unusual about his crossing the bridge until somebody wanted to make it unusual.

"Why would someone want to give him a hard time? Who would benefit? What's the gain and to whom? That's the kind of questions I started to ask. The RCMP was more than willing to talk to me. They told me it wasn't a big deal, they couldn't find any evidence of smuggling. Ernie King knows how much smuggling there is around here. Everybody does. So, now he has to start cracking down by picking on the son of the Warriors' spokesman? Give me a break."

In the late 1960s, when they began protests at the international bridge, Mohawks understood the importance of having their own media outlets, so they put together *Akwesasne Notes*. Throughout the

1970s, the bi-monthly *Notes* carried news, essays, and poetry to Indians across the country. Its contents reflected a wide range of view-
points from the militant ideology of the American Indian Movement,
to the spiritual teachings of traditionalists, to the gung-ho optimism
of capitalists, the musings of socialists, and the findings of archaeolo-
gists. As the *Notes* grew, it could no longer cover the news of the local
community. By the early 1980s, the New York– and Canadian-
chartered councils decided to sponsor the creation of a weekly newspaper, *Indian Time*, and local radio station, CKON, now headquar-
tered in the Quebec portion of the territory.

"They were always looking for volunteers or people to help," Terrance says, "so I went over there and started to do anything I was allowed to do, which was to write for *Indian Time*. This was about four
and a half years ago, when the push for gambling really began. *Indian
Time* and the radio station were governed by a board of directors,
which was very much anti-gambling. Many people, especially on the
New York side, where the casinos were being built, started to get very
tired of this kind of slant. They tried to write letters. Some of the
businesses stopped selling the paper or even advertising in it. But
Mike and the Canadian council were subsidizing it. These guys
wanted to be the kind of Indians who spoke the word of the spirit.
They wanted to hold themselves up as the standards of Mohawk
purity and tradition. They said that casinos would violate the honor
of our ancestors and corrupt our land. The businessmen thought Mike
Mitchell was crazy. They thought that casinos had to do with money
and politics. To the businessmen, Mike and Doug George, the editor
of *Indian Time*, had become preachers.

"The casino owners and the business owners came together with
the idea of starting their own newspaper. I wanted to call it *The
People's Voice* because that's what I think a newspaper around here
should be. I was taught that newspapers should question everything
that's going on and that's what I wanted to do. So I started to work on
finding out what was going on.

"The casino owners were always honest with me. They told me
that they wanted to make money. They told me that they are willing
to work within the law if the police, the feds and everyone else recognize that whites don't have jurisdiction on Mohawk land. When
things got rough, they told me they would defy the law and keep slots.
If the courts wanted the state involved, then the owners said they
would work with the state. To them, this was a business.

"The two elected councils, however, were always trying to lie and keep things from me and the public. In early 1989, I found out about the mismanagement of New York tribal council money at Mohawk Construction Management Enterprises. I published articles that showed how various people had the power to stop the mismanagement but did nothing. When Tony's got trashed on June 6, we printed pictures of them storming the casino. In July, when the police arrested Kakwirakeron, I was there and I saw it happen. Clearly, the police started the violence. In August, when the Lucky Knight got torched, my paper openly printed the names of influential people who led the crowd. Again, I had the pictures. In September, when the Warriors were attacked, I was there, watching people who claimed to be law abiding and peaceful engage in violence.

"So I wasn't going to believe Ernie King about the chase of Sugar Montour. The Warriors are rough and tough, but they do everything to avoid attacking their own. Many of them are smart enough to stay out of trouble until absolutely necessary. The Warriors had reached an understanding with the New York State Police. This so-called group of outlaws showed themselves to be smarter than the people who had the title of grand chief or head chief.

"But I didn't have enough information to run a big story about how Ernie King was being used to stir up trouble and set the stage for another police invasion, this time from Canada. I suspected it and I asked questions about it, but I couldn't make it for the November 10 issue, which didn't have anything controversial in it."

Two days after the newspaper came out, on Sunday evening, November 12, Terrance drove to the converted brick house that served as the office for her newspaper on one side and the pro-gaming Chamber of Commerce on the other. Sitting at her cluttered desk, she scanned the calendar for upcoming meetings and events to cover for the next issue. She typed up a few items, then left around 8:30 p.m. The next morning, she found bullet holes in the office windows.

"Around 9:30 a.m., Cindy Terrance called the barracks in Massena to report that an unoccupied building which houses her newspaper was damaged by overnight gunfire," recalls Sgt. Michael Downs. "When we got to the scene, we discovered that five windows were hit by nine rounds of .22 caliber rifle fire and an empty beer bottle. This was an apparent drive-by shooting."

Standing in front of her office, Terrance answered police questions and spoke to newspaper reporters from Massena, Fort Covington, and

Cornwall, Ontario. "I believed then and still do believe it was the work of the people against gambling," she says. "We're lucky that we weren't there. My assistant and I are sometimes there until three or four in the morning. This is complete stupidity.

"The police said they were going to investigate, but I know there aren't going to be any arrests. I'm not going to let it stop me from writing what I feel to be the truth. You don't mess with someone's life like this and expect them to back down."

At 9:55 a.m., on November 15, Ernie King and Mohawk constable Robert White were on a routine patrol on Borderline Road in St. Regis, Quebec, when they spotted the Chevy Blazer used to ram the cruiser a week earlier. Hitting the lights and siren, King tried to pull it over, but the Blazer didn't stop. King tried to pass on the left, but the Blazer swerved into the cruiser, striking its door. The Blazer raced toward the unmarked border with New York, where King does not have jurisdiction. King pulled to a halt, realizing that several carloads of Warriors were coming toward him. After a brief confrontation, the chief got back into the newly dented cruiser and returned to the Canadian side of Akwesasne.

"In less than two weeks, we were losing our cruisers," says Canadian council Grand Chief Mike Mitchell. "It was physically impossible for us to patrol. The Warriors were taking out our ability to do the job of policing the Canadian side of the reservation."

"We needed a quick, short-term solution," says Doug George, the editor of *Indian Time*, which had openly accused the Warriors of using violence to guarantee the existence of casinos.

Continues Mitchell, "We had won the right to patrol our own land and we knew the Ontario Provincial Police and the Mounties weren't much help when it came to the bridge and Cornwall Island. So I only had one other choice—the Sûreté du Québec, the Quebec provincial police. So I formally requested that they come in and help us."

The next morning, two green-and-white Sûreté du Québec cruisers rolled into the Akwesasne police station. Inside were six officers, assigned to help the constables for 10 days. The patrols were to be conducted in the SQ cars with SQ officers assisted by a local constable. A few hours into the first shift, SQ supervisors were invited to a meeting with the Warriors and Canadian council member David Benedict at the Bear's Den. After the Warriors offered their version of the disputes that led to violence, Benedict supported their argument that the presence of an outside police force could inflame the situation.

"Mike Mitchell and the Canadian council were not aware of this meeting," recalls Doug George. "I found out about it after it had begun because someone saw everybody at the Bear's Den and called the newspaper. It turns out that the Warriors were demanding that the SQ leave because there would be a bloodbath if they didn't. They strong-armed the police, and Benedict went along with it, saying he represented the council."

According to SQ spokesman Roger Mitchell (no relation to Mike Mitchell), the provincial police "re-evaluated" their decision to help the Akwesasne constables. By Thursday morning, November 17, less than 24 hours after they arrived, the Sûreté du Québec withdrew.

The SQ's decision embarrassed Mitchell. "It was lunacy, madness," says L. David Jacobs, a pro-gaming member of the New York–chartered council. "For months, we had been saying over and over again that this was a political problem to be decided among ourselves, and he calls in the Canadian equivalent of the cavalry."

With the support of Tarbell, George, traditional Chief Jake Swamp, and others, Mitchell scheduled a Friday morning press conference. He began by recounting the binge of violence that started on October 30, when Ernie King tried to arrest Art Montour, Jr. Then he spoke about his efforts to enlist help from the OPP, the RCMP and the SQ, all of which declined to send in their officers. "What I feel Canada has done," Mitchell said, "is to say, 'Akwesasne, you're on your own.'"

Explaining that violence could break out at any moment, Mitchell announced his decision to declare a state of emergency and to deputize 30 to 40 Mohawks. "You just don't deputize a posse nowadays—that is for the movies—but I have no choice. Our police force is down to half a car and can't provide for the security of our residents." Mitchell added, "Obviously, they are going to have to be looking at carrying firearms if they want to help the police." As for the posse's authority, Mitchell noted that his council followed Canadian law, which gives a Mohawk-appointed judge the power to swear in the new officers. Would an armed posse help quell the violence? Mitchell replied with a thinly veiled prediction. "I don't know. I hope so. It's one of those weekends," he said. "It's one of those days you can pretty well smell it in the air."

10

THE WARRIORS
WIN THE POT

While the Mohawk constables and the anti-gaming faction fought the
Warriors on the roads of Akwesasne, the U.S. federal government concentrated its attack on the courtroom, in rulings and decisions on the
activities of the casino owners and Kakwirakeron. "The courts were
coming out on matters that the anti-gamblers wanted to use to discredit our position on sovereignty," says Francis Boots. "We didn't
want to get into a debate about white law or courtroom procedures. A
judge's decision was a judge's decision, no more and no less. We didn't
recognize his authority over matters that took place on our land, but
we couldn't just write this process off. We had to be knowledgeable
because the whole point of the antis was to make us look like dumb
thugs."

Stanley Cohen interpreted the rulings handed down in preliminary
hearings. Federal judges rejected the sovereignty and human rights
challenges raised by Kakwirakeron's lawyer, Seth Shapiro; and, Cohen
explained, casino owners failed to persuade judges that Mohawk land
was the equivalent of its own nation within the borders of the United
States. The judges scheduled the gaming trials, dismissing defense
claims that Congress allowed Mohawks to ignore state law and unilat-
erally decide on the type of games and equipment to be allowed on
their territory.

"The Warriors were not really involved in any of the gambling cases," recalls Cohen. "One of the key tactical points was to distance themselves from the casino cases. But everybody knew that the gambling decisions were important."

"These rulings gave the anti-gaming side and people like David Jacobs some ammunition, because the judges clearly said that a sovereign Mohawk nation or territory does not exist," says John Boots. "The antis were happy because that meant trials for the people picked up in the raids of July 20. Dave Jacobs was happy because the judge said that to have legalized casinos we had to work with the state and federal governments. To the people who accept white law and its rule over our territory, this was a victory. To us, it wasn't a victory or a loss, but a continuation of what was going on."

In Kakwirakeron's case, defense lawyer Shapiro moved for dismissal by citing the 1975 Helsinki treaty, which called on all nations to respect the right of all people to work for self-determination. On signing the treaty, Shapiro argued, the United States had pledged not to interfere with the affairs of sovereign states. "I claimed that the Mohawks had been their own nation for thousands of years and continue to be their own nation. This makes the matter a human rights issue," explains Shapiro. "This should not be treated as a matter of law or legal procedure, but a conflict between two different peoples, two different nations. There is nothing criminal or antisocial in Kakwirakeron's behavior."

U.S. District Court Judge Neal McCurn called Shapiro's work "a lovely argument," but ruled that it did not have any weight in a criminal proceeding. He said a jury would have to decide whether Kakwirakeron's actions were the result of a legitimate political protest or the criminal intent to impede an FBI investigation.

"He didn't want to deal with the big issues," Shapiro said. "The judge wanted this to be a neat little trial."

A few days later, Assistant U.S. Attorney John Brunetti asked U.S. Magistrate Gustave DiBianco to revoke Tony Laughing's $300,000 bail because he had violated its terms by taking a short trip to Arizona and New Mexico.

"I said the defendant has clearly demonstrated that he poses a risk of flight," Brunetti recalls. "Here was proof that Tony would take off and skip the trial."

Referring to Laughing's continued operation of the slots despite state police arrest in the raids of July 20, and his refusal to turn himself in, Brunetti adds, "This is the man who does not recognize the jurisdiction of our court and our system of law. He would much rather drag the police on a dangerous, high-speed chase than face the court and make the concession that our law applies to him as a Mohawk. In fact, he claims that our law does not apply to him. If bail is continued, I told the magistrate, then Tony will not have any incentive to show up when a jury is impaneled to hear his case."

In and out of the courthouse corridors, Laughing and his lawyer, Michael Varonese, explained the trip as an emergency due to the ill health of his ex-wife, Eloise, who was recovering from alcohol abuse. "It was something that had to be done," says Laughing. "Anybody who knows me and my business knows I was coming back." The emergency nature of the trip, Varonese says, prevented him from making the appropriate motion to the court. "I didn't have time to file the proper papers," Varonese says. "It was never the intent to flee or violate the conditions of his release."

But Brunetti scoffs at this explanation, citing Eloise Laughing's claim that Tony broke into her house in Arizona, forced her into a pickup truck, and drove for 12 hours. In Gallup, New Mexico, a police officer stopped the truck for a traffic violation, giving Eloise a chance to jump out and complain. Tony sped off, returning to Phoenix, where he abandoned the truck in a parking lot.

"What was Tony going to do next?" asks Brunetti. "Bring his casino into the courtroom and argue that Mohawk sovereignty allows him to run a crap game in the federal courthouse?"

The magistrate, however, doubted Eloise Laughing's account and allowed Tony to remain free on bail. "They tried to make it out like I was kidnapping my ex-wife," Laughing says, "but the police never filed any kidnapping charges. I also understood that this was a close call. I really had to start thinking about my case. Our hope was to beat it before the trials, but of course that didn't happen."

Throughout November and December, federal judges had scheduled trials for Mohawks facing gambling charges. On November 16, after several days of argument and testimony, a jury convicted Roderick Cooke, a partner in the Nighthawk Arcade, for possessing a slot machine on federally recognized Indian territory. A few days later, James Burns was convicted after the jury deliberated less than two hours. By the end of the month, Billy Sears had beaten the rap by successfully disguising his ownership of the slot machines. But the manager of his bingo hall was convicted due to undisputed evidence that he had worked with slots.

"We had to come up with a real good legal strategy," says Eli Tarbell, owner of the Bear's Den, who also faced charges related to slot machines. "We wanted a judge to rule on the law and whether we had the right to have slots and casinos as we see fit. So we started thinking about something we could do together. Something to show the government our intent of getting a firm ruling and settle this. And one of the lawyers came up with an idea of a plea bargain.

"Tony and I would accept a single charge, and the prosecution would drop all the others. Then we had the right to appeal and challenge the law. Our position was that the Indian gaming act gave us the right to have slots and any other form of gambling if it is approved by our community. The whole point was to establish our control over our economy and our land. Let the courts finally rule on that."

On November 27, Tarbell appeared in court and entered his guilty plea. The judge released him pending appeal.

"I got the message," says Laughing. "Everyone knows I run a casino. So let the lawyers deal with the courts, while I stick to my own business. I was planning to do the same thing as Eli. It makes sense."

The legal challenge to gambling and the skirmishes between anti- and pro-gaming factions were creeping across the border. In Kahnawake, just south of Montreal, and Kanesatake, near the pristine town of Oka, Quebec, political splits developed as Canadian Mohawks in favor of bingo games took on elected councils who supported the federal government's strict anti-gaming policies. In late September, six days after the Mohawks of Kanesatake opened a bingo hall offering $1,000 prizes, the Sûreté du Québec launched a raid that included a search of several Mohawk homes. "Our community was divided over bingo and gambling, very much like Akwesasne," says Kanesatake resident Ellen Gabriel. "But the police raid gave the issue a totally different dimension. It's one thing to have division within your own people—we will always have differences like this. It's another thing to be invaded."

At Kahnawake, the opening of a bingo hall also attracted increased police scrutiny as well as heated debate among Mohawks. The tobacco trade and its profitable links to Akwesasne were an open secret in the community, and several prominent Canadian Mohawks questioned the wisdom of a bingo hall if it would prompt a police raid.

"That was the real question," says Joe Deom, a Kahnawake Mohawk who owns an engineering business. "We had kept the police off our land and established a detente, if you want to call it that. If we went forward with bingo, some people felt the situation would be threatened. Others felt it was our land and our right to open whatever business we please."

But the Kahnawake Warriors promised to protect the bingo operation from the police. "It wasn't an issue of gambling," explains Kahnawake Warriors leader Allan Delaronde. "It's the issue of our land, and our people controlling it." At one point, the dispute over gambling in Kahnawake resulted in the firing of gunshots between anti- and pro-gaming Mohawks.

As the problems in Canada intensified, Mohawks from Kahnawake and Kanesatake approached the Akwesasne Warriors for advice and help. "We were more experienced with these kinds of questions," says Francis Boots. "At this point, they were just calling us and asking what could be done. There were legal and political questions both within and without the Mohawk community.

"We consider them part of our nation. An attack or raid at Kahnawake is the same as an attack at Akwesasne. It's one people, one land. We did not want to come on strong and overpower people who asked us for help, but we told them that they should consider legal advice and seek a political resolution, which is what we were doing."

As the Akwesasne Warriors shifted their energies from confronting the police to focusing on political questions, Mark Maracle's combative stance was becoming less relevant to Akwesasne. The patrols effectively ran themselves: the men had divided their shifts and labor, pairing up into teams that drove the territory, manned the base, and operated the radio console. "Mark likes trouble, and when a situation cools down, it is time to quietly slide away," says Minnie Garrow. "Since he was not born and raised here, he knew we could be criticized or discredited for calling on an outsider.

"We were starting to have a positive reputation within the whole Mohawk people, not just the territory known as Akwesasne. We were becoming a political force that could take hold on both sides of the border. We were starting to get support from Kahnawake and Kanesatake. That's why Mark could leave. It wasn't a military situation anymore.

"The threat was political and legal. We were afraid that the antis or the elected chiefs would trick us into something that would give the police an excuse to come in. That's why Stanley was important. He knew the law and he knew what the police could and couldn't do. And he knew what we could do without provoking them. We gave him the job of keeping us out of police trouble and monitoring our strategy. He was a pair of fresh eyes, someone who didn't have to get involved in the personalities. He was a good lawyer who knew how to deal with the white system. He was perfect."

The harassment, bickering, and petty fighting among Warriors and the anti-gaming faction resulted in repeated phone calls between Akwesasne and Cohen's Greenwich Village office. "They were fighting a war for political survival," Cohen says of the Warriors, "and I was practicing law. The work was building up and so was the tension. I had to make a choice between Akwesasne and fighting in the courtroom. I didn't know what to do."

Cohen's decision became easier on December 12. Around 1:20 p.m., near a frozen field that abuts Route 37, a tan Chevette driven by an anti-gambler passed the maroon Bronco used as one of the Warriors patrol cars. From behind, the Bronco was boxed in by a Ford pickup, driven by Canadian Grand Chief Mike Mitchell's nephew, Mark Mitchell. He accelerated, forcing the Warriors either to be hit or to rear-end the Chevette. According to the Warriors, Mark Mitchell rammed the Bronco and sped away.

Mitchell drove to the home of Francis Boots, insisting that the Warriors pay for the damage to his Ford pickup. "I told him I didn't know anything about this," Boots says. "He comes to me five minutes after it happens. What do I know?"

"That's bullshit," shoots back Mark Mitchell. "The Warriors in the maroon Bronco were following me, and I stopped to find out why. When I got out and started going over, they hit my back bumper, then hooked the front bumper, almost pulling it off. I followed them for a bit, then went to my house, thought about it, and figured I'd go over to Francis Boots and tell him to pay up."

"Mitchell was trying to provoke me," continues Boots. "He's yelling that he's gonna smash all of the Warriors' cars if I don't pay. I didn't say a thing, but I called the base."

Around 2:30, a group of antis drove into the parking lot of the Warriors' headquarters with bats in their hands and guns showing through the open doors of their trucks. They threatened to smash the Warriors' cars if they did not pay for the damage caused by the Bronco. Minnie Garrow stepped out of the bingo hall and confronted the men, surrounded by three women supporters of the Warriors, and *People's Voice* reporter Cindy Terrance. "They yelled and screamed at me, and I yelled and screamed back," Garrow says. "I wasn't afraid. No way. What the hell were they gonna do? I said it right to their faces. 'You're chicken. You ain't shit and you couldn't fight the men so you pick on the women. You're wimps. Fuck you.'"

Anti-gambler David Leaf threatened to hit Garrow, while Mark Mitchell's brother Francis, a member of the Akwesasne constabulary, squared off with Warrior Buster Cook, who had come to Garrow's assistance. "It was a minor fight," says Garrow, "some pushing and shoving before the antis got into their trucks and drove away. I knew they wouldn't do anything."

Ten minutes later, as the anti-gaming convoy rolled east on Route 37, another Warrior vehicle locked its brakes on the icy road behind a black Ford pickup driven by a third Mitchell brother, Brian. The Warrior's truck skidded, nicking the rear of Mitchell's truck, sliding into oncoming traffic, and striking a Chevy Camaro driven by Mary Curlyhead, who was traveling with her 11-month-old son, Charlie.

"My car was totally demolished, but we weren't hurt," says Curlyhead. "I saw the Dodge touch the back of the black truck and then come across the yellow line right into my car. You could see that the Dodge just kind of hit the ice and lost control. That was it."

Tommy Square and another Warrior stepped out of the Dodge and saw the group of anti-gamblers pull to a halt. Within two minutes, they claim, the anti-gamblers had converged on the Dodge, wielding bats and smashing the windshield. "Our men ran," says Garrow, "which was the right thing, because we told all our men on patrol to avoid any kind of fight with the antis."

The anti-gamblers saw that the Dodge cab was littered with beer cans and more than 70 rounds for a high-caliber assault rifle. By 3:00, the state police had notified Warriors' headquarters of their intention to investigate. When Garrow called Cohen that afternoon, the lawyer immediately recognized the potential for danger.

"First, you had the possibility of a hit-and-run accident that involved a mother and her child," Cohen recalls. "Miraculously, no one got hurt, but the police have evidence in plain view of drinking and driving and possession of dangerous weapons. The troopers decided to work with the Warriors as long as traffic hazards did not threaten what cops call public safety. To me, this accident clearly looked like it could become a direct threat to public safety. I told Minnie to prepare for an invasion."

Cohen called the state police at Massena and told them that he planned to arrive within the next 24 hours. He asked them not to question any Warriors until he could be present. The troopers agreed.

"The police were calm and assured me there was no urgency," says Cohen. "When I arrived, I spoke with supervisors, and I was told that the troopers had a policy of refusing to intervene in any dispute that could be traced to the gaming controversy. It was a practice started by Major Brooks, who was not going to get his troopers hurt over this. He had had enough of the service and retired in mid-December.

"So they promoted one of his captains, a man named Robert Leu, to be the next major. A few days after the accident, Leu came to Akwesasne and introduced himself to the tribal council. He told the elected chiefs that the Warriors Society should be considered as the policing authority. Those were the words he used, 'policing authority,' to describe the Warriors.

"Of course the anti-gamblers went ape-shit. But the Warriors were ecstatic. Leu told the tribal council that the police could and would work with the Warriors under certain conditions. It was kind of ironic, if not moronic, that other Mohawks couldn't accept that simple proposition."

"The state has walked away from its responsibilities," insists anti-gambling Head Chief Harold Tarbell. "The Warriors have intimidated the police. It's that simple. Their show of force, their tough talk, their thugs—all of that combined has told Albany that this is not a place for peaceful resolution of conflict.

"I'm frustrated. I personally oppose gambling, but I would support it if we arranged a peaceful and legal way of getting a Mohawk government charged with overseeing it. The Warriors, the casino owners, the newspapers think that I am on a crusade against the casinos. Wrong. Very wrong. I want to establish a democracy, a government where we don't need the welfare state and the grant payments of bureaucrats.

"Since the late 1960s, we've had an awakening. You could say the Warriors were part of it, but they went backward to outdated traditions. I went to college and saw how we were always cutting in and out of time and place. One moment, we live in the sixteenth century—hunting and trapping and trading—the next we're stuck in Department of Housing and Development grants, the bowels of the twentieth century.

"I think there is a way to heal these divisions. We have to move toward the development of our own laws, our own institutions. The old ones don't work any more. The Warriors don't want a modern democracy. They want an old-time confederation or association. They want clans. I want our own institutions that go beyond the message of might is right."

Tarbell began to lobby congressional staff members who could influence their legislative bosses to exert pressure. In particular, Tarbell points to the U.S. Senate Select Committee on Indian Affairs, chaired by Sen. Daniel Inouye of Hawaii, an influential lawmaker who came to national prominence for his role in investigating the Watergate and Iran-Contra scandals. After Major Leu suggested that the Warriors be recognized as the "policing authority," Tarbell sent Inouye material highlighting the summer raid by federal authorities and the autumn convictions in federal courts. In his letter to Alan Parker, the committee's top staff member, Tarbell sought congressional action to overcome Albany's passivity.

"I needed action," says Tarbell, "just to show the people of the reservation, and the people opposed to gambling, that this fight was far from over."

Tarbell's moves received unwavering support from his Canadian counterpart, Mike Mitchell, who enlisted the help of the Canadian council's staff. Working out of the Canadian-government subsidized Native American Travelling College, Barbara Barnes coordinated communications between various government agencies on both sides of the border. "We felt that our backs were up against the wall, that the people who worked hard and long and honorably were crowded out by Warriors with guns and Mohawks with dice and blackjack games," says Barnes. "We did not survive white oppression to end up with guns and crap games. We wanted help. We wanted responsible leaders to see that there were and are responsible people in Akwesasne. We appealed to them to recognize us before it was too late, before a real explosion occurred and people were killed."

THE GREAT HUNT FOR THE GREAT LAW

PART II

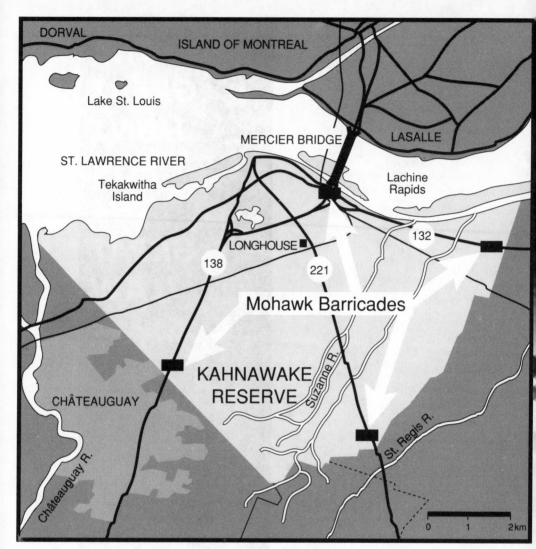

KAHNAWAKE

11

MOOSE ON THE LOOSE

At 12:15 on the frigid afternoon of January 13, Gerald Clinton Mc-Donald stood near the entrance of Tony's Vegas International casino, his back to the glass doors. Mumbling and staggering, McDonald angrily mixed phrases and slogans, curses and dares. Sometimes he referred to himself as Iokenkwaroni, a Mohawk name that designated his membership in the Wolf Clan and his adherence to the traditional religion. Throughout the gaming dispute, he had written letters to *Indian Time* attacking the integrity of the casino owners and Warriors. "We published them because they were articulate and well thought out," says *Indian Time* editor Doug George. "His views were consistent with the paper's stance and an important way of showing the anti-gambling sentiment in the community."

At Tony's, McDonald did not attract a lot of attention, in spite of a blood-stained bandage around his head. He merely looked as if he was in the final stage of an overnight drunk. When he turned toward the door, people first saw the pump-action .12 gauge shotgun. Under his plaid shirt were crisscrossed two rows of shells. "You want to gamble?" he yelled, bracing the wooden stock against his upper body and blasting a shot that shattered the glass door. "Well, you'll have to gamble with me."

At first, the casino's Mohawk security guards thought it was all liquor and bravado. Rumor had it that McDonald had been drinking through the night and morning, and had ended up fighting with a former casino security guard named Gene Hall. "Someone said he was coming here to look for Gene, because Gene kicked his ass and cut open his head," says security guard Muzz McDonald (no relation to Gerald McDonald). "Anyway, we were gonna tell him Gene hadn't worked here for six months."

The security guards, however, never got the chance. Gerald McDonald stepped into the casino, walked up the aisle to the cashiers' windows, and opened fire. The shattered glass showered the petrified workers.

Amid the panic and screaming, McDonald slammed in another two cartridges and headed toward the blackjack room. He hoisted the gun and pumped twice. Two television screens took the shells and burst, jagged edges of glass, metal, and plastic flying with buckshot. He grabbed another two shells and took out another television set and a video-display terminal. A large chunk of glass cut Tony Laughing's girlfriend, Brenda Jock, in the back of the head.

"Where the fuck is Tony?" yelled McDonald. "Somebody's gonna die today. I don't care if I die. Someone's gonna die with me."

Reloading his shotgun, McDonald continued down the blackjack tables as casino security guards and employees led patrons to safety crawling underneath tables. "He saw a couple of people and kicked a guy from Montreal in the head," says security guard Warren Connors. "But I think he really wanted to plug Tony."

Laughing easily escaped by walking outside. "I heard the shots and figured the guy was nuts or drunk. If he was looking for Gene Hall, he was in the wrong place," says Laughing. "If he was looking for me, he never got close."

As McDonald fired an oval pattern of buckshot into the Coke machine, terrified employees ran into the break room and barricaded the door with an air conditioner and an ice machine. A few seconds later, two blasts came through the door; some of the buckshot grazed 22-year-old Scott Loran above the eye. After roaming the casino and firing another round, McDonald broke down and requested to speak with the traditional chiefs and Harold Tarbell.

"It was a potential disaster," says Tarbell. "When I arrived, men who were loyal to the traditional council, not the Warriors, were in control. As I moved toward Gerry, I saw Jake Swamp and Julius Cook standing about 15 feet away from him, talking to him. A couple of his cousins were there. I figured that if he let us get close enough to touch him, we could calm him down, take possession of the gun and lead him out of the building. And that's what we did.

"We led Gerry out, and two things started to happen. First, my rival on the tribal council, L. David Jacobs, insisted that he would go to the police to press charges, which was a smoke screen to further his pro-gaming political agenda. And second, within minutes, they were gambling again."

As the casino and its employees restored order, Tarbell and other anti-gamblers drove McDonald to the hospital, where the cut to his head was treated.

"We could point out to the police that damage was done to property, not bodily injury to people. After all, if Gerry wanted to shoot at someone and kill them, he could have aimed at dozens who were at point-blank range. We wanted to make sure the police knew that Gerry was no longer armed, and he certainly wasn't dangerous. Thankfully, the police understood and were grateful that we would be bringing him in."

"He was a model of decorum," says Sgt. Michael Downs. "He did not show any signs of emotional disturbance or anger. He quietly did what he was told. When asked about the incident, he referred all questions to his lawyer. That's his right and we, of course, respected it." Informed that he was being charged with third-degree assault, reckless endangerment, and criminal mischief, McDonald nodded and told the police that he understood the accusations.

"We were happy that bail was set and Gerry walked out that night," says Tarbell, "but to be frank, we were also worried that a hot-headed Warrior or one of the casino security guards would track him down and shoot him. Gerry isn't a killer or a thug. He's hurt and confused. For a few moments, he lost touch."

"The shooting at Tony's was a warning. It was a sign of deep, deep disturbance in our community," says Warrior strategist Diane Lazore. "The antis were going to come after us. They saw that we were able to hold the line against the police, maybe even win a little respect from white authorities. The antis couldn't have that because it would threaten their way of running things around here."

"We have proved our point that the people support us and the so-called tribal governments are a farce," adds Minnie Garrow. "But that makes it worse because the anti-gamblers now feel that they have nothing left to lose. They have to do something dramatic, bold."

The first step took place on the territory's roads, where the St.

Regis Akwesasne Mohawk Police began to pull over Warrior patrol vehicles, allegedly investigating traffic violations but actually scouting for weapons. At 2:30 a.m., on February 2, 1990, Mohawk constables Steve Lazore and Robbie White spotted the Chevy Blazer that had rammed their police car a few months earlier. Alter a short chase, the Blazer stopped. Lazore, a 12-year veteran of the Mohawk force, got out of the cruiser and explained that the Blazer's rear bumper obstructed the taillight. Believing the incident to be a provocation, the three Warriors, Dewey Lazore, Raymond Lazore (neither related to the constable), and Alwyn Cook offered no resistance, and constables searched the Blazer for guns. They found an AK–47, a .44 caliber Magnum, and a semi-automatic pistol in the car.

"We figured, Let them take us to jail," says Dewey Lazore. "Let them brag about how they disarmed three dangerous Warriors. But it's clear what we had to do: keep cool."

Front-page coverage of the incident in the *Indian Time* gave Mike Mitchell and Harold Tarbell an opportunity to insist that the Warriors were running a heavily armed paramilitary group. Mitchell took a sheaf of newspaper clippings to Canadian bureaucrats and presented himself as the only Mohawk leader who could stand up to the lawless, violent Warriors. In meetings with provincial and federal officials, the Canadian grand chief asked for additional grants of more than $20 million to build a health center and recreation facilities and to establish a Mohawk system of justice that would include local police, courts, and even jails.

"It was a daring and bold concept," says Tom Siddon, the Canadian minister of Indian and Northern Affairs. "Mike Mitchell kept coming up to us with ideas to improve the social and political infrastructure before gambling spread and the Warriors had completely taken control."

On the American side, Tarbell won an invitation to an Oakland, California, conference entitled "Framing a National Indian Agenda for the 1990s." Organized by the staff of the U.S. Senate Select Committee on Indian Affairs, the two-day conference included a lengthy working session with the committee chairman, U.S. Sen. Daniel Inouye, who had called on the federal government to abolish the Bureau of Indian Affairs and channel grants directly to native American communities.

Tarbell's move angered Jacobs, who felt the anti-gaming head chief would distort the situation at Akwesasne. In a counter-move, Jacobs and Tony Laughing presented themselves at the conference, demanding to be seated. "Who the hell is Harold Tarbell to say he speaks for the whole community?" Jacobs says, scowling. "We wanted Harold to talk about how Tony is a thug so we could then show the whole world how Harold Tarbell distorts the truth. Tony is a successful businessman who is working under very trying circumstances. I wanted a chance to explain that."

But the two pro-gaming Mohawks were barred. "He made a fool of himself and he tried to embarrass all of us," Tarbell says of Jacobs. "I was trying to help our community, and this man comes along with a convicted felon. What am I supposed to do? Just accept it? They are a disgrace to our own people."

Jacobs insists that the conference organizers did not bar him, but told him that Tarbell would not let the issue rest if pro-gaming Mohawks were allowed in. "We did not want to disrupt the meeting," Jacobs says. "We just wanted to make the point that Harold Tarbell does not represent a large portion of our community. We clearly succeeded and I was satisfied. So was Tony."

In Akwesasne, editor Doug George trumpeted Jacobs's "eviction" on the front page of the February 16 edition. The increasingly strident tone of *Indian Time*, George says, reflected his deliberate attempt to pressure the pro-gaming faction and the Warriors. "This was the time to exploit our advantage," George says. "I have always been in the forefront of our struggle here in Akwesasne, especially against the casinos.

"But it would be a mistake to say the violence comes from us. I see myself as an activist and an intellectual. Someone who is guiding the movement of our people—that's what I have been doing with *Indian Time* and *Akwesasne Notes*."

George claims his role as an anti-gaming political strategist does not affect his newspaper's coverage. "We are part of the real voice of Akwesasne," he insists, "not hired mercenaries who hold themselves up as heirs to our proud traditions.

"The point is the Warriors are cowards. They hide behind guns and intimidation. They think that other Mohawks will just roll over and not fight back. We are fighting back now, and we will always fight back. I don't see a peaceful solution, even though I support the elected chiefs who are working for one. I don't think the Warriors want to negotiate and disband, which is the only solution.

"The Warriors have to disband because they have corrupted our politics. But the troopers recognized this group and compromised the entire system of elected chiefs. I know that system is flawed and in need of a lot of reform, but it's gone. I don't see the Warriors' giving up their AK–47s without a fight. People don't give up power. You have to take it away from them."

While George's newspaper kept the attack public, Mitchell quietly negotiated a new band council budget package that could dramatically alter the infrastructure of Akwesasne. He won support for a health-care facility, a sports arena, three small recreational facilities, and a criminal justice center. The price tag to the Canadian government was $30 million over five years—almost double his existing funding base. By February, the deal was finalized. "Akwesasne residents do not have the facilities they should have," Mitchell remarked in a front-page story of *Indian Time*. "With the implementation of our priority projects, we will be able to provide new and/or expanded programs to our residents, which will definitely improve the conditions in Akwesasne."

In the early morning hours of March 1, a number of teenagers congregated in the house owned by Richard Thomas, who was not at home. As they played loud music, wandered in and out of the snow-covered yard, danced, made out, and screamed, the crowd's boisterous activities prompted complaints from a number of nearby residents who phoned the constabulary. Several times a cruiser drove by without stopping.

"It was a party," says police chief Ernie King. "We all know that young people can get a little crazy."

By 3:30 a.m., King says, police received complaints of 50 to 60 shots fired from the house. Mohawk cops Louis Mitchell and Peter Francis rushed to the scene, where Mitchell spotted two assault rifles in the back seat of a car belonging to one of the youths.

"I reached in and grabbed them," Mitchell says. "The barrels were still hot."

Mitchell took the weapons and two extra ammunition clips to the Akwesasne police station, where they were identified as an AKS semi-automatic .223 rifle, the bayonet attached, and a .223 Mini–14 assault rifle, the collapsible shoulder stock and night scope in place.

"We knew they were fired right before we got there," says King, "but we didn't know by who." Despite this disclaimer and the fact that the police did not find any discharged shells, the March 2 edition of *Indian Time* reported without attribution that the weapons belonged to several young Warriors, who attended the party and fired the rounds. No arrests were made.

That night, Mitchell's wife, Doreen, and his two daughters were asleep in their River Road home when shotgun blasts thundered through the neighborhood. Doreen went outside, the police say, and discovered several spent shotgun shells on the road. Neighbor David George, Jr., brother of Doug George, came to help.

"They hit the back of the car," David George says. "Right above the license plate, in the middle of the trunk. I think there were three that hit the house. One came in right under the window where one of the girls was sleeping."

Within a minute of that shooting, the police say, shots from a high-powered rifle pierced the Akwesasne station house in St. Regis. One bullet lodged in the wall less than 10 feet from Mitchell, who was on duty and had yet to hear of the gunfire at his home. King blamed the Warriors: "It was clear that this was retribution for taking their guns. They don't care about family and children. They care about their guns. If you take them away, they'll come back and get you. Well, we were not going to be intimidated at all."

Two days later, before dawn, the Mohawk police say a red pickup truck pulled up to the station and stopped; men opened fire with automatic weapons. One bullet entered the building and the cops returned the fire, squeezing off more than 80 rounds before the truck drove away. The cops claimed they missed their target.

On the morning of March 6, Mike Mitchell called a press conference. Pointing to the AK-47s, night scopes, bullets, and pistols displayed on the table, Mitchell gestured for the cameras, then posed with an assault rifle in front of his satin parka while he explained that the guns were seized from Warriors by the Mohawk constabulary.

"The police are trying to serve their community and provide law and order. They're issued .38 caliber weapons, but we might as well give them BB guns compared to the artillery they have to go up against," he said.

"Being a border community, we have always had factions and feuds but we've always been able to sit down and talk out our differences. This is the first time in Mohawk history, to my memory, where it hasn't stopped escalating. Our elders didn't teach us that this is the way. The Great Law of the Iroquois Confederacy is based on unity and non-violence. I didn't become a leader to pick up a gun and kill. Many Mohawks are fed up and want this very volatile situation resolved peacefully before someone gets killed. We're still at the stage where we can take one step backward."

To reach a peaceful settlement, Mitchell insisted, the Warriors had to surrender their weapons. Then he played a tape, purportedly of a Warrior radio transmission. "Mike is trying to get us to lay down our arms," said one voice.

"We'll lay down our arms if he cuts his head off," replied another voice on the tape.

"This is nonsense," Mitchell cut in, stopping the tape to challenge the Warriors. "If you're going to kill someone, then kill me."

A reporter pressed Mitchell to outline his next step. With a wave of his hand, Mitchell unveiled a threat to use Mohawk-manned blockades and roadblocks to keep gamblers out of Akwesasne and the Warriors off their patrols. "The ironworkers would stay home. The children would stay home and non-Indians would be prevented from entering the reservation," the grand chief said. "A reserve-wide shutdown until safety, law and order can be restored."

12

A CHIEF LOOKS
FOR GAME

Although prepared for a campaign of arrests and petty harassment, the Warriors were taken completely by surprise by Mike Mitchell's threat to blockade Akwesasne. "At first, we couldn't believe this," says Francis Boots. "It was deliberately creating a fight that did not have to be fought. I told other Warriors that Mike was only talking. They said, 'No, Francis, don't be stupid. We have to get ready.'

"They were right. First, we had to show that we were not involved in any of the shootings. That was something we were ready for. Second, we had to have the force to get people, food and other supplies in and out. Third, we had to establish communication with the outside world, especially if we were to be surrounded and blockaded. And fourth, perhaps most important, we had to make sure that our people understood our position, what we were doing and why."

Throughout that first week in March, the Warriors met around the clock, gathering information, forming plans of action, and assessing their financial position. Boots pulled the leadership together; but Kakwirakeron, one of the Warriors' biggest public relations assets, and his lawyer, Seth Shapiro, were tied up in final preparations for their trial. "This was an important political event," continues Boots. "Of course we wanted him to be cleared, but that was not how we were going to measure success. We had to use the trial to shape the politics of our situation.

111

"He had to fight to stay out of jail and we had to support him. I think that's one of the reasons that the antis moved at this time. They knew that we could not rely on him for his advice and help, especially in dealing with the news media. He was too busy to deal with reporters and be the effective spokesman he is."

According to Boots, Mitchell's press conference triggered an explosion of media attention. "The antis gave the news media great pictures of guns. We saw it on our own TV sets and it looked like we were the terrorists and the antis were the peace-loving, reasonable folks. We knew we had to answer this, but we didn't know who to use as our spokesman.

"We thought about Minnie, Diane or myself; but that would leave us with no time to take care of the other jobs that we were doing. At one point, the phone rang and my older brother, John, answered and he was doing fine, talking to the reporter. We listened and watched him. I think it was Minnie who suggested that he take this job."

"There are always going to be these allegations brought against us," John Boots begins in a deep, gravelly voice that carries traces of anger and resentment, warning and foreboding. "But where is the proof or evidence to support them? There is none. We've stated over and over again that we will not let political differences spur us toward violence. That is how the antis work, not the Warriors.

"At the party on March 1, Ernie King and the police admit that they never heard the shots fired. Where are the spent shells to prove that 50 or 60 bullets went flying into the air? We doubt that they exist. Instead, the police ask the people of our nation to believe that some kids shoot off the guns and then are dumb enough to openly stash them in the back seat. This doesn't make sense. Where are the arrests and the suspects? There had to be witnesses, but we never hear about them because there can't be real witnesses to a made-up shooting.

"They created this shooting to fit the political purpose of making the Warriors look like thugs. The police say Louie Mitchell's house was shot up because we didn't like him taking our weapons. It sounds good and can read well in the newspaper, but it's not true. He didn't take our weapons because we didn't shoot any weapons on March 1. He didn't embarrass us or anyone else on the night of the parry. So we had no reason to shoot at him or his house during the morning of March 2.

"At Louie Mitchell's home, they found several spent shotgun shells and some damage to the family car or the side of the house. Same thing at the police station. How come nothing gets hit and nobody gets hurt even though people are supposed to be firing these dangerous automatic weapons?

"Our answers to these questions are simple: it didn't happen that way. The police are looking for ways to discredit us so the band council can get money from the Canadian government, so the tribal council can regain its credibility in Washington."

As John Boots worked to spin public opinion back toward the Warriors, he received some unexpected help from Tarbell, who prevented *People's Voice* reporter Cindy Terrance from videotaping the regular public meeting of the tribal council. "When the meeting started, I began to record and I had been taping for about an hour and a half," explains Terrance. "And all of a sudden one man got up, pointed to me and said, 'Stop recording.' Harold Tarbell noticed him and recognized him, giving him the floor. This man said that I was making this tape so the Warriors could have it. He was afraid the Warriors would look at the tape, see who supports the council, and then harass them.

"I told the man I don't give my tapes to the Warriors or anybody else. I also reminded him of a motion that allowed the Mohawk press to record the meeting. The crowd and Harold Tarbell just grew louder and demanded that I stop taping, and I was afraid, so I did. Then someone yelled, 'What about the tape she has in there? What are we going to do with it?' The crowd came back chanting, 'Destroy it. Destroy it.' The tribal council secretary, Carol Herne, demanded that I go into her office with the camcorder. I was scared shitless, so I did.

"Tarbell comes into the office and demands that I give him the tape. I do and he steps out in front of the crowd, which is now yelling, 'Break it, break it.' He flipped open the door of the cassette and grabbed the tape and ripped it, which made the crowd cheer and yell. They even started banging the walls of the building. A few moments later, Tarbell returned to his seat and told the crowd to cool down."

After Terrance described the incident in the March edition of *The People's Voice* and filed a formal complaint of assault with the state police, Tarbell declined to comment, but he did tell reporters about a plan to suspend or expel his rival, L. David Jacobs, from the tribal council: Tarbell intended to ask state and federal authorities to conduct a criminal investigation to determine whether bribes had been paid to Jacobs by casino owners. Though he didn't cite any hard evidence, Tarbell said, "If he is under investigation, he should be suspended until the cloud of suspicion is removed."

Tarbell prevailed on Alan Parker, staff director for the U.S. Senate Select Committee on Indian Affairs, to persuade the chairman, U.S. Sen. Daniel Inouye, to write a letter urging the U.S. Bureau of Indian Affairs to launch a corruption probe into Jacobs's continuing support of illegal gambling.

Jacobs denounced the move as "ludicrous and transparent" and promised to cooperate with any investigator. "I have nothing to hide," he says. "I represent my constituents out in the open. They may disagree with me on some issues, but I do not hide from them. Harold didn't understand that he was showing the weakness of his own position. And that weakness started to spill over onto others in the antigaming faction, especially Mike Mitchell, who kept pushing his threat to blockade the territory. Everybody understood that the blockade was the real threat, not Harold's move to get pencil-pushers from Washington looking for tall tales about a chief getting paid off."

The bickering on the tribal council gave John Boots and the Warriors their first break in countering the aggressive campaign to discredit them. While Mitchell and the Akwesasne police worked hard to provide evidence that disgraced the Warriors, Tarbell's political ineptitude quickly diverted public attention from the shootings at Louis Mitchell's and the police station. "By March 10, everybody was talking about Harold taking Cindy Terrance's tape or the pissing match between him and Dave Jacobs," says Boots. "They were tripping all over each other. We had to stick to our work.

"The antis wanted to isolate us and we had to prevent that. So we started to reach out to Mohawks in other communities. We wanted to show our people that by attacking us, the antis were attacking the entire Mohawk nation. Mike Mitchell and Harold Tarbell thought they could beat us by going to the white governments of Canada and America. Well, we knew we could beat the antis by going to our brothers and sisters in other territories."

They immediately won a pledge of support from the Kahnawake Warriors Society, whose members had invested in, worked for, and defended a newly constructed $3.3 million super bingo hall, the largest in Canada and the fourth largest on the continent. Many of the Kahnawake Warriors admit that proceeds from the illicit trade in tobacco, fuel, or building supplies formed the bulk of the initial cash investment that built the hall, which sits on a 15-acre tract and employs more than 100 people.

"That's what our business is all about," says Earl Cross, the manager of Kahnawake Super Bingo. "We side with the Warriors in Akwesasne. We draw strength from them and their abilities to keep the police off their land, and keep away from the co-opted politics of the elected chiefs. The Akwesasne Warriors are our family. They have our help."

According to Diane Lazore, the Warriors in Akwesasne struck a deal with their counterparts in Kahnawake. Working through Kahnawake Mohawks active in a tobacco network that stretches from Montreal to Syracuse, the Akwesasne Warriors were to receive 25 cents for every carton of contraband cigarettes brought in and out of the territory. With that, the Warriors were to pay for supplies, new equipment, office expenses, and other needs.

Collection of the money and transportation of the cigarettes were arranged on a week-to-week basis. "This wasn't a permanent business relationship," says Lazore. "It was something that got done when it had to be done. A few people would take off and drive to Kahnawake or wherever there was a meeting or something to do, then they would come back and some money and tobacco might have changed hands. We never had any real desire for any long-range plan.

"We were not looking for an enormous amount of money, just enough to keep us going in case of the blockade. We were worried about not having enough money to buy gas for our patrols, or parts to fix cars or radios."

Nevertheless, Minnie Garrow says, the Warriors were unable to keep ahead. "If we got money, it was always to pay for things that we bought or needed yesterday. Whatever we took in was spent immediately. We were living one day to the next."

As the Akwesasne Warriors reached out to Kahnawake, they received a plea for help from the bitterly divided Mohawk community of Kanesatake, near the small town of Oka. Several factions of men and women at Kanesatake were battling over their unique system of using government-sanctioned clan mothers to appoint band councilors, a proposed bingo hall, and resistance to the municipality's plan to expand a golf course into a grove of towering pines that contains a Mohawk burial ground. "To us, there were four other factions. The Group for Change and the League for Democracy went to Ottawa and sought reform of the laws, then two others, one led by Clarence Simon, the other led by George Martin, fought for leadership of the band council.

It was just one clique trying to replace another," says Ellen Gabriel, who was part of a fifth faction, working out of the Kanesatake Cultural Centre. These men and women reject the white-sponsored government and adhere to the Mohawks' traditional religion. "The real fight was about the Pines and the forest land. Will the Québécois and their town have it for a bigger golf course or will we have it?

"To us, the Pines are sacred, a cemetery of our ancestors. The town and the members of the golf club have said they want that land to expand from nine to 18 holes. There are more plans for a resort, which means further shearing our land to provide access to the river.

"When the townspeople and their mayor announced their plans for this land, we said no way. Last year, we led a protest through the village, which included representatives from the Assembly of First Nations, which brought people from native groups across Canada. The deputy premier of Quebec wrote a letter on our behalf. Then the federal and provincial governments forced negotiating sessions. The mayor was very, very upset. It went on throughout the fall of 1989. Then, all of a sudden, in January of this year, the band council splits because they cannot agree on expenditures. So, a few dozen Mohawks try to oust the existing grand chief, Simon, and replace him with Martin. No one can figure out why this happened, except to speculate that one side wants to undercut our position in the negotiations over the Pines. We suspect that it was a setup, but no one can say for sure."

As a result of the split, the band council found itself unable to make decisions concerning the Pines. Frustrated with Mohawk squabbling that held up proposed development, Mayor Jean Ouellette, a member of the golf club, refused to participate in any more discussions. "All we do is wait. Wait for Ottawa and then wait for the Mohawks," Ouellette says. "This is not how you treat the municipality and the people of our community. I can understand there is a dispute, but let's resolve it. If not, we'll go forward. The new golf season is coming and it would be wonderful for our community to look forward to the prospect of increased business and the development of a resort to take advantage of the view and the river as it passes by."

By early March, the golf club had scheduled its annual meeting, which included a vote on a proposal to give the town $90,000 to be designated as an advance on 35 years' rent for 22 hectares of the Pines. "The club would not own the land," explains Ouellette. "That was never the intent. The municipality would charge the club the price of clearing the land and making it part of the golf course. Then there would be a lease arrangement with a yearly fee."

"They were going to take the Pines and make it a golf course—our holy place goes for their recreation," shoots back Denise Tolley, who works with Gabriel at the Kanesatake Cultural Centre. "Can you imagine what would happen if we wanted to take a church cemetery and turn it into a lacrosse field or sweat lodge? At first, we went to the Warriors at Kahnawake. They said that they were learning from the Warriors at Akwesasne, where the Warriors are fighting divisions within their community to protect the land. They patrolled the Mohawk land and protected it from outsiders and traitors.

"So we called the Warriors at Akwesasne."

The Mohawks from Kanesatake met with Francis Boots, asking for advice on tactics, how to set up a patrol, and the best way of implementing their plan to build a barricade on a dirt path leading to the Pines. On the morning of March 10, the men and women of the traditional faction dragged a fishing shack onto the path and began a formal occupation of the disputed tract. "We supported them," recalls Boots. "Hold the land. Move back off the road, but hold the trees and the forests, which are on a ridge overlooking the provincial highway. To keep people in communication with each other, they asked for the radios because they figured the mayor would call the police. We had some old equipment that was working and we gave it to them.

"For us, this was a very important move. We had formed alliances with people in Mohawk territories and we could show our people that the white border will not divide us, that the governments of Canada and the United States will not be used as a wall to keep the Mohawks apart. While the antis went and asked the white authorities to help discredit us, other Mohawks came to us and expressed their faith and belief in our nation.

"Though we didn't help very much and we always needed money, we showed our people that we were not going to abandon Mohawks who believe in our sovereignty. Whether it's a fight over bingo with the antis or a dispute over a golf course or a way of sharing tobacco money, we are not going to accept the rule of white law over our land. Here in Akwesasne, Mike Mitchell and the antis are the ones who want to step on the Mohawk nation. In Kahnawake, it has been the Sûreté du Québec, launching raids against the tobacco trade or the new bingo hall. In Kanesatake, it's the town of Oka looking to make a golf course out of the Pines.

"But take it back one step and you will find all of this activity benefits the Canadian government, which wants to extend its law to our land. The officials in Ottawa and Quebec City are funding Mike

Mitchell, just as they are directing the police to raid the Kahnawake bingo or letting the mayor of Oka cut down our pines for his golf game. Canada wants to stamp us out many way—paying other Mohawks great sums of money to set up puppet band-council governments that will divide us, calling the police to intimidate us, or using the force of local officials to take our land. Right now, Canada is using the fist, while the Americans are tying us up in the legal system, using the courts to grind us down and choke us. Our response is the same it has always been—we are mounting an organized resistance."

On Saturday, March 10, Mike Mitchell convened a meeting of nearly 400 residents at the Akwesasne Mohawk School on Cornwall Island. Insisting that peace would come only when gambling and tobacco smuggling were run out of Akwesasne, Mitchell asked the crowd if it would support closing the territory to all "non-residential and unnecessary traffic." He received an enthusiastic response.

"Many of the people at this meeting were employed through the Canadian council," says Harold Tarbell, who also attended, "but that doesn't make much of a difference because we were ready to do something to get the rule of law back in our community."

Harold Tarbell attended as a concerned Akwesasne resident and as head chief of the New York tribal council, though he admits he was not an official representative. Also playing a key role at the meeting was Doug George, the editor of *Indian Time*, and his brothers, who openly advocated roadblocks and barricades to prevent busloads of gamblers from entering the territory and patronizing the casinos.

"That's how the casinos really make their money," says Doug George. "Look at their parking lots and you see bus after bus. We have the right to control the road just as much as the Warriors do. It's about time we thought about using that power."

"We were fully aware of plans to shut the roads, including Route 37," says state police Maj. Robert Leu, the commander in charge of Troop B, which covers the area. "Right now, the situation at the reserve is like a family, where two sides are yelling and shouting at each other, getting out all their aggression, but no one is getting hurt. The worst thing would be for an outsider to come in there and force them to get along. This has to be solved by the Mohawks, not the police or the politicians."

Three days after the meeting, the anti-gaming faction released a report prepared by Alan Parker, of the U.S. Senate Select Committee on Indian Affairs. The document describes the St. Regis reservation as "the worst situation in Indian Country." Based on a brief visit to Akwesasne in January and subsequent discussions with Tarbell and other Mohawks who oppose gaming, Parker's report makes three additional points: the casinos are "unequivocally in violation" of federal laws that regulate gambling on Indian territories; the casino owners and pro-gaming Mohawks "are cloaking themselves in the flag of sovereignty" for their own gain; the territory's nine traditional chiefs, ostensibly representing the Mohawk religion, are against gambling. "Every single one of them abhors what is going on," the report states.

Earning front-page coverage from Syracuse to Montreal, this melodramatic report gave the anti-gaming faction another opportunity to trumpet their threatened blockade. Mike Mitchell claimed that dozens of Mohawks were planning to mount checkpoints to stop white gamblers from entering the territory. "No one wants violence," he said. "But we want the lawful resolution of this matter. We have been patient and suffered for too long. Expect our passions to be high."

Tarbell claimed Parker's report provided strong evidence of the need to make laws that apply to both sides of the reservation. He also noted that Senate committee staff held out the possibility of increased federal aid if the Mohawks were able to resolve their differences and follow the spirit of federal law. "That's really what the committee wants us to do," Tarbell says, "evolve into a democracy, where there are elections and an orderly exercise of power without violence and intimidation. There is support for us if we find a lawful way to settle our differences."

In Albany, bureaucrats and top-ranking police brass took notice when Parker's report made the capital's newspapers. "You can say it slid over the line from a public-safety matter to a potential political or inter-governmental matter," says Cuomo's director of State Operations, Dr. Henrik Dullea. "We felt that our troopers had a very good handle on what was going on. To our mind, the Senate committee was not getting the full picture, but it could shape the issue. We worked the phones, talking to everyone, making sure that they knew we were available but not willing to storm in there.

"We wanted to do everything we could to prevent an international incident that brought into play conflicting laws, conflicting sets of cops, border patrols, customs agents, and who knows what else. If negotiations were needed and the time came for a political solution, then we wanted the discussions to come straight to our office. By offering his office as the mediator, the governor tried to prevent bloodshed."

Shortly after 9:30 on the morning of March 23, Mitchell and Tarbell announced the temporary closing of offices belonging to the Canadian- and New York–chartered councils, the first step toward mounting the blockade. By 9:45, anti-gamblers had parked their cars across Route 37 and told motorists that the casinos would no longer be allowed to open. A few minutes later, another group of anti-gamblers set up a similar roadblock near four corners in Hogansburg.

"It was a squeeze play. They wanted to control access within the territory," says state police Sgt. Michael Downs. "They rightly figured that we would not go in after them. At the international bridge and at points outside Mohawk land, we set up our own roadblocks to warn all motorists about the gambling checkpoints. Canadian authorities stopped everyone on the bridge and made sure people knew what they could be driving into. We publicly told the media that we had no intention of going onto the Mohawk territory. The governor's office issued a statement backing us up, emphasizing that this had to be settled by the people who lived on the St. Regis reservation."

By the end of the first afternoon, the Warriors had received reports of more than a dozen skirmishes, angry exchanges, and shoving matches at each roadblock. "We are just going to take it one incident at a time. Our patrols are out and watching. The people know we are here," says Francis Boots. "The true Mohawk people will not be tricked into fighting each other for the glory of puppet governments."

13

MANY BRANCHES LYING ON THE GROUND

During the first days of the blockade, Mike Mitchell dropped hints that provincial and federal officials would approve a new form of Mohawk government if the band council at Akwesasne joined with its counterpart in Kahnawake. Approaching Kahnawake council Grand Chief Joseph Norton, Mitchell suggested that Mohawk communities seek "municipal" status under Canadian law. "We would be our own government, our own territory that would not have to rely on the bureaucracy and its grants," Mitchell said. "We would enact our own laws, empower our own police to enforce them."

Though Norton remained aloof, the proposal served its purpose, which was to cast Mitchell as a leader focusing on issues much larger than gambling. To distance himself from the angry exchanges on the barricades, Mitchell entertained all media inquiries about sovereignty and inter-governmental relations, but referred all questions about the blockade to Brian Cole, the New York–chartered tribal council employee who led the September 1989 showdown between antis and Minnie Garrow outside the Warriors' headquarters. Standing near a makeshift barricade across Route 37, Cole identified himself as the blockade's official spokesman. "We will be ruled by our lawful leaders and our traditions," he says. "We are appealing to the white world as well as our brothers and sisters among the Mohawks here in Akwesasne and other communities. We are going to continue the blockade until there are no casinos and our government has the ability and power to carry out the laws of our people."

Standing beside Cole were three young men who would not identify themselves except to say they received paychecks from the Canadian band council controlled by Mitchell. One of them adds, "We have to clean out the Warriors. It's really that simple. If we don't get them out of here, they're gonna come and kick our ass."

"The Warriors and the antis traded accusations back and forth," says Sgt. Michael Downs, "and we weren't going to get involved in that kind of baiting and provocation. We didn't patrol Route 37 or force the barricades. We had a helicopter or two checking on what was happening. It was a lot safer to be in the sky."

Both sides noticed the helicopters and resented their presence. "The police are afraid and intimidated to come here," says Cole. "We have to man these blockades because the police won't act. Instead, they go around in their whirlybirds watching everybody."

"Right now, both sides hate us," quips Downs. "That means we're doing something right."

Throughout Akwesasne, the blockade hiked the already high tension and further polarized the community into pro- and anti-gaming camps. On the New York–chartered tribal council, the three elected chiefs became openly hostile. "Harold Tarbell was making it very clear that the barricades were part of his idea of what leadership should be," says Tarbell's arch rival, David Jacobs. "This was destructive and divisive. He encouraged Mohawks to battle their own, to choke the roads of our community. This was not a difference of opinion or a dispute about policy. This was directly hurting people. He engaged in an act of sabotage against Mohawks.

"I got together with the third chief on the council, Lincoln White, and we proposed a resolution to expel Harold. And it carried by a vote of two to nothing. We kicked him out. Of course he said it didn't carry any weight. Well, I don't give a shit. Harold had to be told his kind of behavior was not acceptable. I wanted to slap some sense into him."

"This is the kind of manipulative, behind-the-back move we can expect of Dave Jacobs," Tarbell retorts. "Just like the gamblers and casino owners, he has no respect. We stand up and encourage the people to peacefully honor the rule of law by stopping cars, and he tries to mow us down because we stand in the way of his friends' making big money at their illegal casinos. If he can't come at us face-to-face, he'll try knifing us in the back. His resolution is just a desperate ploy for power. It won't work."

On Sunday afternoon, March 25, a bulldozer rumbled down Route 37, pushing snow, dirt, and bales of hay together to make a wall that would help block the road and screen the anti-gambling men and women from the late-winter wind. Then the men at the barricade directed the machine east on Route 37 to perform a similar task near four corners in Hogansburg. As the dozer approached the Bear's Den and Tony's Vegas International, security guards from the casinos piled out into the parking lot and brandished their rifles, yelling at the driver to stop.

From behind the Bear's Den, the engine of a second bulldozer kicked over. "It was like a really bad movie," says Doug George, who supported the blockade. "You had the bulldozers squaring off like they were rusted, mechanized monsters. As the casino's bulldozer came out toward the road, ours kept coming. We were just going on the road, and then Tony's guards started to fire warning shots."

Laughing concedes that his men fired over the approaching bulldozer. He also claims that the anti-gaming faction "sent that machine to try and knock my casino over. Let's face it, that's what they want and I'm gonna protect my business. I don't want to hurt anybody, but if that dozer would have come any closer, those bullets might not have just gone over people's heads."

Several patrons in the Bear's Den who witnessed the episode confirm the approach of the bulldozer, the warning shots, and the emergence of a pickup truck and a sedan from behind the anti-gaming bulldozer. The truck and the car dramatically accelerated, witnesses say, and then three bursts of automatic-weapons' fire were heard going toward the guards at Tony's casino. "This was a new development," says Francis Boots. "This wasn't random or done in darkness or driving by. This was gunfire in the pattern of attack and response—very dangerous. When we heard about this, we called our people on patrol. We tried to get the word to them to be careful, that they could not fire first. Under no circumstances could that happen."

After Boots tipped off the six to eight Warriors who were actually patrolling, Dewey Lazore began to chatter into the radio. "Frosted Bear to Rabbit Six," he said, giving his conversation an aura of coded importance. "Sector Three-Five to Zone Two," or "Six cars at Zone One, heading east, Rabbit, do you read me?" The patrols responded with equal gusto: "Roger, Colonel" or "Affirmative, Big Eagle Three" or "Ten-four, Base One, westbound on three seven at 13:35."

"We knew the antis were listening," explains Lazore, "and we figured that the shooting at Tony's would give them reason to be looking for us and make things worse. So I wanted them to think that we had a whole bunch of people behind us if they started to mess with us. They heard it and believed us."

Adds Stanley Cohen, who was at the Onkwe Bingo Jack when the shots were fired, "This deception worked like a dream. The antis want to believe that the Warriors are terrorists, so they would want to believe in these coded conversations.

"We just had two or three cars going back and forth to check out what was going on. We would say that we had a patrol in Raquette Point when no one was there. Or we'd say Cornwall Island or Hogansburg. We just wanted the antis to think that we were constantly moving people around. And they wanted to believe that we were a group of guerrillas sneaking around the territory with AK-47s and waiting to stage a raid. Nothing could have been further from the truth, but the myth worked to our advantage."

On Monday, March 26, the Akwesasne Warriors hosted a day-long "Mohawk National Warriors Council" with representatives of the Warriors Societies from Kahnawake; Ganienkeh, northwest of Plattsburgh, New York; the Grand River territory in southern Ontario; and Tuscarora Nation that straddles New York and Canada near Buffalo. "We wanted them to come down to look and see for themselves," says Boots. "We wanted whatever help in terms of equipment and money because our deal with cigarettes was shaky, but we weren't ready to ask for manpower. At the same time, we wanted others to know the real story and be prepared to come here if things got worse."

According to Minnie Garrow, the gathering gave the Akwesasne Warriors the opportunity to showcase their political program. Instead of dwelling on gambling and the cigarette trade, the Warriors focused on how the American and Canadian governments sought to impose their versions of self-government on the Mohawk nation. "We walked everyone through this," Garrow says, "starting with the raids of June 6. We explained to the people from other communities that the Warriors united and formed organized resistance within a political context. We told people that band councils and tribal councils are important to understand, but their purpose is to cripple our people, to make us think according to white rules and structures."

In describing that context, the Akwesasne Warriors steered the conversation toward the upcoming legal battle involving Kakwirakeron. "His trial was scheduled to start any day," says Garrow, "and we believe that any attempt to get the Warriors involved in violence would be used to discredit us in the courtroom. It would be beneath us to fight the roadblocks with violence. They are manned by puppets who are only doing the dirty work of white governments. We will not give our adversaries the satisfaction of that kind of response.

"While the people from other communities were here, the police and the reporters started to call about a meeting to end the blockade. They said that Brian Cole and some of the antis were going to meet with casino employees in the late afternoon. The next day, the tribal council, the band council, and traditional council were also going to meet. We said, 'Let them meet. We want the roads to be free, but we will not get involved in this kind of politics. We do not recognize the authority of clowns who block the roads.'

"The police and the reporters expected us to jump at the opportunity to sit at the table and play power broker. But we are not interested in becoming another tribal council or band council. We weren't interested in puppet politics. The people from the other communities had a chance to see us go around the table, make a decision, then communicate it. Our message got across."

Later that day, administrators of the Salmon River School District, which serves Akwesasne and the surrounding towns, canceled bus service for students living on Mohawk territory. Superintendent Robert Jaeger vowed to keep schools open and encouraged parents to bring their children to class, but insisted that the volatile situation in Akwesasne could not guarantee the safe passage of buses.

"Life was starting to fall apart around here," says Warrior spokesman John Boots. "We had to really work hard to stay calm."

On the evening of March 28, Kakwirakeron and his wife, Verna Montour, were at their Bombay farmhouse, making last-minute preparations for their trip the next morning—a three-hour drive to Syracuse, where they were to meet Seth Shapiro at the Holiday Inn. "We had been working with Seth off and on ever since the arrest and the bail hearings in July and August," says Verna. "From the beginning, I didn't trust him, but he got Kakwirakeron out on bail, and that made a strong and favorable impression. My husband wanted to stay with him."

Both Kakwirakeron and Shapiro anticipated a straightforward prosecution, which would set the gambling scene at Akwesasne, present the efforts by the state police to control the slots by making arrests, establish the legitimacy of the federal warrants for July 20, and then allege that Kakwirakeron directed the Warriors to block the road. To defend himself, Kakwirakeron would take the stand and explain his version of the events, the purpose of the Warriors Society, the claim of Mohawk sovereignty and its history. In addition, Shapiro planned to call two police officials for the defense: Robert Charland, a retired state police major who commanded troopers at Moss Lake in the 1970s, and Leigh Hunt, the Syracuse police chief who knew Kakwirakeron and saw him as an effective mediator and advocate, not a man of violence.

"It was a substantial defense," says John Duncan, the assistant U.S. Attorney assigned to present the case to a jury. "I could not pin any act of violence on him. We didn't have a witness who could say that Kakwirakeron ever possessed a gun. My witnesses talked to him, saw him in the road, then they saw Warriors forming barricades. I didn't have any direct evidence that he stood in the road with a gun and threatened to blow someone's brains out. To the contrary, he was talking to a lot of people, including state police supervisors. The defense could make a claim that he was trying to defuse the situation, not inflame it. That's how I expected the trial to go."

"My best shot was a motion that the court should not hear this case because it involves the relations of sovereign nations," says Shapiro. "On July 20, my client took these non-violent actions to protect what he considers to be a sovereign land, the homeland of his people. From our point of view, the entire system of government has conspired to obstruct justice for the Mohawks. But we knew the judge didn't want to hear it. He wanted the case to stick to the narrow charges against Kakwirakeron."

As Kakwirakeron and his wife spent their last evening at home together, Shapiro arrived in Syracuse. There he encountered a woman who was unknowingly under investigation for being part of a prostitution ring. Alter they met and separated, the woman was corralled by an Onondaga County sheriff, who demanded information. A few minutes later, Shapiro heard a knock on his door. When he answered it, he found the woman beside a plainclothes deputy sheriff, who flashed his badge. Then the woman identified Shapiro as having offered to pay for sex; the cop placed them both under arrest, charging her with prostitution and him with soliciting a prostitute.

"It was embarrassing and I never thought it could happen that way," he says, refusing to discuss the details of the incident. A few weeks later, the charges were dropped; the court ruled there was no convincing evidence that they were together.

"I'll never forget when the phone rang in our room and it was Seth," adds Verna Montour. "We had just arrived in Syracuse and my husband answered. You could see his face, and his head jump back. 'What?' he said. I could see Kakwirakeron calm himself down, take a deep breath, and listen. He's a good listener and, boy, did he listen. The conversation took a minute or two. Seth told him that he had been arrested. Kakwirakeron said okay and hung up. Then he told me.

"I was really mad. I didn't like Seth from the beginning, and I thought this was the breaking point. I know that you can't always trust the police. I know that we were all worried about the FBI doing something to knock us out or whatever. But this was not right, and I told Kakwirakeron.

"I asked if he wanted to stop the trial and get a new lawyer. He just looked at me and shrugged. I couldn't believe it, but then that's who he is. He put his trust in Seth, and he wasn't going to take it away even though he knew this was a very bad omen. We didn't expect to win in the white man's court, and that's how we left it. Kakwirakeron figured that he had given his word to Seth, which was more important to him than the procedures of the court or the laws of white people."

That same morning, FBI agent John McEligot called prosecutor Duncan to tell him the news. "I said, 'This couldn't happen.' I didn't believe it. Even I thought that the Syracuse police might have set him up or something," says Duncan. "I have been in the system for a long time, and nothing like this has ever gone on. But it was true. Seth got picked up, and when we got to court, he had to go into the judge's chambers and tell him.

"Oh, did he have to swallow his pride. I felt bad for the guy. This was on the opening day of what he was building up to be a big political trial."

The incident must have caused Kakwirakeron to doubt his lawyer. So if the arrest was a setup, it worked in that regard.

A delegation of Warriors came to court to support Kakwirakeron and Verna, but they were openly furious with Shapiro. "It was totally outrageous," says Rowena General. "Kakwirakeron told us to take it easy. Kakwirakeron was a peacemaker. He would always ride things out and rely on his intelligence. We went into this expecting him to lose and go to jail, but we wanted to challenge the law and the authority of the court. How could we do that with a lawyer who we felt was compromised? We felt our strategy was spoiled."

14

A BEAST FALLS
FROM THE SKY

The next day, March 30, bizarre events on the northern edge of the Adirondacks overshadowed Shapiro's arrest. Around 10:15 a.m., as a heavy snow swirled in the winds that rolled over the mountains and into the St. Lawrence Valley, the Warriors received a phone call reporting the presence of a helicopter flying low over Akwesasne. A few minutes later, the Warriors' radio console crackled with air-to-air transmissions and reports of at least one more chopper, showing the drab green markings of the National Guard.

"We were used to the state police flying overhead, but the National Guard was a whole different matter," says Minnie Garrow. "That immediately made us think about the possibility of an invasion or some kind of military plan being hatched. We got really worried and we started to put out the word.

"We knew the police would fly over once or twice because of the anti-gambling barricades. We could handle that, but no one should hover over our land and fly low, especially helicopters with military markings.

"We were convinced that someone was trying to get us to behave violently and create the need for an invasion and occupation. The helicopters were there to help the police and even the National Guard take over our land.

"Our leaders reached out to Kahnawake and Ganienkeh, telling Warriors in those locations that we expected an armed invasion."

Eleven miles away at the Massena General Hospital, the snow-storm threatened plans to transfer an elderly heart patient to a cardiac intensive care ward in Burlington, Vermont. A National Guard mede-vac helicopter was to leave Vermont and fly to Massena, pick up the patient, and return. When National Guard pilot Chris Samples and his civilian passenger, Dr. James Van Kirk, took off, they figured he could fly in and out of the mountains; but the storm turned progressively worse. According to Samples's flight transmissions, the chopper flew over the 3,800 foot peak of Lyon Mountain and curved northward to-ward the lowlands. The strong snow squalls, however, forced Samples to less than 500 feet as he passed the crossroads at Ellenburg Center, heading west.

Barely flying above the snow-capped forest, Samples lost his bear-ings and could not pinpoint his own location. Following the roads and the wood-frame houses built in the clearings, Samples saw several people on the ground, including a man with a shoulder weapon. He never heard the bullets.

One shot tore through the door. It hit Van Kirk in the elbow and a piece of metal grazed his neck. A second or third shot severed the hy-draulic line that controlled the helicopter's rudder and steering mech-anism. Spotting the blacktop of Route 190, Samples desperately wrestled with the throttle. He swerved the falling chopper away from the forest and onto the shoulder of the road, near the wooden fence and sign that reads "Repossessed Area of Ganienkeh Territory East. 50,000 B.C."

Samples sent out radio distress signals that were immediately picked up by the local ambulance corps and state troopers assigned to the Troop B outpost in nearby Plattsburgh. The Mohawks at Ganien-keh first came to the aid of Samples and Van Kirk, then paramedics and troopers arrived to transport them to the hospital.

"It was miraculous that they got down without crashing," says Ken-neth Cook, the state police officer in charge of the investigation. (Lieutenant Cook had played a key role in the Akwesasne raids of June 6 and July 20, 1989. Now a captain, he supervised the regional branch of the state police Bureau of Criminal Investigation.) "The pilot made it very clear why he was flying and the route he took. He had no idea about Ganienkeh and the Mohawk troubles at the St. Regis reserva-tion. This pilot is some kind of hero. That chopper should have crashed, but he saved it. It's amazing."

The police secured the landing site as a crime scene, ringing the copter with troopers and beginning the search for bullet slugs and other evidence. "Dr. Van Kirk was clearly shot, which is clearly an assault, maybe an attempted murder, crimes under our jurisdiction as state police," Cook notes. "And then there was the shooting down of a military helicopter. That's a federal crime, which falls under the jurisdiction of the FBI, and we called them right away. And of course the National Guard didn't take too kindly to the fact that one of their medical helicopters was fired on."

Cook and a contingent of troopers walked up to the gates of Ganienkeh, announcing their intent to search the nearby encampment and buildings for weapons.

"No way," says Darryl Martin, one of approximately 50 year-round residents of Ganienkeh, where a high-stakes bingo hall is the only commercial establishment. "This is our sovereign territory, which we won back through the struggle of Moss Lake. And we will not give up what we fought for, especially at the time when our brothers and sisters and cousins at Akwesasne are fighting for the sovereignty that is ours by natural law."

Later, a handful of men masked their faces with bandanas and closed the wooden gate. Then a car was pulled across the ice-covered access road, and guards showed their AK–47s.

Cook called for more troopers and encircled the territory's formal entrance. By day's end, state and federal authorities established a command post within 100 yards of the helicopter, having brought uniformed troopers, SWAT teams, FBI agents, and military personnel to the scene. "No one was going anywhere," Cook says. "We wanted to search the Mohawk encampment."

Recognizing their predicament, the handful of armed men in Ganienkeh used a cellular telephone to call the Warriors Society in Akwesasne to ask for help. "We were convinced that this was the beginning of the big attack," says Minnie Garrow. "When the helicopter went down, it gave the authorities the perfect chance to blame us for something violent. We expected the police, the FBI, and the military to open up on us. We figured that they wanted us to fight on three fronts spread out across New York—the barricades here in Akwesasne, the courts in Syracuse, and the standoff in Ganienkeh. The Mohawk nation was under siege from within and without.

"When we got the call, we didn't know what to do next; face the roadblocks, support Kakwirakeron, help Ganienkeh stand up to the police, the FBI, and the military. So much was going on. The men at Ganienkeh told us they never saw a helicopter until it landed, insisting that they did not shoot it down. That made some sense. It was possible that the helicopter made it as far as Akwesasne and got shot somewhere around here, where there are all kinds of people walking around with guns—both Warriors and anti-gamblers on the barricades. At Ganienkeh, they had no reason to shoot, but here people were in the middle of an intense conflict."

"When the helicopter went down, we recognized that the circumstances around us had really, really changed," says Francis Boots. "We knew we were being thrown up against the wall. We weren't thinking strategy—the time for that was over. We had to be fighting."

In the Onkwe Bingo Jack, the Warriors organized themselves into three overlapping battle groups, each with a specific political and military mission: the first centered on John Boots, who quickly mounted a protest march to dismantle the anti-gaming barricades at Twin Bridges on Route 37; the second, led by Rowena General, marshaled support for Kakwirakeron and the effort to ensure that his trial furthered the Warriors' political goals; the third smuggled men, food, fuel, weapons, and other necessities in and out of the thick forests surrounding Ganienkeh.

"We have to remind the police and the antis that we are willing to fight for our beliefs," says Diane Lazore. "If this was only about the blockades, we could use the low-key approach and embarrass the antis. But the helicopter downing and the big state police move at Ganienkeh gave us the feeling that the cops were coming in at any moment. And what we learned from the raids of June 6 and July 20 is that we cannot let the police move first.

"For the past few months we have been wanting to show some response after Gerry McDonald shot up Tony's or Mike Mitchell made his asinine public statements. But we kept ourselves in check. With the helicopter down and the roads blocked, we were afraid that doing nothing would be seen as a sign of weakness. The trick was to do something so the police would continue to stay out of Mohawk land. That's why we had to make some noise on the roadblocks and support the resistance at Ganienkeh. If the troopers came in at either location, then we would have lost a big battle."

While the police and Mohawks agreed to an uneasy ceasefire as the prelude to negotiations at Ganienkeh, the pro- and anti-gaming factions at Akwesasne continued to move toward confrontation. The day after the helicopter went down, more than 400 people gathered inside the Mohawk Bingo Palace to discuss the anti-gaming roadblock. This meeting, organized by pro-gaming chiefs L. David Jacobs and Lincoln White, was designed to force negotiations that would allow the free flow of traffic. But the Warriors sent men and women to the meeting with a slightly different agenda—to round up support for a march on the barricade.

"The people had jobs in casinos that were closed. They had jobs off the reservation, but had to drive miles to avoid the threat of violence from the antis. These people were angry, especially the women. They were tired of this kind of harassment when they went back and forth to their jobs, the grocery store, the schools."

After the pro-gaming chiefs spoke, James Ransom, an ally of anti-gaming Chief Harold Tarbell, expressed his support for the blockade, only to be hissed and jeered. "The people were ready to do something and that's exactly what we wanted," Warrior spokesman John Boots says. "Our plan was to get as many of them behind us, walk out of the Bingo Palace arm-in-arm, and confront the people at the roadblock."

"We can do this," Minnie Garrow told the crowd. "We do not have to be held hostage on our own land. This isn't about gambling or morality. Mohawks do not have to do this to their own people. It's time we show our numbers."

Within 20 minutes, more than 300 people had filtered out of the hall and formed a column across both lanes of Route 37. Linking arms and waving a few quickly made placards demanding an end to the roadblocks, the men and women walked straight toward the barricades without encountering any opposition.

"I went right up to the bales of hay and started to pull them down, toss them to the side," says John Boots. "Another group spotted Dave Rourke and surrounded him as he stood beside his pickup. Looking into the cab, someone saw that Dave had stashed 15 baseball bats or thick pieces of wood to use as clubs. We took them out and showed them to the crowd. Remember this was supposed to be the group of people who proclaimed themselves to be non-violent.

"On the other side of the road, in position to be pulled over to block it, there was a school bus from the Canadian side. You know, a token of Mike Mitchell's support. The bus had Mohawk Council of Akwesasne, the formal name of his council, painted on the side. One of us got in and just drove it away into the Bingo Palace parking lot. Man, there was a great cheer. Then across the road, about 10 yards up from the hay, were uprooted guardrails and logs. We just began to clear that to the side. The antis had even put a portable toilet out there and we moved that. Very carefully.

"Then, a few yards farther up, I saw a van belonging to one of the anti leaders, Roger Thomas, being pushed off the road by a few antis. I thought they were pushing it away to save it, but then I saw them pull out a gas can, pour it over the van, and light it up. They just torched it. We were shocked. The crowd watched in disbelief. How could they do that? What was it going to accomplish?

"Then Minnie told me, 'They're going to try and blame us for it.' And I knew she was right. We had to stop because of the fire, but we loaded up whatever we could. After a while, we took the truck and the bus to the parking lot outside the tribal council office. By 6:00 p.m., the road was free and open. We left."

Three hours later, the anti-gaming faction set up another barricade and announced their intent to continue the blockade until the casinos agreed to a permanent shutdown. "The Warriors were organizing a serious attack on us," says Doug George, the editor of the *Indian Time* newspaper and anti-gaming strategist. "They wanted the public to believe that the National Guard medevac helicopter was shot down by us. They tore down our barricades and set Roger Thomas's van on fire. Our protests were not violent. The Warriors were being violent to protect the casinos. We were standing up for our principles."

Canadian Grand Chief Mike Mitchell and his American counterpart, Head Chief Harold Tarbell, combined their influence to support barricades positioned on the U.S. side of the border. Band and tribal council employees served as "roadblock commanders" to oversee the interruption of traffic and the construction of obstacles. A typewritten copy of their roster was discovered in the school bus driven away from the barricades: among the 16 names were Akwesasne police Chief Ernie King, who was commander from 11 a.m. to 4 a.m., constable Louis Mitchell and his brothers Brian and Ernest, each of whom supervised a four-hour shift. Four people, including Doug George, were listed as spokesmen authorized to write and issue press releases and respond to reporters. Another five employees of the Mohawk Council of Akwesasne were listed as "the people to see if you have to get reimbursement for damages to your vehicles, personal injuries, etc. . . . Please bring estimates to the roadblock commanders or to the Mohawk Council of Akwesasne/Mike Mitchell." The roster notes "Checks are issued every two weeks; the next one will be 4/12/90."

"Sure, we were using people employed by local governments to man the roadblocks and keep up this pressure," explains George. "We had no choice. The conviction of the casino owners, the trial of Art Montour—or, as the Warriors say, the great patriot Kakwirakeron — will only increase the number of white laws that we are subject to. The Warriors were drawing the attention of white authorities, daring them to come in here and regulate our lives even more.

"The way to win sovereignty is to show the world that we can form our own government, that we can forge our own democracy without gunplay and without beatings. That's why the roadblocks are important. This is our best chance to stand up and loudly tell everyone that there is a movement for Mohawk government and self-rule. Sovereignty means a government, not a rumble that kicks out the police. We need these roadblocks because we need a government. The Warriors want to destroy the roadblocks because they want to destroy our government and take power without any real program or plan."

Mike Mitchell denounced the Warriors and began direct negotiations with white officials. From Ottawa he sought the establishment of one central government in Akwesasne. "We are not seeking to become Canadian or American citizens," he says. "We are not accepting municipalization. Our discussions with the Canadian government only involve Akwesasne. The council is looking for one indivisible land and one indivisible government, not a constitutional or statutory solution, but complete recognition of our sovereign rights."

A spokesperson for Tom Siddon, the Canadian minister of Indian and Northern Affairs, confirmed that Mitchell had presented a wide array of changes aimed at the creation of a single council that would administer the entire territory. His proposals also included plans for a Mohawk criminal justice system complete with courts, prosecutors, police, and jails. In consultation with the provincial authorities in Ontario and Quebec, Siddon's aide said, federal officials had begun "preliminary" negotiations with the Mohawk Council of Akwesasne.

Mitchell's tough rhetoric spurred his American counterpart, Tarbell, to arrange a meeting with Dr. Edward Brown, the director of the U.S. Bureau of Indian Affairs. Held in Brown's office in Washington, D.C., the April 2 session involved seven Mohawks—three anti-gaming officials—Head Chief Tarbell, Subchiefs James Ransom and Hilda Smoke; and four pro-gaming officials—Chiefs Jacobs and Lincoln White, Subchief Agnes Pyke, and clerk Carol Herne. "Brown saw that we were divided and totally unable to reach any kind of consen-

sus," says Tarbell. "But he was intent on getting us to agree on something. The man was steamed. He wanted a deal.

"After a couple of hours, Brown finally said that he was thinking of
pulling out all federal funds if we couldn't find some common ground.
He said the council was showing itself to be incapable of governing
the territory. He said it was clear that the casinos were out of business
until there was a formal gaming compact as prescribed by the law. I
could live with that. I was happy because Brown was finally using his
clout. He knew that Dave Jacobs, Lincoln White, and the Warriors
were just fronting for the casinos, who were making a fortune. So
Brown laid it out in hardball terms—'Get together or else.'"

"The man knew that we had yet to comply with the law and reach
a formal agreement about gambling on our territory," counters Jacobs.
"He also knew that I had contacted state officials a few months ago
and informed them of our desire to start negotiations for a formal
agreement. That's the first step toward compliance. Christ, I had been
saying this all along. I want the Mohawks to get full rights as guaranteed by acts of the U.S. Congress. Harold doesn't want the threat
posed by all of this money.

"White people want to come to our land and drop their cash. What's
wrong with that? For the first time in hundreds of years, we would
have something other than land that whites want and we would control it. This opens up the possibility of dramatic change. But Tarbell
wants to continue his hold on the meager means of government that
we have. He calls it democracy. I call it begging and handouts."

After Brown issued his threat, Tarbell's ally, Ransom, proposed
three major objectives: removal of the existing roadblocks; the cessa-
tion of all illegal gambling; and the re-establishment of daily patrols
by the New York State Police, who would protect all inhabitants of
the reservation. Ransom's terms became the basis of an agreement
between the council's anti- and pro-gaming factions.

The agreement was signed in the presence of Brown, who said the
BIA would help the council find a mediator to hear all sides of the
various disputes and issue recommendations for solutions.

Though Brown declined to comment, BIA spokesperson Carl Shaw
was quite blunt: "The council is on the verge of disintegration and the
mediator is the only way out."

In Akwesasne, however, the BIA agreement took a back seat to the
April 3 announcement by the operators of the Mohawk Bingo Palace,
Guilford White and Basil "Buddy" Cook: 180 employees were to be

laid off. "Buddy and I are partners with the tribal council, which calls Harold Tarbell the head chief," says White. "I don't find it funny that Tarbell is working to close the business that his council profits from. It's kind of sick. Technically, the council owns 51 percent of the Palace and we send to the tribe a monthly percentage. Six, seven, eight weeks ago, when business was booming, we were making payments of more than $50,000 to the tribal council accounts. Then 10 days ago, Tarbell and Mike Mitchell launch the blockade on the start of the weekend, which is our biggest time. As soon as the blockade began and the roadblocks went up, we were shut down.

"We aren't a casino. We are a legal bingo hall. All we do is play bingo. And we are the only gambling parlor that has a formal arrangement to give something back to the tribe. But the roadblocks are up and we can't do business. We can't make our payroll unless people are allowed to come in here and play. This is sad. Our own people taking away some of the few jobs that we have around here."

"If the roadblocks continue and more people lose their jobs or more businesses are forced to close, people will get angrier. They will want to fight, not march," says John Boots. "That is always a pretext for the police to come in here. Right now, we are holding them off at Ganienkeh. It's tense and any flare of violence could prompt them to move on both Mohawk communities. That's how it always starts—an isolated incident flares up into a big confrontation. When the antis start doing things that take away jobs, they are starting something dangerous because the casinos have given people a place to work, a true sense of security that they did not have before.

"If the antis want to take that away, they should be careful. The Warriors are organized and we will resist nonviolently. But we cannot control the actions and feelings of people who have just lost their income and are angry and upset. Look around you—all over our territory, there is growing resentment. You can't expect Mohawks to sit down and strike an agreement that will close casinos and give away their jobs. The mediator has to understand this. The morality of gambling is one issue. The legality of it is another. But the hard fact remains that people are making a living in these casinos.

"The antis are taking away the livelihood of Mohawks who will now have difficulty getting work elsewhere. The mediator has got to see that this is about our life, not about gambling."

15
LOST IN THE
WILDERNESS

Stanley Cohen was barely awake when the phone rang around 9:00 a.m. After a late return from a Florida vacation, Cohen had planned on a day off. "The last thing I wanted was to go back to work," he says, "but Minnie called and told me what was going on. It was like having a bucket of cold water dumped all over me. A helicopter shot down, Harold Tarbell meeting with the BIA, Mike Mitchell talking to the Canadians, people losing their jobs because there wasn't any traffic. All hell broke loose. Minnie asked me to go up there right away. She had never made that kind of request before."

"We didn't know what to do next," continues Garrow. "We had the barricades and the antis pretty much under control. We knew that the BIA meetings and Mike Mitchell's talks with Canadians were bullshit, but those kinds of moves allowed the antis to frame the issues in terms of Warrior thugs joining with outlaw casino owners to terrorize the community.

"On top of this, we had a major crisis in Ganienkeh. Over the first two days, Mohawks had closed the gate and stood face-to-face with the cops. On the second night, we organized our convoy. Having hunted on that land, the Warrior men knew the woods and the paths through the trees and they walked into the encampment with weapons and ammunition, packs of food, canisters of fuel, and a cellular telephone. When they got there, they found out that Mohawks from

Kahnawake had come down to arrange a deal that would seek a police pledge of leniency or amnesty in exchange for letting detectives and FBI agents search Mohawk land.

"And that's when it became clear to us that some old problems were cropping up. After the founding of Ganienkeh in the 1970s, Kakwirakeron split with Paul and Allan Delaronde, who became the leaders of the Warriors in Kahnawake. Over the years, they grew apart over politics and personal matters," says Garrow.

"But we suspected that the Delarondes were saying let the police search because it would undermine the position of Kakwirakeron and people from Akwesasne. All along, we had been clear—our sovereignty and our dignity could not be bargained away. If others did it, then we wanted our lawyer present to make sure we in Akwesasne were not sold out."

Garrow, Francis Boots, Rowena General, and other Akwesasne Warriors also point out that the helicopter downing and the authorities' belief in their right to search Ganienkeh reflected the issues being presented in Kakwirakeron's trial.

"How would it look in the middle of the trial if the same men who joined Kakwirakeron at Moss Lake suddenly decided that they could bargain with the police and grant detectives access to Mohawk land?" asked Francis Boots.

"This was clearly the wrong message, the wrong strategy at the wrong time. We called Stanley because we trusted his judgment. We could get him in there and he could help us. As an outsider, he could give us a different, less involved view of why people were making these decisions. Maybe it was the pressure, maybe they were misinformed. Or worse, maybe they did not understand what we had been fighting for."

Though Cohen came to negotiate, the police insisted on a search. "We found a bullet still lodged in the helicopter and ballistics tests determined that it was a .223 caliber slug similar to those used in AK-47 rifles. We had a man shot through the arm. I wanted to look for a match in the bullets and guns," says Capt. Kenneth Cook, the highest-ranking state police officer on the scene.

"I wanted my troopers to get in there and behave like professionals. I was convinced that the shooting took place around the Ganienkeh encampment. The Mohawks tried to tell me that it took place much farther west by the St. Regis reservation, but Chris Samples—the helicopter pilot—said he never made it that far. The Mohawks closed the gate and posted armed guards. So we got a warrant, and the feds got a warrant, and we brought in enough troopers and agents to secure the crime scene. This wasn't about sovereignty. This was about the crime of shooting at a helicopter and wounding a person. To me, that's assault, not politics."

According to Cook and FBI documents filed in U.S. District Court in Albany, Mohawks from Ganienkeh were initially against a deal while those from Kahnawake considered it. "The Mohawks were split," says Cook. "Just when we thought one side had the upper hand, the other side fought back and we would get nowhere."

Cohen adamantly argued against any deal with the police. He warned that the state could decline to press charges, but the FBI had broad jurisdiction because a military helicopter had been damaged. In exchange for allowing a search of Mohawk land, Cohen pleaded, the Mohawk negotiators should win recognition that federal and state law do not apply on Mohawk land.

"Stanley made some of the issues very, very clear," says Ganienkeh Mohawk Darryl Martin, who felt that the Delarondes and others did not fully grasp the significance of a police or FBI search. "Though the men from Kahnawake played an important part in our past struggles, this is not their home. They can go back north, but I have to stay here and live with the consequences of whatever is decided."

Criminal charges were only one concern of the Mohawks from Ganienkeh. They also feared police would use the pretext of a criminal probe to threaten their successful bingo hall, which had already attracted the attention of State Attorney General Robert Abrams for failing to comply with regulations that limit the size of a jackpot. Cook says that police and FBI promised Mohawks that they were not interested in the gaming operation but could not rule out a search of the bingo hall. "We wanted to look everywhere," says Cook. "They had to understand that we were looking for evidence of a crime and we had the law on our side."

After eight and a half days, Martin and others from Ganienkeh showed fatigue and stress. "When the helicopter first came down, we were the first ones there to help when the ambulance came to treat the wounded man," Martin snaps. "Do you think we would do that if we had shot it down? We are always available for the police. We just want some recognition that this is our land, that the police cannot storm onto it as if it were white man's territory. All they have to do is acknowledge that their law does not apply. We all want to live in peace, but give us our dignity and respect our way of doing things.

"There are some disagreements among us. Some of the Mohawks

might believe that the police could be restricted to only searching the houses, where they would find no evidence and then leave. These Mohawks say, 'It's days after the shooting, so what could the police find?' And I say, 'This has nothing to do with crime, but everything to do with principle and our identity.' Other Mohawks argue back, 'We did not see anybody shoot at the helicopter. The police could not have any evidence against us. Why put all this energy into something that might go away real fast and we could go back to our businesses?'"

Martin concedes that continuing had dire financial consequences for Ganienkeh, as its lucrative bingo business was shut down. In order to go on defying the police, the Ganienkeh Mohawks needed another source of income, but the Mohawks from Akwesasne and Kahnawake could not offer money.

On the afternoon of April 9, the tenth day of the standoff, a deal emerged: Mohawks said they would give state and federal authorities permission to search the homes built close to Route 190. To protect against authorities' planting evidence or falsifying reports, Cohen proposed that the police and FBI allow a Mohawk-appointed forensic expert to observe as troopers and FBI agents entered the territory and went through dwellings; the authorities agreed. That evening, more than two dozen armed Mohawk men packed up their weapons and disappeared through the woods. On the morning of April 10, a forensic expert from New York City flew to Plattsburgh, met a state police escort, and was driven to Ganienkeh.

"We went house to house, walked around and looked in corners and closets and wherever we could, but nothing was there," says Cook. "We have no suspects and no leads. We've talked to many Mohawks, but all of them say they never saw anybody hold a gun and they never heard any gunshots. I have my own personal thoughts as to what happened, but the New York State Police doesn't have any evidence to support the arrest of anyone."

Hours after the search was concluded, a team of FBI agents returned, formally notifying Martin of warrants for the arrest of 14 Mohawks on charges that they obstructed justice by interfering with the execution of a search warrant. Martin could barely speak. "I was numb," he says. "I knew we shouldn't have taken any deal whatsoever. Look what happens."

"These were almost exactly the same charges that they used against Kakwirakeron," Francis Boots says. "We call it defending our rights and our land; the FBI says it's obstructing justice."

. . .

A couple of hours after the FBI served the arrest warrants in Ganien-keh, U.S. District Court Judge Neal McCurn called for order in his Syracuse courtroom and directed the jury to announce its decision: on the most serious charge, that Kakwirakeron used a deadly weapon to block execution of the search warrant, the jury voted for acquittal. A cheer erupted from the gallery. On the lesser charges of interfering with the execution of a search warrant and conspiring to interfere by helping mount the Warriors roadblocks of July 20, 1989, the jury voted for conviction. Kakwirakeron silenced the jeers and taunts with one sweeping motion of his large hands. Then McCurn allowed Kakwirakeron to remain free until his sentencing as long as he did not enter Mohawk land to participate in Warriors Society activities.

"I expected to be found guilty even though I am innocent," said Kakwirakeron.

"I was disappointed about the conviction on the lower charges," said Shapiro, musing on his first major criminal case, "but I felt that I had done a good job in beating the count of using a deadly weapon. I interpreted that as a victory by split decision."

The different perspectives reflected the growing chasm between lawyer and client. Kakwirakeron realized that Shapiro lacked the experience to handle a major political defense. "He handled the bail hearing and got Kakwirakeron out. He did a very good job," says Verna Montour, "but at the trial Seth could not hold it together."

"From the beginning, I told everybody to expect the worst," Shapiro says. "Then the prosecution started its case and it became very clear that the prosecutor clearly fell short on the top count. The gallery started to whisper about beating the entire rap. Well, I tried to explain to them that the law doesn't work that way. But I don't think I got through."

Rowena General, who monitored the trial on behalf of the Warriors Society, had a different view. "We figured that Kakwirakeron could have won this case," she says, "but Seth Shapiro got in the way." Wounded by such bitterness, Shapiro explains that to win an acquittal, Kakwirakeron would have to convince the jury that the roadblocks were a spontaneous protest aimed at protecting Mohawk land, not the casinos. "That's a pretty big step," says Shapiro, "and I don't know if the Mohawks realize that. The prosecution wanted to show that Kakwirakeron was the leader of the Warriors Society and we were successful in debunking the prosecution myth that Kakwirakeron is the man who calls the shots.

"That part of the defense succeeded, but two facts were indisputable and they hurt us: the Warriors took action to show their defiance of the FBI and police, and Kakwirakeron is an important member of the group."

According to prosecutor John Duncan, the case hinged on Kakwirakeron's ability to cast the Warriors as men with a legitimate political grievance. "I don't think that there is any question that this group of people resisted or encouraged resistance to the FBI and state police," he says. "On July 20, the Warriors and Kakwirakeron undertook certain actions to block the road. The defense got trapped into thinking that the trial was about big political issues. But it was really about a narrow issue—how the Warriors' roadblock delayed the execution of a search warrant.

"It was easy to establish the facts. The warrant was issued, the road was blocked, and so on. But the defense was quite colorful. First, the Mohawks refused to swear an oath to a Judeo-Christian God and the judge allowed them to conduct their own oath ceremony to the eagle and the Creator. It was moving. It showed the jury that these are people who really believe in their culture, and it showed their determination to hold on, even in the midst of a courtroom of what they would call a hostile or foreign power.

"Second, Kakwirakeron was a very, very strong witness. His physical stature, his command of the language, his calm but firm demeanor made a very strong impression on the jury. Compared to Kakwirakeron's testimony, my witnesses were boring. I had to figure out a way to pull the rug out from under him."

Duncan says the opportunity presented itself when Kakwirakeron testified that he did not know the police and FBI teams came to the territory to execute search warrants. "That was a terrible, terrible blunder," says Duncan. "Here is this imposing, intelligent man taking control of the courtroom and then asking the jury to believe that he did not know the authorities were there for a purpose.

"When he said that, I knew I had an effective opening for cross-examination, but Seth didn't get it. He kept drawing attention to the implausible circumstances of Kakwirakeron talking to the cops on a cellular phone, actively negotiating with a major and lieutenants, but not knowing about the search warrants. I exploited it.

"Kakwirakeron understood the trap he was in. He started to reach for answers and lost his positive impact on the jury. At one point, during a recess, he walked past me and leaned over to say, 'Do you make visits?' I looked at him and answered, 'I don't know if it's proper for me to speak to you.' I was suspicious, but then he grinned and said, 'I just want to know if you'll visit me in prison.' Even I had to laugh with him. He knew that his testimony had not held up."

16

THE ANTIS STALK
THEIR PREY

The helicopter downing and Kakwirakeron's trial may have knocked the Akwesasne barricades off the front page of local newspapers, but anti-gaming Mohawks continued their campaign. The verdict in Syracuse and the search in Ganienkeh were perceived as defeats for the Warriors; and tension at Akwesasne mounted again.

"The gunshots are common now, all too common," says Margaret Peters, an anti-gaming Mohawk who continued the campaign of blocking traffic at the Twin Bridges on Route 37. Fingering a piece of paper listing the times and dates of confrontations, she continues, "I will not deny that our people have armed themselves with baseball bats on occasion, but I'm sure those bats will not stop the bullets from a rifle or AK-47, which is what the Warriors have.

"On April 5, there was a bomb threat at Mike Mitchell's office. Two days later, shots are fired at the house of Tom Porter, one of the leaders of the anti-gambling movement. A few hours later, three Warriors arrive at the Hogansburg roadblock and smash a car windshield. Less than an hour later, shots are fired as a car goes through this blockade. To cap it off, another round of gunfire is heard near the Mohawk Bingo Palace.

"On April 8, we hear of four separate incidents of shots being discharged—two at the barricades, one on Route 37 and one in front of Tom Porter's house. The next day, it gets worse. The people on this roadblock see Art Montour, Jr., and Stacey Boots speeding by and they hear shots. By the evening, we are told that the state police want to arrest Art Montour, Jr., for shooting at the troopers parked off the territory. Right before 11:00 p.m., a car tries to run this roadblock by smashing three other cars parked in a line. An hour later, right before midnight, shots are fired at the Hogansburg roadblock.

"The anti-gaming faction has been blamed for many things—the breakup of families, the increase in violence, drinking and car rammings, even the helicopter shooting—but it's absurd. People have to start admitting their own participation in the turmoil here on the reservation. The Warriors have to stop blaming everything on Mike Mitchell or Harold Tarbell, the Canadian or the United States government. All of the chaos began when the casinos and the bingo halls came here to Akwesasne."

To protect their political position, the anti-gaming faction prepared for the arrival of the intermediary promised by the U.S. Bureau of Indian Affairs. "We wanted to keep up the pressure," says anti-gaming Chief Harold Tarbell. When the BIA selected John Vance, a professor at the Bridgeport University School of Law in Connecticut to be mediator, Tarbell said, "The position we will present remains the same. We are consistent—the blockade will stop once the Warriors agree to disband and illegal gambling stops."

The Warriors found themselves in an ideological and tactical quandary, outmaneuvered by the anti-gaming faction. Francis and John Boots feared that the Warriors were losing the advantage they had gained during 10 months of battling the police, the FBI, and the government-sponsored councils. Moreover, Vance represented a new initiative to solve the gambling dispute. Instead of using the police or the FBI to vilify the Warriors, the government temporarily changed tactics, assigning a professional negotiator to address all parties and bring them together at the bargaining table.

"It looks like we have only two options," says John Boots. "Fight at the barricades and take back our territory from the antis, or join the negotiations set up by the white governments we do not trust."

No one wanted to pursue either option.

"We wanted to find a way to outmaneuver the antis without getting involved in physical attacks," says Minnie Garrow. "We asked ourselves if there was a way that we could send Vance a sign of our willingness to be part of a dialogue or discussion. The idea was to show everyone involved that we can use words to explain our position. We do not have to flash rifles to make our point.

"But we could not let Vance dictate the agenda. According to the antis, Vance was here to mediate what they call the 'gambling problem.' To get involved on that level was to let Washington set the rules. Instead, we thought of writing him a letter explaining our philosophical objections to the American and Canadian systems. We were going to focus on the Great Law of the Iroquois Confederacy and how it guides us to be skeptical of chiefs who encourage Mohawks to blockade other Mohawks."

On the evening of April 10, Garrow, Lazore, Francis and John Boots began drafting a three-page, single-spaced, typewritten letter to be presented as an official communication of the Warriors. "We appreciate your position as federal mediator, and respect your hopes of restoring order in the Mohawk territory of Akwesasne," the letter began. "Prior to mediation, it is imperative that you completely understand and respect our history, our concerns, our laws, and position. The Mohawk Warriors Society is a non-negotiable issue. All of the traditional males within the Iroquois Confederacy are Warriors. . . .

"The responsibilities of the men include acting as brothers, uncles, fathers, and grandfathers to all of the people, from the youngest to the oldest. The men must build. They must educate. They must work to provide for the people. Today, that has meant a shift from the land-based projects such as agriculture, hunting, etc. that are now insufficient. . . .

"We are also the protectors of the Haudenosaunee—the people of the Longhouse, the protectors of the Kaienerenkows—the Iroquois constitution. It is our collective responsibility to our future generations that our ways always continue. We govern ourselves consensually, based on the Iroquois constitution, which was established by the Creator."

After setting out the Warriors' claim to legitimacy under Mohawk law, the letter detailed demands that roadblocks be removed, that Mike Mitchell's expenditure of government funds to support the roadblocks be investigated, and a probe of the violent incidents involving employees of the American- and Canadian-chartered councils be undertaken. Garrow, Lazore, Rowena General, John and Francis Boots presented the letter to Vance on April 12.

"I told him that the traditional group of people in Akwesasne are reluctant to come forth," says Francis Boots, "because our constitution, which we call the Great Law, forbids us to participate in any activities of the tribal government and the band council, which are arms of the foreign governments of Canada and the United States. Though we do not recognize his authority, we see the need for discussion and mediation, not violence.

"I wanted him to see us as people who want to speak, but he had to know that we cannot alienate ourselves from the Great Law and lose our identity. We wanted Vance to see us as the Mohawks who will talk and listen to everyone if we receive the respect that we deserve."

While Vance found the letter to be a chilling rejection of the American legal and political system, pro-gaming chief L. David Jacobs saw it as a sign that the Warriors were eager to join the negotiating process. From his reading of the text, Jacobs believed he could form an alliance with the Warriors against the anti-gaming faction that was mounting barricades and demanding the closure of casinos. "Neither the Warriors nor I wanted the blockade to succeed," says Jacobs. "We didn't and still do not agree on many things, but we knew that the roadblocks could not be allowed to stand and close down the biggest businesses we had."

Jacobs has never had any moral or philosophical objection to casinos as long as they do not serve liquor. To him, the gaming halls were the territory's first steps toward bringing real economic power to the Mohawks. "I'll be the one to say it. This is all about money and power," he declares. "The roadblocks and barricades show everyone that the antis are only interested in protecting a clique led by Harold Tarbell and Mike Mitchell.

"If I were an accountant, I'd say that the casinos bring assets into a place that has been filled with liabilities. I understand that there are inequities in how this money is distributed. I know that some of the casino owners defy the state and federal laws, but I also know that this is the first time that Mohawks are generating large amounts of cash right here on our land.

"To get a paycheck to pay for houses and food for their children, our men and women do not have to walk the high steel. Those days are gone. The building boom is over. It's an economy that we don't control. The casinos threatened people like Mike Mitchell and Harold Tarbell, who use the councils to build a political-patronage machine. The casinos grow richer and stronger than their governments.

"As for the Warriors, these are the true believers in the Mohawk nation. They don't care about money as much as they care about pride and tradition. They want to prove that Mohawks are the noble victims of a Christian religion which only justifies the brutality and thievery of whites. The Warriors are convinced that our defeats will be avenged—if not this generation, then the next.

"As for me, I'm different. I think we got our asses kicked by whites and we have to change—not lose our identity, but change."

Jacobs met with Vance and formally presented the pro-gaming position of seeking compliance with federal laws that allow casinos on reservations. Citing the August referendum when Akwesasne residents backed gaming by a nine-to-one margin, Jacobs insisted that gambling had popular support. When asked about slots, he indicated that casino owners would give them up if state and federal governments authorized a Mohawk-run gaming commission.

Jacobs then asked the casino owners to tell the Warriors that they would be formally recognized by the two pro-gaming members of the tribal council in exchange for their cooperation in beating the blockade. As relayed by Tony Laughing and Eli Tarbell to Kakwirakeron, Jacobs said he and Lincoln White would guarantee passage of a tribal council resolution legitimizing the Warriors if they supported a call for the state police to dismantle the roadblocks.

Harold Tarbell's submission to Vance stridently reiterated his calls for an end to the casinos and the Warriors, with no sign of flexibility or compromise. Recognizing his advantage with the mediator, Jacobs kept chipping away, presenting himself as the man willing to talk with all parties. "The Warriors were tired and on the run," he says. "I couldn't beat the blockade on my own and neither could they. So my idea was to form an alliance. The Warriors would have direct access to the mediation and negotiation process to get rid of the blockades."

The Warriors balked at any arrangement that could be interpreted as making an agreement with the state police, but they were receptive to discussions with anyone who opposed the blockade. "At least the Warriors understood that I was a player and they could help themselves by dealing with me," says Jacobs. To test his progress, Jacobs introduced a tribal council resolution calling on the state police to enter the territory, dismantle the roadblocks, and arrest men and women who participated in the blockade. The resolution won the overwhelming support of a packed meeting at the Mohawk Bingo Palace. Members of the Warriors Society told the meeting they would welcome the police into Akwesasne if troopers confined their activities to clearing Route 37 and making sure traffic could flow without interruption. As a signal of good faith and to show the Warriors' support on this issue, Francis Boots and Kakwirakeron agreed to sign a protocol that said the tribal council and the Warriors were committed to initiatives aimed at ending the blockade and restoring peace to Akwesasne. It was the first time that the New York–chartered council officially acknowledged the legitimacy of the Warriors.

"This is a great moment for me," says Jacobs, "because it shows that Mohawks can come together and start a dialogue. There's hope for negotiation."

Boots explained the Warriors' decision to sign the protocol: "We are not participating in the tribal council and we are not saying it is a true representative of the Mohawk nation. The council is not asking us to participate in their affairs and we won't. All they want is for us to see their point of view and discuss ways of coming together. That's reasonable. In return, we have asked for the same consideration.

"Now, when Mohawks of all political and religious beliefs are being threatened by this group of anti-gambling terrorists who claim to be true heirs to our ancestors, the Warriors will stand with anyone who sincerely wants an end to this threat. The Mohawk people want the roadblocks taken down. Dave Jacobs knows that and so do we."

The fragile new alliance did nothing to curtail the violence. Shortly after midnight on April 18, a pro-gaming Mohawk named Richard Adams came to a halt at the anti-gaming roadblock at Twin Bridges. He was pulled from his car, beaten, and dragged through the muddy median strip. At that point Minnie Garrow drove by with her two teenage daughters and her grandson asleep in the back of her van.

"I'd decided to leave the territory for a few hours and visit some people in Plattsburgh," says Garrow. "I was on my way home—the road to my house is right near the bridge. And that's when I saw antis on the roadblock beating a Mohawk man.

"You know me. I went right in their circle and tried to pull them away. I tried to push my way through and I got to Richard and held him. I figured that they wouldn't hit a woman. Well, the antis started punching me in the shoulders, and they slugged me with a flashlight. Someone hit me with a stick or something.

"By this time, my daughter came running out of the car. But someone jumped in her way and put her in a bear hug for a moment, slapped her, then ran. I don't know how Richard got free and I was yelling at him to get in my car. When Richard opened the door, he jumped in and slammed it. I saw someone pull open a back door and yell or maybe he kicked the car, but my grandson was awake and crying. I don't know how my daughter got back to the car, but I just kept pushing people away and made it back to the car, then took off to the Warriors' base at the Onkwe Bingo Jack."

Less than an hour later, more than 40 Warriors marched straight into the barricade of hay bales, cars, plywood, and metal railings. As the antis ran for safety, flames engulfed the hay and plywood. The dented cars used to block the road were doused with gasoline and set ablaze. Around 2:15 a.m., a "liberated" New York Department of Transportation dump truck rumbled down Route 37, its steel snow plow pushing the blackened cars into the mud. With the road open the Warriors left.

After daybreak on April 19, the antis once again set up the road-block, with concrete blocks paid for by the Mohawk Council of Akwesasne and delivered to the site. Later, more than 300 local whites protested the closure of Route 37, by blocking the junction of Routes 37 and 122 at Westville, a hamlet just outside the reservation on the way to Fort Covington. When word of the protest reached the anti-gaming barricades, four key allies of Mike Mitchell's drove to the protest and offered to explain.

"We're here to tell you why we blocked the roads," said Canadian-elected chief Louis Lazore.

"That's an internal problem of your community," shot back protest leader Tom Latreille. "We don't want to get involved and we don't want you to punish us for divisions in your community. Your road-blocks are damaging our businesses and lives in this area. It has hurt us all because traffic cannot go through. Do you get our message?"

About 90 minutes after the white barricade went up, the state police arrived and ordered it removed. Many of the residents refused but troopers calmly took down the bales of hay, and asked pedestrians and motorists to disperse. "We didn't like it, but we weren't going to fight the cops," said Latreille. "But we did feel that there were two separate standards of law—the Indians can block the roads for three weeks and the cops do nothing. When we do the same thing, the cops are on us in a couple of hours. It doesn't seem fair, does it?"

Replies Troop B commander Maj. Robert Leu, "The people who live there are upset and I can understand that. But the blockades on the reservation are a totally different problem. The Mohawks are a divided people. If we go in, we're worried that they'll immediately close ranks against us. And they have an enormous amount of firepower."

Shortly after midnight on April 21, David Terrance heard a strange noise outside his trailer, located near the house of Warrior strategist Diane Lazore, who lived on River Road in Syne. Walking around the far corner of his home, Terrance, who did not belong to any political faction, saw flames crawling up the back wall. He ran inside, wakened his wife and bundled their sleeping children out through the front, while a neighbor called the Hogansburg Volunteer Fire Department. By the time the first truck arrived, the flames had roared through the roof, hallway, and back bedrooms. The Warriors saw the burning of the trailer as an attack meant for Lazore, a woman who lived alone with her infirm mother and children.

Throughout April 21 and April 22, spurts of gunfire from both sides filled the air. When the antis fortified their barricades, building sandbags and wooden obstacles, the Warriors pulled back to consider the effect of the Westville roadblock. "As the prospect of negotiations got further away, we thought about Westville, how they made their point without serious violence," says Minnie Garrow. "People wanted to do something, almost anything, to get the roadblocks down and show the antis how much their stupid barricades hurt the community. So we started calling people. We figured that we had a couple hundred people who were ready to go into the roads."

But the plan was almost derailed in the early morning hours of Monday, April 23, when firefighters received a call about a blaze tearing through the North American Indian Travelling College on Cornwall Island. Home to educational programs that employ a number of anti-gaming activists, the college was completely destroyed in a fire that began around 5:20 a.m. Authorities immediately suspected the Warriors.

"We thought about calling our barricades off because we didn't want to press the situation," says John Boots. "We knew the antis thought we set the fire, and of course that's not true. We took a couple of hours to think it through and then we realized that we shouldn't be intimidated by them. Our position was clear—we would set up the barricades, but we would never attack."

Throughout the sunny spring morning, dozens of small obstacles were placed on the winding roads along the St. Regis and Raquette rivers. "It worked like a dream," continues Boots. "We didn't have anything heavy or big, just a few people and some wood at each location. We harassed the antis, just as they were harassing us. People came out in support of us. Soon we had dozens of people stopping everybody and serving notice that we would no longer tolerate the antis."

At nightfall, the antis struck back. Around 8:10, anti-gaming activist Regis Lazore sped into a spontaneous protest against a month of blockades in Hogansburg. His car hit 26-year-old Louis Thomas, who was tossed up on the hood, then rolled off onto the road. Miraculously, he was able to stand, but within an hour, a core group of demonstrators had armed themselves with Molotov cocktails and stood in the back of a dump truck rolling straight for the anti-gaming barricade at Hogansburg. When the antis refused to leave, the demonstrators started throwing the firebombs, causing minor damage.

On the other side of the reservation, at the Twin Bridges anti-gaming barricade, a Warrior patrol was rammed. Warriors claimed that a melee followed and they were beaten by Richard Mitchell, his son Francis, and other antis. The Warriors also said that Richard Mitchell hit several Warriors in the thighs and groin with the nightstick he used in his job as an Akwesasne constable. Other antis punched the captives in the face and sprayed cleaning fluid and other chemicals all over their bodies.

Warrior Tommy Square was beaten unconscious. The antis then tied his hands and feet and threw him into the trunk of a car. He was taken to the Route 37 traffic circle and dumped at the feet of the state police. Troopers called it "a citizen's arrest."

17

THE WARRIORS CHARGE

"After the attack on Tommy Square, many of us were convinced that this was it," says John Boots. "The antis tried to kill him. They broke his bones. The police had the nerve to file weapons possession charges against Tommy. That sent us a clear message. The antis could do this and go unpunished.

"We told everyone about Tommy Square because we wanted all of our people to know that the antis are the ones who turn Mohawk against Mohawk. Our numbers grew and we spoke of obtaining justice. We had numbers on our side and the next day we were ready to dismantle the roadblocks."

As darkness settled over the Raquette River at 7:00 p.m. on April 24th, Warriors gathered near the Twin Bridges. According to anti-gaming activist Angela Barnes, the Warriors and their supporters unleashed a torrent of screams and shouts, threats and dares. At one point, several dozen men and women with bats and sticks marched toward the barricade. Three Molotov cocktails backed them off.

"That's how the violence started," Boots claims. "We were ready to move forward and confront them face-to-face, pull apart their fortifications, and chase them away. But they wanted to drive us back with homemade explosives."

The antis insist that the Warriors were the first to toss firebombs. "We had two bunkers and we split into two groups," says Barnes.

"Each group had water and would pour it on the flames if a firebomb crashed inside the bunker."

Over the next hour, the police would later claim, a large group of Warriors remained in front of the barricades, while Dewey Lazore, Louis Bush, Frank Mitchell, Alwyn Cook, Stacey Boots, Anthony David, Bruce Johnson, Dudley King, Stanley Thompson, Ray Herne, Chick Wheeler, Tony Wheeler, and Chuck Cole took up positions on either side of the bridge. "There were a number of weapons at the bridge," says Francis Boots. "We were not going to fire first, but we were going to make sure that our people were protected. We would not let the antis come out with their weapons and capture people like they did Tommy Square. We were ready to defend ourselves."

Around 9:00 p.m., the police report, the first volley of gunfire ripped through the night. Both sides blamed the other for starting the battle. "The antis saw more and more people gathering on the bridge and the antis were afraid," says Minnie Garrow, who was told of the shootout. "To keep them back," Garrow adds, "the antis would shoot off into the air or even on the bridge."

One anti, Richard Jacobs, claims that thousands of rounds were exchanged in an hour of shooting. Others say the Warriors continuously fired their AK-47s into the sandbags and parked cars. "There were upward of 300 to 500 rounds fired at people who were behind the barricades," says Kevin King, the "roadblock commander." King says he heard the Warriors threaten to storm the barricades with their automatic weapons. "They were yelling, 'We're gonna kill you motherfuckers.'"

During the gunfight, anti Ellen Herne telephoned Gov. Mario Cuomo's aide, Jeff Cohen. She even put the phone out her window so Cohen could hear the gunshots and press Cuomo to order intervention by the state police. But the gubernatorial aide remained low-key, unwilling to be drawn into a panic. Then the antis dialed Washington-based staff members of the U.S. Senate's Select Committee on Indian Affairs to say that Cuomo had ignored their pleas for help while an intense firefight was under way.

"Everybody knows there were guns out here, but if all that gunfire took place, someone would have been hit," says John Boots. "The antis threw firebombs at us. We threw them back and waited for our numbers to hit full strength. They saw a big crowd and they shot in the air, trying to scare us. That didn't work. So they shot again. We answered with warning shots in the air.

"That's how it went, back and forth for maybe an hour and a half. People will always say that this was a firefight or massive shootout. Not true. There were automatic weapons and you could hear them snap off the rounds. But we are talking about less than 200 rounds going into the air, not even that.

"Around 10:30, we were ready to move forward. We had more than a hundred people on the bridge. Again, they threw firebombs and I heard shots coming our way. Our people just started to run right at the hay bales and the sandbags. We had sticks and bats. The antis started to run. A few of them shot at us, the bullets kicking up the mud or flying way over our heads."

Behind the barricade, the Warriors found gasoline, kerosene, firebombs, ammunition, guns, and clubs. They doused the cars parked along the side of the road and set them and the hay bales on fire. Some of the Warriors celebrated their victory by shooting into the burning hulks.

From her living room window off Route 37, Bea White could see the entire riot. "I called the police barracks in Massena and asked them if they had any contingency plans for anyone caught in the attack," says White, who has avoided the extremes of both factions. "They said unless someone was killed, they could do nothing at all."

Around midnight, the Warriors turned their attention to the abandoned barricade on the other side of the territory near four corners in Hogansburg. Using flammable material the antis had left behind, the Warriors set fire to cars, wood and hay, destroyed the bunkers of sandbags and smashed the plywood screens and shields. Within 15 minutes, the eastern barricade was a pile of smoldering trash littering the roadbed. After 33 days, Route 37 was open.

At dawn April 25, when the sun's glimmer slid along the Raquette River, two pumper trucks from the Hogansburg Volunteer Fire Department arrived at the bridges. Fire Chief Frank Lacerneza just shook his head and said, "It looks like a war zone."

Four hours later, Harold Tarbell spoke to Alan Parker, the staff director for the U.S. Senate Select Committee on Indian Affairs. Tarbell claimed the Warriors had used sophisticated weapons to fire at homes and attack a school bus filled with women and children. When Parker asked if he had relayed this information to state officials, Tarbell replied that key aides to Governor Cuomo had repeatedly rejected requests for help and/or police intervention. "We had to go to the feds," insists Tarbell, "to up the ante and get the governor directly involved."

His Canadian counterpart, Mike Mitchell, worked the phones, telling provincial and federal officials there was an impending bloodbath. Mitchell claimed the Warriors' attack against the barricades involved thousands of rounds of automatic weapons' fire, coordinated fire-bombings and arsons, beatings, rammings, and a continued program of vengeance. He suggested the possibility of Warriors going house to house, seeking to punish men and women opposed to the casinos.

Provincial and federal officials agreed to help plan and pay for the evacuation of Mohawks to a temporary shelter run by the Canadian department of Transport in Cornwall. After being notified by officials of the ministry of Indian and Northern Affairs, supervisors of the RCMP, the OPP, and the Sûreté du Québec agreed to increase the number of officers available for duty on the Canadian side of the reserve. If needed, provincial officials said, they would recommend sending troops to Cornwall to bolster the police presence.

"That's the kind of response we wanted from Albany," says Tarbell, "but Cuomo wouldn't move."

That afternoon, however, U.S. Sen. Daniel Inouye, chairman of the Senate Select Committee on Indian Affairs, sent Cuomo a heated appeal on behalf of the antis:

My staff has received telephone reports last night and this morning from Head Chief Tarbell and his associates that the so-called Warriors Society group have literally surrounded the homes and barricades where members of the anti-gaming faction have assembled. Following the attack with a grenade and automatic weapons' fire of Tuesday night, it was reported that the Warriors Society personnel fired in excess of 1,000 rounds in the direction of homes of those who oppose the illegal gaming and at barricades, including a school bus occupied by women and children. The latest report is that members of the Warriors Society continue to fire in the direction of anyone venturing outside their homes and that Warriors Society members have been observed drinking heavily and congregating at several of the casinos.

I am aware that certain elected tribal officials have been opposed to federal and state intervention and have expressed support for maintaining casino operations on the reservation notwithstanding their illegal status under both federal and state law. Apparently, this latest escalation of violence by the Warriors Society has been seen by others, at least in part, as a response to the tribal government resolution signed by two of the chiefs designating the Warriors Society as a police force and requesting that the state police work with them. However, the majority of the elected tribal officials, under the leadership of Chief Tarbell, have opposed any such proposal and are urgently and unequivocally requesting the intervention of the state police or the National Guard.

Cuomo knew that he had to make a firm but low-profile defense of his policy of holding back the troopers. Instead of a personal appearance, he opted for a written statement to the press, acknowledging receipt of the letter and thanking Inouye for showing concern about such "a grave issue." The governor then went on to dissect the letter and its claims, carefully pointing out that the antis had repeatedly exaggerated the level of violence in an effort to draw the state police onto Mohawk territory. Cuomo emphasized the political nature of the gambling dispute and his belief that a strong police presence would not encourage Mohawks to solve their differences.

"First," says Dr. Henrik Dullea, Cuomo's director of State Operations, "we could not get into a fight with the chairman of a Senate committee. The whole point is to get a political, not a police or military, solution to this problem. We want dialogue, not guns."

"He's a chicken," Tarbell says of Cuomo. "How many times do we have to tell him that we are in danger? He'll let us get blown away."

"After talking to Ottawa, we seriously started to think about declaring an emergency and suggesting that families seek shelter in Cornwall," says Mike Mitchell. "The Warriors are terrorists and if they are going to have control of Akwesasne, then our land is not safe for anybody who wants gambling to stop and our people to lead normal lives."

"It was very clear that the Canadian government understood the threat to public safety, while Cuomo just shrugged," says Tarbell.

On the morning of April 26, Inouye's letter and Mitchell's discussions with Canadian officials made local headlines. The Warriors expected the antis to seek help from the federal governments, but they were startled by Inouye's references to the National Guard and reports that Canadians were considering sending troops to support an increased police presence. "We weren't going to panic and say that the army was on its way, but we understood Tarbell and Mitchell wanted tanks to roll in here and blow us away," says Francis Boots. "They were still figuring out ways to continue the battle. They didn't want to give up."

That afternoon, Brian Cole and a small group of antis tried to rebuild a barricade at Hogansburg. "Brian was making a very stupid move," says Cindy Terrance of *The People's Voice.* "It took about 15 minutes for a crowd to form. There were a few Warriors, but most were just the nearby residents who were sick and tired of this. Some people had bats and threatened to use them if Brian didn't stop with the roadblock. Well, he didn't. He grabbed his bat and off we went.

"It was pretty bad. The antis got stomped. It was a small riot. The people went crazy, yelling and screaming. You could hear them pounding on a parked truck and they just kept hitting on Brian and he was left lying there with broken bones and all kinds of internal damage. I hate to say it, but not too many people feel sorry for him."

Word of the vicious beating triggered rumors that the Warriors were compiling a hit list and that Cole was the first victim. "The antis said we were running a torture operation and a goon squad," says Minnie Garrow. "We told the reporters to come up here and drive around, watch the territory return to normal. This was the first time in more than a month that there weren't any roadblocks and people were enjoying it.

"When Brian Cole tried to build a new barricade—that's the only time a problem came up. And it was the people of that area, not the Warriors, who rushed to that corner. People were tired of this kind of shit and he got hurt. That sent a pretty good warning to the other antis. The Mohawk people—not just the Warriors—were not going to tolerate the roadblocks. It was over. The only way they could win was to make us into criminals and hope that the police or troops would come here to occupy the land."

Mike Mitchell made his move on the morning of April 27. He summoned reporters to the Canadian council offices and formally announced, "We can no longer guarantee the safety of our residents. I am encouraging people to seek safety and shelter in Cornwall, where the Canadian government will help us."

By noon, a caravan of trucks and cars carrying women and children was streaming out of the territory, through the city of Cornwall and on to the shelter, which offered cots and canned food, television and cards, cigarettes and magazines. "Everybody knew or felt that something was going to happen," recalls Doug George, the outspoken anti-gaming editor of *Indian Time.* "We were looking for the Warriors to attack at any moment. We had to defend ourselves, which meant guns and other weapons. We weren't going to go out in the open, but we were ready to fight if we had to."

At the Akwesasne police station, a detail of specially trained, heavily armed officers of the Sûreté du Québec arrived in their green-and-white cruisers. On Cornwall Island, Ontario, the Royal Canadian Mounted Police and the Ontario Provincial Police dispatched teams of officers to patrol the roads. On the New York side, Harold Tarbell informed members of Cuomo's staff of the evacuation plans and pressed for a contingent of National Guardsmen. Insisting that the Warriors had plans to wage a firefight, Tarbell said he expected violence by nightfall. Again, Cuomo's staff rejected the appeal, but reporters from national television and big-city newspapers were on hand to broadcast Tarbell's sharp denunciation of the governor.

Cuomo responded by meeting the Albany press corps. Choosing his words carefully, Cuomo praised the state police, noting that the troopers' restraint had helped contain the situation. Cuomo then cast doubt on claims in Inouye's letter that thousands of rounds were fired, noting that not one of those purported rounds wounded anyone. Finally, he pointed out that troopers stationed at the edge of the reservation had excellent access to information about the use of weapons and the threat to people not involved in the controversy. When asked why he would not send the troopers onto Mohawk territory, he echoed the police position that any intervention would ignite more violence.

"Nobody has said here's what you should do: paratroop in pointmen," Cuomo said in a somber baritone. "Everyone is saying the same thing, 'We want this situation resolved.' That's true. People want the Middle East resolved. And I want this resolved, and we're working very hard to figure out how to do it."

That evening, news broadcasts juxtaposed Cuomo's and Tarbell's comments with images of Mohawk women leaving their homes and Mohawk men brandishing AK-47s or Mini-14 assault rifles. Television also showed casinos open for business and drawing in hundreds of customers. But the viewers did not see the heavily armed Warriors and antis who followed each other's patrols up and down Route 37. "We were watching them and they were watching us," says Francis Boots. "Something didn't feel right. You could feel it, but you couldn't touch it. Even when dawn came, no one was relieved. It just meant another day of waiting."

18
THE KILL

"My brother Gordon and my 12-year-old son were watching TV," says Diane Lazore of Saturday afternoon, April 28. "The phone rang and Gordon got up to get it. He was walking right in front of the picture window. The sound of a shot—*clack*—rang out and then the bullet came crashing through the double pane. It was going for his head and it just missed him. They were trying to kill him. Less than 10 seconds later, *Frat-a-tat-tat.* They must have fired more than 500 rounds. My son and brother hit the floor and they crawled out the back, through the bushes and over the hill. I saw them on the road and they told me not to go home."

For Francis Boots and Minnie Garrow, the attack called for a strategy, not vengeance. But other Warriors disagreed, saying the time was ripe for a tumble or ambush. "It was very hard to hold back," Boots says, "but I had been telling people that the antis wanted us to fight. They wanted confusion and chaos to prove that the Warriors were violent and untrustworthy. That was our biggest test."

"If the antis had their way, my brother or son would be dead," Lazore says. "But they are very much alive, and so am I. Score one for us"—she stops to flash a grin —"but this has shaken me up. I see them lying on the floor, bleeding and yelling, no one hearing them. It's hard not to think about it. I went back to the house and you could see the holes in the walls, in the floor, the windows shattered. On the front siding, on the outside of the living room wall, you could see an arc of bullet holes and then the small clusters concentrated on particular spots."

"This was desperation and hate," Minnie Garrow says. "Though this was a declaration of war, we could choose the battlefield. We did not have to give in to other Mohawks who wanted to see our nation destroyed from within."

"The antis believed that we were so violent, so out of control, that we would be compelled to retaliate with a massive show of force," says John Boots. He went on to observe that if the Warriors used violence, they would be playing directly into the hands of the antis. Boots believed the antis were trying to demonstrate that the Warriors were out of control. "An act of violence," Boots claimed, "would give the antis a chance to parade in front of Cuomo or the Canadians and say, 'Look at how awful these Warriors are. We told you they were killers and you didn't believe us.'

"That's how cynical and childish they are"— Boots pauses, musing— "the antis wanted the police and the army to come on our land and force us to disband. What they didn't know was that we are so much better than their little game."

"I'd been up for two days worrying about the violence," Lazore says, standing in her living room. "Friday night, when we thought there would be a retaliation for Brian Cole, we figured the antis were waiting for the early morning light. But that passed and the day stretched until noon. I thought we were in the clear. Then came this. I look at the couch and think my son was sitting there. I wonder if these days will ever end."

Asked why she plans to stay overnight at the damaged house, Lazore replies, "My father built this house 50 years ago. It's my home."

The next day, a barricade of rocks, logs and tree stumps appeared on River Road, 300 yards from Lazore's house and directly in front of that of David George, Jr., brother of *Indian Time* editor Doug George. Davey had decided to create and man his own barricade so Warrior patrols could not circle through Snye and come out near Hogansburg.

"There was no choice," says Davey. "The Warriors aren't interested in peace or talking things out. They're interested in fighting and kicking our ass. They want casino money and cigarette money and they don't want to share any of it. They talk about being Mohawks, but do they hunt? Do they fish? No, they gamble and smuggle."

With the support of his brother Doug, Mike Mitchell, Barbara

Barnes, Akwesasne Police Chief Ernie King and his constables, Davey announced his intention to close the road until forced to leave or the casinos close. Since his house is on the Canadian side of the reserve, his barricade fell under the jurisdiction of King's police force. He believed that he could gain control of the River Road and force the Warriors away from this part of the territory.

"It's a real good strategy to stick to the Canadian side, where our police have the authority and the provincial and federal governments have said they would support our police," says Doug George. "Our fight with the Warriors has gone way beyond the councils and the casinos. This is about our identity as a people. We believe in democracy. They believe in thuggery. They want to push us around, to force us to have casinos and the frontier economy. I want something else and that's why we're fighting. If Governor Cuomo were interested in our safety, then there would be troopers all over Route 37. But he's not. It's cheaper to let us kill each other and impose a tax on whoever is left. If this happened in a town like Malone or Potsdam, do you think he would hesitate to call in the police? I don't."

For the next two and a half days, a fragile peace held. At the Onkwe Bingo Jack, the Warriors maintained their vigil around the Formica table, downing cup after cup of coffee and smoking an endless number of cigarettes. From the tribal council office, Harold Tarbell repeated his requests for state police or National Guard intervention; the politicians and bureaucrats listened politely and then refused. On their makeshift barricades, the antis grew nervous, convinced that a major Warrior attack could come at any minute.

On the night of April 30, a small crowd gathered at Davey George's house. Sometime after 9:00 p.m., Doug George says, the group received a phone call notifying them that Governor Cuomo was the guest on a statewide call-in show broadcast over a Plattsburgh television station. "That's when the first shots came in. The first volley was fast, almost like a warning," says Davey George, claiming that Warriors were hiding in the trees less than 100 yards to the west.

Instead of firing back, the George brothers say, Doug dialed the call-in show and explained his predicament to an associate producer, who immediately understood the potential for newsmaking drama. "It didn't take long," Doug recalls, "and I heard the voice. He said, 'This is Mario Cuomo.' I introduced myself and said, 'Governor, we are here being shot at and fighting for our lives. When will the police come and restore order so we can have peace?'

"He told me that I was exaggerating the problem. Can you believe that? You could almost hear the gunfire on the air. He offered the same old thing—the police will only make matters worse. He said, 'There are two sides to this. Sort it out.'"

According to Doug, the next burst of incoming gunfire began a few minutes after he hung up. "We knew the Warriors were out there," Doug says, "and they knew we were in here. We shot a few rounds back, but we couldn't get a clear view. This was going to be one hell of a night. I took a handful of caffeine pills and prepared myself."

"You really couldn't figure out what was going on out there," Davey says. "So we hung back."

Around 4:00 a.m., members of the Akwesasne police force knocked on the door of Teddy Thompson's house, less than 200 yards east of Davey George's and Louis Mitchell's homes. "The cops were in uniform and they tell him he's got to get out, evacuate, because it's not safe," says Teddy's son, Peabody. "He gets into the car with his nephew and drives away, but the cops stay behind."

At daybreak, the antis heard the distant hum of a speedboat running up the St. Regis River as it curves behind Davey George's house. Davey says he suspected that the group of men standing in the hollowed hull were Warriors evading the barricades to launch an attack. Less than a minute later, as the boat came closer to shore, the antis claim automatic weapons' fire flew across the water. After the boat passed, the George brothers say, a second volley came from the grove to the left.

"We had people in the woods, but not on the water," says Francis Boots. "The night before, we knew that the antis had gathered at Davey George's. They had a whole bunch of guns and we suspected they were going to move on what was left of Diane Lazore's house. So we had people out there to protect her. When the antis fired at the boat, some of our people figured the gunfire would come their way next. They did not want to wait. So they shot high as a warning."

Minutes later the rapid fire of AK–47s and AR–15 assault rifles again tore through the trees, then stopped. "That's how it went," says John Boots. "Whenever they made a threatening move toward us, we fired into the air."

In the midst of what the antis call a "pitched battle," they received additional ammunition from an Akwesasne police officer, whom they will not identify.

From the east of Davey George's house, near the edge of the river as it curved past Teddy Thompson's house, the George brothers say they spotted someone. Camouflaged in military fatigues, his shoulders hunched, running low to the ground, the young man appeared to be heading toward the grove allegedly controlled by the Warriors. Another volley of automatic weapons' fire exploded and a scream pierced the air.

Around 6:00 on the morning of May 1, anti-gaming activist Barbara Barnes received a phone call, telling her that someone had been shot near the barricade at Davey George's house. Instead of notifying the ambulance or the provincial police, Barnes called Bruce Roundpoint, a general contractor who had done jobs for the Canadian council controlled by Mike Mitchell. Roundpoint left his home on Cornwall Island in the pickup that he frequently used for work. Crossing the international bridge into New York, he followed Route 37 into Hogansburg and onto River Road in Snye. By the time he arrived, Akwesasne police Chief Ernie King and constables were on the scene, attending to a skinny young man who had been shot in the stomach.

Roundpoint lowered the gate of his truck and the bleeding man was placed in the back. As police officers began to pick up ejected shells scattered on the ground, Roundpoint was told to drive the wounded man to the fire station in Fort Covington. From there, a volunteer ambulance crew would transport the victim to the emergency room at Alice Hyde Hospital in Malone.

At 6:30 a.m., Beverley Papineau, who lives in Snye, saw a sight she will never forget. "I came across Bruce Roundpoint's truck," she says. "I could plainly see that Bruce was driving. A second car was behind Roundpoint's. In this car sat Louis Lazore, elected to serve on the Canadian council. In plain view in the back of Bruce Roundpoint's truck were two men. There was also a body lying in the truck. The head and the shoulders were covered with a camouflage jacket and I could only see the legs protruding."

Approximately 10 minutes later, Roundpoint arrived at the fire station and the wounded man was transferred by ambulance more than 20 miles to Malone. The emergency doctors and nurses received a patient who had lost a tremendous amount of blood; he was shivering because of a rapid drop in temperature. At first, surgery and transfusions were effective and his vital signs strengthened. Then an undetected clot choked the supply of blood. Around 9 a.m., Matthew Pyke, 22, was pronounced dead.

"It was murder and Doug George and his goons wanted to blame us. They didn't even stop to think of poor Matthew Pyke, lying there and then thrown on the back of a truck," says Minnie Garrow. "His suffering had to be put into their scheme. And they worked real hard to do it.

"Many of us met at the Bingo Jack—John Boots, Rowena General, Diane Lazore, Larry Thompson, Dana Leigh Bush, Dewey Lazore. All of us believed that the police would be coming at any moment, but we were wrong and we soon found out why."

Since the body was found in Quebec, Canadian law gave Akwesasne police Chief Ernie King and his constables jurisdiction over the crime scene. Instead of seizing weapons and isolating each of the participants and witnesses so they could make independent statements, the Mohawk cops milled around River Road. "They said that Matthew was found about 50 yards from my house," says Diane Lazore, "and after the shooting no one could get near there except for the antis and Ernie King's cops. People saw the Akwesasne police and the antis walking back and forth, pointing and talking as if nothing had really happened. The antis still had their guns. The police were picking up the bullet casings and throwing them away.

"Then we started to hear how Bruce Roundpoint's truck came from Cornwall and took the body down the back road. The antis didn't even call the ambulance service at Akwesasne, which was less than 10 minutes away. Instead, this truck has to come around the long way to Snye and then goes to the farthest hospital in Malone. The Akwesasne ambulance corps would have taken Matthew to the hospital in Cornwall and he would have been in surgery within a half hour.

"And then we found out that Matthew's brother, Larry, was the Akwesasne ambulance crew chief on duty at the time of the shooting. Can you believe that? He would have driven the ambulance to save his brother's life."

Garrow, Lazore, and John Boots understood that their first move had to be a press release denouncing the violence, thereby pre-empting any effort to claim the killing was the result of trigger-happy Warriors. "Matthew was known to be against the casinos," says Boots, "and we figured that the antis would claim we killed him to intimidate our political opponents. We had to show that we were not involved in any way."

For Boots, the most important task lay in reconstructing the early morning gunfire that climaxed with Pyke's wounding. Speaking to the Warrior men who were in the woods, checking the Warriors' log of radio dispatches and confrontations, Boots discovered that the base received reports of gunfire from River Road. "People called us up to tell us that they heard some gunfire during the night," says Boots. "They told us that the George brothers were up all night and wanted action. The calls came from the River Road area, from people who live there. And our own people in the woods say the antis fired off and on through the night, but the real heavy gunfire came in the morning."

As Garrow and Lazore worked on a press release that "denies, absolutely, any involvement" with the fatal gunplay, Boots and other Warrior men began to consider the possibility that Pyke might have been shot by mistake. The men sketched a map that indicated a direct line of fire from Louis Mitchell's house to the spot where the body was found. "Matthew Pyke came right into their sights," notes Boots. "I don't know why he was there or where he was going, but it looks like he was easily seen. Somebody on the anti side could have panicked and thought he was a Warrior leading an attack."

"It was a mistake. This was the only way we could explain why the antis couldn't let the ambulance corps handle it," says Garrow. "They had to keep the shooting away from any outsider because they had to create a story and keep to it.

"I mean, if they had evidence that a Warrior shot Matthew Pyke, we would have known about it. A whole army of policemen would have stormed our headquarters, searched us up and down. No, we figured that the antis couldn't have any evidence against us. But we were very scared."

At noon, the Akwesasne police still controlled the crime scene. "We had received calls about gunfire that morning," says state police spokesman Sgt. Michael Downs, "but it was difficult to get a handle on what was going on. When we called the Quebec authorities, they said they were also unsure about what happened."

Around 2:00 p.m., the Warriors received a phone call telling them that a fire had engulfed Diane Lazore's house. "I was screaming and we raced down there, but we had to go all the way across the territory. By the time I got there, nothing was left. The firemen were spraying water on a collapsed house. They told me that the antis had blocked the road. They said they had to wait for 10 minutes while my house burned and burned."

Less than an hour later, Joe Gray left the office of the Massena *Daily Courier Observer* and drove east on Route 37 toward the reservation. After parking his car within sight of the barricade set up in front of Davey George's house, he wandered around. "I got there around three and everything was pretty quiet," says Gray. "I could see some smoke and smell that something had burned, but I didn't know about the fire. I was just there to look around."

Walking through a lightly wooded section, Gray noticed a body lying on the ground next to the cinder-block chimney of a house on the south side of River Road. "You could see the blood smeared on the siding and the guy lying on the ground, face up," says Gray. "He wasn't moving. I went for the barricade, where I met this husky guy in a hunter's jacket and a cap. It was Davey George, and I told him, 'Hey, there's a guy lying down there who needs some help.'

"Davey says, 'Did he have a camouflage jacket on? I'm looking for a guy with a camouflage jacket.'

"I said, 'No, I don't think so, but I'm not sure.'

"'Well,' he says, 'I think you should get out of here. The Warriors might start shooting again.'

"I tried to tell him again that the guy needed help, but he said, 'Get out of here. This isn't very safe. The Warriors could start shooting at any time.'

"It was clear that he wasn't going to help. I had a short telephoto lens on my camera and I wanted to take a picture and double-check if the guy had a camouflage jacket. Then I would get help. I figured there was a pretty good story here.

"I followed the road to a bend where I saw a man working outside on his house. He had a cast. I just walked up and said, 'Hey, there's somebody lying over there and it looks like he's been shot.'

"Well, this guy tells me his name is Tommy Square. He was a Warrior and he was just beaten up a few days ago. He said he had heard a lot of gunshots that morning, but the Warriors weren't around. He figured the antis were shooting, but the bullets were going in the air.

"We got to the body and it was clear that the man was dead. Tommy Square went back to make a phone call. I went down the road to find Davey George, but he was gone. A few minutes later, the first group of Warriors started to arrive. I guessed Tommy Square called them. Soon there was a small crowd around the body, and I just watched the show. I had my pictures and my story."

While the Warriors gathered off River Road, reporters traveled to where Canadian Grand Chief Mike Mitchell and his American counterpart, Harold Tarbell, held a press conference to declare Pyke a martyr, viciously gunned down by men who cloak themselves in political argument but settle debates with bullets. The chiefs repeatedly called for outside police help, if not military assistance to quell what they called "the roving bands of terrorists who shoot and kill" to further their political aims. Mitchell and Tarbell noted that more than 1,000 Canadian troops stood ready at a garrison outside Cornwall, about 18 miles away from the territory.

"We hope it doesn't get to the point that the army is needed," Mitchell said. "But we have to restore order and the only way to restore order is to have the Warriors disband. I don't know if we can negotiate this, but I'm willing to try. In our nation, on our land, we have one big dispute over gambling, but we have two different white responses. The Canadians are very clear. They will not allow gambling and they will not allow the Warriors to front for gambling. The New York response is to wait and see, let the Mohawks shoot themselves up first, then maybe do something."

Adds Tarbell, "There is long, detailed public record of my request for police assistance and police protection. Well, now it was too late. To have shootings over a disagreement over casinos is far too high a price. But Governor Cuomo, the state police, and the Bureau of Indian Affairs—they don't listen, do they? There's no votes up here. We're just Mohawks. Why send in the troopers? We're not worth it."

After the press conference, Tarbell went to visit his friend Brian Cole, still hospitalized as a result of the April 26 beating that followed his attempt to re-establish the anti-gaming barricades. "I was painting a pretty ugly picture," recounts Tarbell. "I told him that I didn't expect any help, that this would just go on. He tried to make a joke. He wanted to cheer me up. Isn't that something? I was sitting there complaining and the guy with the broken bones is trying to make me feel better. And then the phone rings. Since Brian's in bed, I answer.

"The voice on the other end sounds real official and says, 'Hello, may I please speak with Chief Tarbell?'

"I'm pretty surprised. I mean how did someone find me over here. So I say, 'This is Chief Tarbell.'

"Then I'm told, 'Please wait, Governor Cuomo will get on the line.' "Then you can hear the voice, you know it, and he says, 'Chief Tarbell, this is Mario Cuomo.'

"He wanted me to wilt or become intimidated and I wasn't. He said that the Sûreté du Québec wanted to travel over the international bridge at Cornwall, come into the traffic circle, drive into Akwesasne on Route 37, go into Hogansburg, and take the back roads to the crime scene in Quebec."

"I said, 'That's fine.'

"'But,' Cuomo said, 'I'm ordering the New York State Police to escort them. You'll see a long line of Canadian and New York police.'

"I told him it was about time. And he said he was sending up Dr. Henrik Dullea, his director of State Operations, to serve as his personal envoy and mediator. I asked him if this meant his office would be available to mediate. He answered, 'Absolutely.'

"When I hung up, I told Brian and he smiled. It was late, maybe too late, but now the Warriors and the casino owners would have to deal with the state. When I got back to Akwesasne, I heard about the second body, who had been identified as Harry Edwards, Jr. I don't know if he was a Warrior, but he certainly was in favor of the casinos."

Minnie Garrow knew J. R. Edwards as an easygoing, almost happy-go-lucky man, neither political nor strident. The 32-year-old had pieced together a living by walking steel and returning to Akwesasne between jobs. "I think he might have played a card game in the casino here or there. Maybe he joined a pro-gambling march when Tony's was ransacked. But that was it," says Garrow. "And now this. There was no need for these people to die. They are young men."

By the early evening, the Warriors had evidence supporting their claim that Matthew Pyke was mistakenly shot by antis: after the shootings, when he was allowed back in his father's house, Peabody Thompson discovered a box of bullets and two baseball caps—one with "Steve" over the bill, the other with "Mike."

As interpreted by Thompson and the Warriors, this discovery indicates that the Akwesasne police cleared the Thompson house and then used it as a firing position for the antis. "It makes sense to us that they believed that Warriors were gathered at Diane Lazore's," says John Boots. "So they would want to take over Teddy Thompson's house, which has a straight shot at Diane's. Then, early in the morning, when the light was bad, Matthew Pyke was running near Teddy's trying to get in on the action. In the bad light, they didn't know who he was—he looked like a Warrior—and they shot him. That's the only way it makes sense to us. As for J. R. Edwards, we can't figure it out. Matthew Pyke was found east of the barricade and J. R. was found west. J. R. was shot in the back and he wasn't armed. It looks like he was running or hiding or something. Nobody knows."

Shortly after 6:00 p.m., as the Warriors collected information for another statement to be released to the press, the phone rang. "I expected a reporter looking for information about the shootings," Boots said. "They were calling all day. So I answer, 'Warriors' base.' The voice on the other end says, 'This is Mario Cuomo.'

"I take a moment and say, 'Hello, Governor. This is John Boots.'

"He says hello, then asks if he could speak to someone in authority. I told him, 'We don't have someone in authority. We work by consensus.' Then he says, 'I have instructed the state police to escort the Sûreté du Québec along Route 37 as they drive into the scene of the killings. Will you guarantee their safety?'

"I told him, 'With all due respect, I can't guarantee anything. No one wants more violence, but we have to talk about this. Give us a few minutes.'

"He said he understood and hung up. Our immediate response was to cooperate and show appreciation for the fact that the governor called us and, in his way, asked for our help. I think it was Minnie who came up with the idea of our patrols meeting the state police at the border to our territory and escorting them through.

"When he called back, we told him that. He appreciated our position and he told me specifically that the troopers were coming through just to escort the Canadian authorities to the crime scene. To me, it was very, very clear that he was asking for a limited police presence that would end within hours."

At 8:00 p.m., a line of blue-and-yellow state police cruisers started to roll down Route 37, accompanying the green-and-white vehicles of the Sûreté du Québec. For more than 90 minutes, the police cars kept coming. When it was over, the New York State Police had once again set up roadblocks, while the Sûreté du Québec established a command center in the middle of St. Regis village. One police spokesman estimated that more than 400 New York and Canadian officers were stationed along the roads that connected Cornwall, Hogansburg, St. Regis, and Snye.

"It was an absolute invasion," says Francis Boots. "We were tricked and deceived. The police just rolled in and took over."

19
THE RULES OF EVIDENCE

"We were not very pleased," says Dr. Henrik Dullea, director of State Operations for New York, in something of an understatement. "The state police mentioned that the body was found 'over there,' meaning on the Canadian side. I understood immediately that this was a rite of passage. The situation at the St. Regis Indian Reservation had gone into a totally new phase. The biggest threat to public safety was the concentration of firepower, the weaponry believed to be in the hands of the Warriors and other Mohawks. We were worried about revenge and continued escalation of violence."

Within minutes, Cuomo and Dullea contacted state police Superintendent Thomas Constantine, ordering him to devise a plan for possible intervention. The governor also instructed Constantine to begin discussions with the Sûreté du Québec, which was responsible for the investigation of the killing. "This was an international incident involving a complicated protocol and a number of governments and their departments," said Dullea. "My job was to represent New York State."

Throughout the day of the killings, Constantine and SQ officials spoke over the telephone as did Dullea and John Passarella, the chief of staff to Quebec Premier Robert Bourassa. Although Canadian and American law-enforcement officials had conducted face-to-face, informal discussions about Akwesasne since the middle of April, no one had formulated a plan of action. "When the anti-gaming barricades were up, we spoke about what to do if the situation warranted a joint Canadian and American response," Dullea points out. "But until the killings of May 1, we had never received any official communication requesting us to deploy troopers or the National Guard. The provincial police were very concerned that they would be fired on if they drove through the American side of the territory. The Sûreté du Québec asked Constantine if our state police would escort the provincial authorities along the road. We agreed."

That escort role became the cornerstone of the New York State Police plan, notes Dullea. "When the Sûreté du Québec said they were ready, Constantine went to the Massena barracks, stood in front of the troopers and personally gave them their instructions, telling them in very clear terms what was expected and how our role was to avoid violence. Once the decision was made to send the troopers along Route 37, Constantine wanted a lot of manpower. He was afraid of heavily armed Mohawks surrounding one or two police cruisers and hurting his troopers. So the first 40 went in with the long convoy of Sûreté du Québec officers and then additional New York State troopers arrived. By the middle of the next day, we had set up a rotation that involved close to 200 troopers."

At the same time, the Quebec authorities planned an international meeting to be held on May 3 at a hotel near Montreal's Dorval airport. In Toronto, then Ontario premier David Peterson also scheduled a special session with Cuomo, when both were to attend a conference of Great Lakes premiers and governors held in Buffalo. From Albany, Dullea was dispatched to Akwesasne, where he received a state police tour of the territory and then settled into office space above the Bear's Den. His first meetings included separate sessions with Harold Tarbell, L. David Jacobs, and Lincoln White, followed by a delegation of Warriors and their lawyer, Stanley Cohen.

"Chief Tarbell was obviously relieved that the police had taken their positions on the territory," recalls Dullea. "Chiefs Jacobs and White expressed their desire to meet with me and negotiate, but they openly wondered about the police presence. As for the Warriors, I met Francis Boots, Rowena General, Minnie Garrow, and Stanley. They were polite and cordial, but they made it very clear that they would not participate as long as the police were on the territory. I wanted to let them know that I was available and we exchanged phone numbers, both my home and my office. Then they left. The next morning, I was on my way to Dorval."

As delegations of officials juggled meetings, they desperately tried to overcome problems of split jurisdictions. High-ranking Canadians claimed Cuomo's repeated refusals since January to dispatch police or National Guard troops amounted to an official acceptance of illegal gambling and the Warriors. In the House of Commons, the minister of Indian and Northern Affairs, Tom Siddon, launched a thinly veiled attack on Cuomo, saying the Americans spurned earlier offers of a joint police or military response to the violence. "It is our desire to see the State of New York cooperate and assist in dealing with the element that appears to be provoking this incident," Siddon said, implying that the governor was reluctant to deal with the Warriors, thereby encouraging the group to pursue violence.

Siddon's sentiments were echoed by then Canadian solicitor general Pierre Cadieux, who insisted that his government had repeatedly sought American assurances that the state police or FBI would be sent to Akwesasne if the Sûreté du Québec, the Ontario Provincial Police, or the RCMP moved in. Cadieux claimed that Canadian officials were poised to order a large-scale police operation weeks before the killings, but were held back by the Americans' unwillingness to launch a similar move on their side of the border. "We have been after a concerted effort from the start," said Cadieux.

At the Great Lakes conference, Cuomo rebutted Canadian claims that his restraint contributed to the explosive atmosphere: "The bodies were found on the Canadian side and our state police do not go on the Canadian side." When the reporters asked Peterson if he felt New York's policy contributed to the violence, he was diplomatic: "We have our responsibilities, and to the best of our abilities, we have fulfilled those. I don't think it's constructive for me to just sit here and cast blame. I am looking for constructive solutions."

At the meeting in Montreal, however, sharp rhetoric continued. Speaking to more than 30 representatives of New York, Ontario, Quebec, and the federal governments of Canada and the United States, the Canadian deputy minister for Indian and Northern Affairs, Harry Swain, said his government was willing to consider a role for the military and he sought a similar commitment from the Americans, who openly resisted any troop deployment. "We worked to set up a system to cooperate among the police agencies," says Dullea, who indicated that New York did not see the Mohawks as a military menace, but a loosely organized group threatening public safety. "Though we knew that the Canadians had positioned troops in that area, it was never our desire or intent to follow that lead and we didn't."

All the talk about police and troops skirted the major difference among governments—gambling. The American federal government clearly encouraged all tribes to work with state officials in starting businesses such as bingo halls and casinos, a move adamantly opposed by the Canadians. When Dr. Edward Brown, the director of the U.S. Bureau of Indian Affairs, pointed out that American federal law gives Mohawks the right to gamble on their land, the Canadians countered that fast cash from gaming could easily flow across the border and encourage smuggling in cigarettes, fuel oil, and building supplies.

"In many ways, that is the nub of the intra-government approach to this problem," says Carl Shaw, the BIA's spokesman. "Our laws do not agree with the Canadian laws. They do not want gambling of any kind and we want regulated, controlled gambling that brings money into the territory."

While the American and Canadian police worked together to stop the spread of weapons, the bureaucrats and government officials pursued opposing political strategies: the Canadians openly encouraged Mike Mitchell and his anti-gaming council, while the Americans tried to broker an agreement that would legalize gambling as proposed by tribal chief L. David Jacobs.

"After the meeting in Dorval broke up, I went back to Akwesasne to meet with the Tarbell faction and the Jacobs faction," says Dullea. "It is a matter of law. Whether I want gambling or not, the federal law is crystal clear: a state that allows certain forms of gambling must negotiate with Indians seeking to have the same rights. That's why I went back."

Dullea spent several days in Akwesasne trying to negotiate an agreement, but the Warriors held to their decision to reject negotiations while the state and provincial police forces occupied Mohawk land. "We do not talk with a gun pointed at our head," says Minnie Garrow. "We understand that New York has different interests than Ontario or Quebec and we are willing to work with all three governments. But they must be willing to work with us. You cannot work with us when you're sitting on top of us, when we cannot breathe. The police had to go if we were to negotiate."

"We had to figure out a way to show our defiance and our resistance," says Francis Boots. "First, we would not accept Dullea as the man to define the agenda. If he said, let's work out rules for living side by side, then we might have something to talk about. But he was only interested in saying, how can we get you to have casinos in compliance with our laws? That has nothing to do with what we are about. Second, we have to show Mohawks that we can stand up and say no. We can stand on our own traditions, and it is up to us to decide how we live. Our people have to see this political alternative to living under occupation."

Hours after the killings on May 1, Doug George went underground—as would his brother Davey. Telling Eric Siblin of the Canadian Press that the Warriors had put together a hit list of 200 anti-gaming Mohawks, Doug George said, "There is no police force, whether it's Mohawk or state troopers, that can guarantee my safety. I would rather leave than put my friends and family in the position of having to avenge my death."

George's claim of a hit list made headlines, but the Ontario Provincial Police, the Sûreté du Québec, and the New York State Police doubted its existence. Indeed, as they took control of the territory, the police discovered that the Warriors had opted to avoid all confrontation. New York State Police spokesman Sgt. Michael Downs reported that when police contacted the Warriors Society they received the stiff but cordial treatment they expected. "We knew that the Warriors did not want us anywhere near the territory," says Downs, "but they were polite and honest. There was no deception, or any hint of any plan to commit violence."

On Cornwall Island, the OPP officers and RCMP secured the international border and the bridge spanning the St. Lawrence River with roadblocks and searches for weapons. The Mohawks complied with a stern and distant demeanor. "The whole point was not to give any cop an excuse to make the situation worse," says Garrow.

On River Road, the Sûreté du Québec had taken control of the crime scene, and investigators were piecing together the events on the evening of April 30 and the morning of May 1. Police uncovered a trail of clues that raised serious questions about Doug George, his decision to flee, the role of the St. Regis Akwesasne Mohawk Police, and the anti-gaming faction's attempt to blame the Warriors for the deaths of Matthew Pyke and Harry Edwards, Jr.

While Doug and Davey George disappeared, allegedly to protect themselves from the Warriors, Akwesasne police officers slipped across the St. Lawrence River to the Holiday Inn in Cornwall. With the approval of their boss, Akwesasne police Chief Ernie King, and Canadian Grand Chief Mike Mitchell, the Mohawk constables kept away from the crime scene, as Mitchell issued press releases urging the Sûreté du Québec to concentrate their probe on the Warriors.

Police investigators patiently stitched together statements that detailed how the George brothers had mounted the roadblock with the express consent of the Akwesasne police and how Mohawk constables had used their private vehicles and weapons to resupply the men hunkered down at Davey George's. Peabody and Teddy Thompson came forward to tell the SQ that Mohawk constables took over the house at 4:00 a.m., approximately two hours before the heavy shooting began. In their statements, the Thompsons emphasized that the constables left their hats and a box of ammunition, .30-06 shells, which could be used in the rifle that belonged to anti Ken Lazore.

When the Sûreté du Québec approached the Warriors, lawyer Stanley Cohen advised his clients to request that the Canadians comply with the established protocol of contacting their American counterparts and setting up an interview under the auspices of the state police. "Because I am not licensed to practice in Canada, this guaranteed my presence," says Cohen. "And we wanted as many official witnesses as possible. We had no direct information about the killings and we wanted as many police officers as possible to hear it straight so we could end their suspicions of us."

By the end of the first week in May, the Sûreté du Québec had focused their probe on the men at Davey George's, approaching them one by one, asking questions. According to Constable Roger Mitchell, the police developed a portrait of 10 to 15 men clustered in and out of the house, each man having access to a small arsenal that included .38 caliber police service revolvers, 9 mm automatic pistols, .380 caliber automatic pistols, hunting rifles including one .30-06, an AK-47 assault rifle, a .22 caliber rifle and shotguns. Mitchell and other constables claimed the antis were firing east, in the direction of Yellow Island, an uninhabited strip of land sitting in the middle of the St. Regis River, from where Warriors were shooting.

But the Sûreté du Québec could not find any definitive evidence to place the Warriors on the island. Indeed, the SQ detectives received statements indicating that the antis were firing in the opposite direction, toward the scene of the killings. At least two constables admitted that they saw Matthew Pyke drive up to the Thompson residence, get out of his car, and run around the corner of the house.

A moment later, Roger Mitchell told investigators, he heard Pyke yell, "I been hit."

Mitchell and fellow constables Steve Lazore and Kenny Lazore later testified in Quebec provincial court that they did not call an ambulance even though they were on the scene when Pyke fell. They waited with other constables and Chief Ernie King for Bruce Roundpoint to bring his truck. Then Mitchell and Steve Lazore left the scene, traveling to the home of St. Regis Akwesasne Mohawk Police dispatcher Elizabeth Sunday, where they made several phone calls, including one to Ernie King at Davey George's and to members of the Canadian band council, who used cellular phones to keep in contact with the men on the barricade.

Mitchell further testified that he saw Davey George point a rifle at Arthur Yopps, a River Road resident who walked out of the forest holding a white flag. He said he also saw Doug George wandering around the roadblock looking to borrow a gun. Virtually all of the men who testified said they witnessed shots being fired from Davey George's toward the Thompson house where Pyke was found.

By Friday, May 11, the SQ had presented their findings to Crown Prosecutor Raynald Sauvage assigned to the Palais de Justice at Valleyfield. With his approval, the Sûreté du Québec wanted Kenny Lazore and Roger Mitchell taken in for questioning; Davey George was to be arrested on misdemeanor charges of weapons possession. As for Doug George, the authorities sought his arrest on second-degree murder for the killing of Edwards. "All the evidence is circumstantial," said Sauvage.

Lazore, Mitchell, and Davey George were eventually released, but Doug George surrendered and was jailed in lieu of $15,000 bail. Upon his release a few days later, he said, "The prosecutor will never be able to prove that the bullet that killed Edwards was fired from a gun in my hands."

Five months later, a judge dismissed the murder charge against George.

FREEDOM FIGHTERS AT THE COUNTRY CLUB

PART III

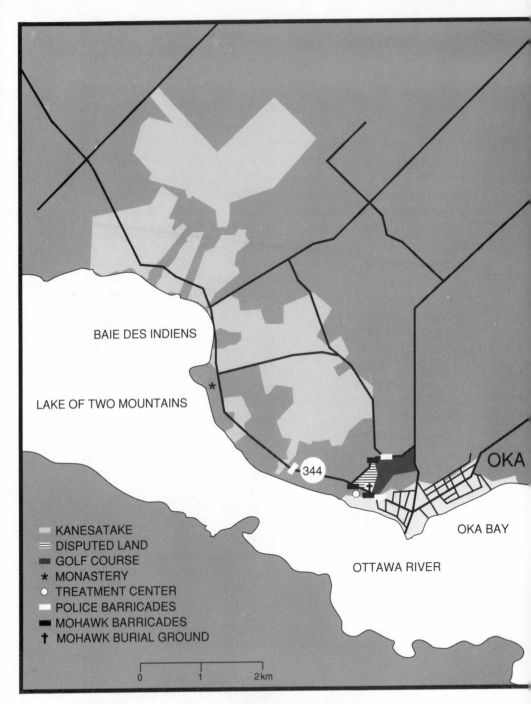

BAIE DES INDIENS

LAKE OF TWO MOUNTAINS

*

344

OKA

OKA BAY

OTTAWA RIVER

KANESATAKE
DISPUTED LAND
GOLF COURSE
* MONASTERY
○ TREATMENT CENTER
POLICE BARRICADES
MOHAWK BARRICADES
† MOHAWK BURIAL GROUND

0   1   2km

KANESATAKE

20
THE LEISURE CLASS
TEES OFF

The arrest of Doug George changed the political landscape: though the Warriors took it as a small but important vindication, the Canadian authorities saw it as a sign of increasing civil disorder. While the Warriors grudgingly conceded that cops had conducted a fair inquiry, they knew they were now dealing with a government that had already placed troops on standby if police could not contain the situation.

"We were pleased that the Sûreté du Québec did not trump up a case to arrest any of us," says Francis Boots. "But once Doug George was arrested we did not want to be involved in any way. To us, the arrest was used to show that the police were needed to restore and maintain order. And that is not good for any Mohawk."

As the Sûreté du Québec and New York State Police tightened their grip on Akwesasne, the predominantly white press portrayed the Warriors as unwilling to compromise; however, this view merely strengthened their support among Mohawks throughout northern New York and Canada. "The media was one of their best weapons," says pro-gaming tribal Chief L. David Jacobs. "Every day, the papers and the television stations were filled with stories and pictures of Warriors, bold and dramatic. Their high profile captured the imagination of our territory. While I had to deal with reality and negotiate with bureaucrats, the Warriors could become the stuff of mythology— self-made legends in their own time. You could see them every morning, noon, and night. Just turn on the tube and pick up a paper."

At Kahnawake, where Mohawks believed the government was looking to clamp down on bingo and buttlegging, the Akwesasne Warriors became symbols of pride and independence. Francis and John Boots, Minnie Garrow, and Diane Lazore were hailed as leaders of an uprising against the elected councils and chiefs such as Mike Mitchell and Harold Tarbell, and against the white authorities who stood behind them. At Kanesatake, where Mohawks were fighting the expansion of a golf course onto an ancestral burial ground, the Akwesasne Warriors were a source of strength and inspiration.

"When we first started to stand up and resist in March, building our barricade on the ninth, the people of Akwesasne stood with us and answered our requests for help," says Denise Tolley, a member of the traditionalist faction working out of the Kanesatake Cultural Centre. "They came to our barricade and supported our actions, saying we were all part of one Mohawk nation and an attack upon one part is an attack upon us all. By April, they were under attack, with the antis blocking the roads and terrorizing Akwesasne, so they could not devote their attention to us. But we kept talking to them, offering our help or seeking their advice."

Triggered by the threat to the pine grove, the dispute in Kanesatake also involved a fight over the Canadian government–sanctioned band council. On April 6, after weeks of stormy meetings, loud speeches, and sporadic sit-ins, the faction loyal to George Martin occupied the council office. His rival, Grand Chief Clarence Simon, called in the Sûreté du Québec, which dragged Martin and 10 of his followers down the stairs of the two-story brick office as angry Mohawks taunted the green-clad authorities with jeers of "Teenage Mutant Ninja Turtles." Though there were no serious injuries, the presence of the police further incited the community, especially those concerned about the small barricade of an old aluminum fishing shack, tree stumps, branches, and logs pulled across the dirt path leading to pines coveted by the golf course.

"Once the police showed up to clear the band council office, we figured that we were next," says Tolley. On April 26, the Quebec Superior Court in St. Jerome granted the town of Oka's request for an injunction to bar Mohawks from continuing their protest.

Outside the courthouse, the lawyer for the town of Oka, Luc Carbonneau, added, "We are working in concert with the Sûreté du Québec. If there are any problems, they are ready to intervene."

When word of the injunction reached Kanesatake, the people at the barricade vowed to continue their vigil. "The Québécois have been on our territory for more than 300 years," said protester Robert Gabriel, "and this is the first time the Mohawk people have stood up to the encroachment. One injunction is not going to stop us."

During the next three days, Mohawk protesters and Oka officials traded barbs, as the Sûreté du Québec were deployed along Highway 344. Nevertheless, both sides agreed to a May 1 negotiating session under a cluster of pine, oak, and, cedar trees in the middle of the disputed land. Oka councilor Gilles Landreville and Carbonneau were accompanied by Pierre Coulombe, representing Quebec Premier Robert Bourassa and then–Indian Affairs minister John Ciaccia. Though Landreville insisted that the land belonged to the municipality of Oka, the provincial officials showed signs of compromise, including a letter from the Quebec Environment department, calling for a full environmental impact study before any change was made to the forest.

As a sign of good faith, the Mohawks proposed a 15-day moratorium, followed by the removal of the barricade if they controlled access to the forest. "As long as we survey the people who enter the forest," said Mohawk spokesman Johnny Cree, "we would be willing to take down the barricade."

Carbonneau deemed the proposal "a very good" start, but Landreville remained adamant that the town had the right to lease the land to the Oka Golf Club. As the negotiations continued through a second day, the signs of discord became more evident. Coulombe was joined by a federal official, Yves Desilets of the ministry of Indian and Northern Affairs, who could not understand why the Mohawks refused to accept provincial and federal assurances that the expanded golf course would not be built if the barricade was removed. "We were ready to order a moratorium in exchange for removal of the barricade," Desilets said. "But the Mohawks would not back down from holding the forest."

Shortly before noon on May 2, the Mohawks discovered that the Sûreté du Québec was accompanying men carrying long boxes into the clubhouse of the Oka Golf Club. To the men and women on the barricade, the police-sanctioned transport looked like preparations for an attack.

Less than two hours later, the Sûreté du Québec flew a helicopter very low over the barricade, increasing Mohawk suspicions that the police were preparing an invasion. By the end of the afternoon, young men in khaki and camouflage fatigues were appearing along the path and at the barricade. Pulling bandanas over their faces, they spoke of armed resistance and defiance, echoing the words of Warriors from Akwesasne. Walter David, Jr., a soft-spoken traditionalist and economic-development officer for the band council, predicted disaster. "It might turn into war if the Sûreté du Québec comes here," he said. "Our people have the right to defend themselves on our territory:"

Amid the rising tensions, the Mohawks broke off negotiations. When Desilets walked out of the forest, he described the situation as "total confusion."

That night, the Warriors at Akwesasne received an urgent call from Kanesatake. Listening to the description of the Sûreté du Québec maneuvers, the Warriors agreed that a large-scale police invasion could take place at any moment. "The more we discussed it, the more we realized that the situation had stabilized at Akwesasne," says Francis Boots. "We weren't going to openly fight with the police, nor were we going to get involved with Dullea. The forces of New York, Ontario, and Quebec had overwhelmed us. Our form of resistance was to avoid participation in their process. We had pulled back and settled in.

"The people at Kanesatake needed help and we could give it. They still had the chance to prevent an invasion, and that's why they were calling us. They believed that we could help them stand up to the police and stand up for our nation."

As the New York State Police settled into their occupation of Akwesasne, the local officials in Oka and the Sûreté du Québec continued to show signs of using force to gain control of the Pines. As the Akwesasne Warriors mulled over the request for help, John and Francis Boots, Minnie Garrow, Larry and Loran Thompson, Diane Lazore, and others openly considered the growing conflict over the golf course as part of a coordinated campaign to undermine the Mohawk nation.

"I have to think that the Sûreté du Québec headquarters consider Akwesasne and Kanesatake as part of one Mohawk problem in Canada," says Minnie Garrow. "And to some extent they are right. We are one people.

"I can't tell you that it is the same officer giving one set of orders. But I can tell you the SQ and the Quebec politicians want to contain us, just as the New York politicians and police want to contain us. Here they set up negotiations with Dullea, an attempt to draw us into the system.

"In Canada, the mayor of Oka, the provincial and federal authorities all tell Mohawks to pull down the barricade and accept a compromise in which the federal government or Quebec buys the land and puts it aside. They don't understand: the land is not for sale. Our sovereignty is not for sale. The Creator gave us this land. The Creator gave us our law and our rights. We negotiate on political differences, not rights.

"As the Warriors Society, we have a purpose to protect our identity, and now we have been asked to help other Mohawks who face the same kind of force that has been imposed upon us at Akwesasne—to stand up and tell the world that we will not be compromised. This is what we have left of our nation. We will not give it up."

According to Francis Boots and Garrow, the Warriors' restraint at Akwesasne allowed them to help at Kanesatake. On May 8, Oka Mayor Jean Ouellette presided over a rowdy meeting in which Québécois and Mohawks squared off. Led by Guy Dubé, some townspeople had formed an ad hoc committee called the Regroupement des citoyens d'Oka, which demanded that the municipality take title to the forest and immediately begin expansion of the golf course. "The citizens and the council have been taken hostage by the Mohawks," Dubé shouted into the crowd of 200 who packed the council chambers.

Councilor Landreville accused the Mohawks of intimidation and harassment of local residents when they approached the barricade to express their displeasure with the protest. Mayor Ouellette added, "We've reached the limits of our endurance. We're stuck with a situation which becomes increasingly poisoned as each day passes."

In response, Mohawk Allen Gabriel accused the mayor and council of promoting "a campaign of racial slurs and misinformation," and insisted that the golf club could expand in a different direction. When Dubé urged the council to seek a court injunction that would force the Mohawks from the barricade, Gabriel warned, "We will not back down, even if the provincial police move in."

A week later, the Regroupement voted to support Ouellette's plans to have the municipality buy the forest and lease it to the golf-course developers. Though the federal Indian Affairs negotiator, Yves Desilets, and the provincial native affairs representative, Pierre Coulombe, continued to meet with both sides, the Regroupement took an increasingly hard line.

This combative tone alarmed the Kanesatake Mohawks, and they appealed to the Akwesasne Warriors for help in constructing a stronger barricade, establishing a thorough system of communications and organizing a 24-hour patrol to monitor the territory's perimeter. "The people were very worried about an attack," says Francis Boots, who led a delegation of Akwesasne Warriors to Kanesatake. "It could have come from the police or some of the people of Oka.

"You have to understand that we felt anything was possible. When I first came to Kanesatake in March, the issue was the Pines, and the people of Kanesatake made their position known by setting up the barricade. To many white people, this small, peaceful barricade became part of the picture that spread from Akwesasne. When Canadian officials heard of any barricade, they thought of guns.

"At Kanesatake, the barricade was in an open field that did not carry any traffic. There weren't any guns, just a walkie-talkie. We performed Mohawk spiritual ceremonies—the burning of tobacco, chants, and dances. Our patrol was just people in cars driving around certain sections of the territory, side by side with people from Kanesatake, so they could get a feel for this kind of job.

"This wasn't state Route 37 or an asphalt street built by the province. This was a dirt path leading to our lacrosse field and our old cemetery, not a strip for casinos. But the governments could not see that. It was a holy place, and we did not want to defile it with violence or golf or anything else."

"I can trace my ancestors to this land for seven generations," says Johnny Cree, sitting on a patch of faded grass before the grove of 100-foot pines that stretch the entire kilometer north from the edge of Highway 344 to Centre Road in Oka. "When I was a boy, my parents and grandmother and grandfather told me how my great-grandparents and great-great-grandparents told them about the cemetery and the priests ordering these trees planted." He pauses, walking up the gentle ridge that commands a clear view of the blue-green water of Lac des Deux Montagnes. "It was my mother and father and my grandparents who took me up here, and with other Mohawks we made it part of our tradition." He pauses again, pointing to a clearing that includes a battered plywood lacrosse box that also doubles as a softball field.

"Lacrosse is a ceremonial game and a chance to bring the community together or visit with other Mohawks from Kahnawake or even as far away as Akwesasne or Six Nations. Lacrosse originally was a way to settle arguments or find cures for illnesses. As young men, we were told it was a way to honor this place and the bravery of our ancestors.

"I laugh at the Canadians who have turned it into a sport for babies with padding. If you are good with the stick and you are fast, then it is not a game of flattening others, like hockey. It's a game of skill and speed, the way our men hunted and fished."

As for the mayor's threat of forcing the Mohawks to abandon the barricade, Cree shakes his head. "Their guns may move us or shoot us, but this—" he stamps his boot on the soft turf "—is ours. Always was and always will be.

"I agree with the Warriors who urge us to build barricades and help us mount patrols to watch for attacks," adds Cree, a father of four and faithkeeper of the Longhouse. "I agree that we are one Mohawk nation that demands and deserves sovereignty. I agree with their resistance to any expansion on our land, but guns—I don't think they help the situation."

The Warriors initially honored these sentiments, refraining from bringing weapons or ammunition into Kanesatake during May and early June, when the possibility of a negotiated settlement appeared strong. Though Mayor Jean Ouellette, his council, and the Regroupement des citoyens d'Oka pressed for a second court injunction to force the Mohawks out of the Pines, a Quebec Superior Court judge refused to make such a ruling. "There is no urgency because the provincial and federal governments have their mediators and we are willing to continue discussions," said Jacques Lacaille, the lawyer representing the Kanesatake band council. "This is not the time for force or definitive rulings. It's time for dialogue."

Following the court decision, Ouellette and his council proposed a three-month moratorium on plans for golf-course expansion in exchange for removal of the barricade. "This buys some peace for a time," added Lacaille, "but in three months, we were back at the same situation."

To Johnny Cree and other Mohawks, the mayor's proposal only emphasized the need for direct action. "Don't they see that the land is not a negotiable issue?" asks Cree. "It is ours. We were willing to take our barricade down immediately and never put it up here again if the government could guarantee that the Pines would not be taken. It's very simple. To get rid of the barricade, expand the golf course someplace else."

Quebec Premier Robert Bourassa considered the dispute at Oka to be merely a small, nagging controversy. The real battles were for hydro-electric power, oil, and timber on native lands, billions of dollars' worth of natural resources. The resolution in Oka would not require extensive government expenditures, just patience and determination. For the first time in many years, the Mohawks were asking the government to endorse the status quo rather than to create new programs or administrative structures. "All they wanted was for us to guarantee the Pines, just as they were," says a top-level aide to Bourassa. "That would not have cost us anything."

Throughout the early months of the Oka barricade, the Bourassa government urged restraint as the most likely way for Mayor Ouellette to produce a settlement. The killings at Akwesasne forced Bourassa to consider the potential for Mohawk-sponsored violence; yet he believed that the Mohawks understood it was in their interest to remain calm. If guns appeared on the barricade, the Quebec officials reasoned, then the Mohawks could easily lose their claim on the public's sympathy as the dispossessed struggling against the greedy leisure class. "All we wanted was time," says the Bourassa aide. "We figured a few months would give this a chance to be settled."

But the national debate over Quebec's future and the Canadian constitution dramatically undercut the patience required to resolve the golf-course dispute. As the Mohawks of the village spent the spring and early summer digging in, Canada's first ministers were discussing the Meech Lake accord, an initiative of Prime Minister Brian Mulroney's intended to provide recognition of the special status of Quebec under the Canadian constitution. On June 9, Mulroney summoned Bourassa and his counterparts to Ottawa for a marathon negotiating session to finalize the accord, which would then have to be ratified by each of the country's 10 provincial legislatures.

The aboriginal population of Manitoba launched a campaign to block the deal. Led by Elijah Harper, a member of the provincial legislature who was once the elected chief of the Ojibway-Cree at Red Sucker Lake, the Manitoba natives were angered by the omission in Meech of aboriginal rights and its emphasis on the English and French. Harper tied up business in the legislature until it became impossible for Manitoba to complete the approval process in time to meet the deadline of June 23 agreed to by the federal and provincial negotiators. Like most Canadian politicians, Bourassa believed Harper and his allies made their move to further the cause of Canada's 700,000 aboriginal people. In his efforts to entice Harper to support the Meech Lake Accord and thereby entrench recognition of Quebec as a distinct society in Canada's multiplicity, Bourassa vowed that he would personally champion native rights to self-government if the Manitoba chiefs allowed Meech to pass in Manitoba.

Harper barely acknowledged Bourassa's ploy, but the Mohawks saw an opening. "For the first time," says Ellen Gabriel, who helped organize religious ceremonies at the Kanesatake barricade, "it looked like the Quebec government was trying to please the people who were here first, not the other way around. This showed us that we had more power than we thought."

For months, Bourassa had carefully crafted a strategy designed to give Quebec broad areas of autonomy within a federal Canada. But the failure of Meech underscored a weakness that has haunted Bourassa since 1971, when he announced Quebec's plan to build the James Bay hydroelectric dam by flooding Cree land. Trumpeting the dam as "the project of the century," Bourassa and his government made glossy presentations to investors, the press, bureaucrats, and engineers. The Crees heard the news over the radio. After waiting nine months to see construction maps and blueprints, the Crees organized their eight villages into an alliance that eventually won a court injunction against the project. Led by Chief Billy Diamond, the Crees won $225 million in compensation for giving Quebec the right to build the dam.

Thirteen years later, in 1988, Bourassa unveiled plans for a second phase of the project: dams on a different section of Cree land that would supply power to New York and other parts of the U.S. Bourassa insisted that the original agreement gave Quebec the right to locate electricity plants on any section of territory claimed by the natives of James Bay. But the Crees were ready, and have tied up the project in a lengthy court battle.

"Bourassa doesn't see us until it costs him money or power," says Ellen Gabriel. "As long as the barricade at Kanesatake was quiet and we were talking to the mediators, he didn't want to hear about us."

Meanwhile, Mayor Ouellette was growing impatient as day after-day Mohawks dominated the news. One evening Ouellette was denounced on television as a racist; the next morning the newspapers depicted him as a greedy opportunist. What started as an unusual real estate deal had become a test of valor and integrity. Ouellette could not back down.

He tried to explain this to provincial officials, supposedly his political allies; but to Ouellette and the Regroupement des citoyens d'Oka, the provincial government betrayed them to avoid a few days of embarrassing publicity. "We aren't asking for special treatment," says Dubé of the Regroupement. "We do not want government money. We want the right to make our decisions about our land."

Ouellette won the village council's support to continue the pursuit of an injunction. "The land does not belong to the Mohawks and the courts will recognize that," Ouellette said, referring to eighteenth-century land grants and claims given to the Sulpician order by Louis XV. "The law is on our side, and once the judge rules that, we can go forward with our plans. That is the proper course of action and we will act within the law."

By Saturday morning, June 30, the town's lawyer, Luc Carbonneau, won an injunction that ordered Mohawks to dismantle the barricade. Carbonneau told federal and provincial mediators that Oka would participate in extended discussions only about vacating the property. In a last-ditch effort to continue negotiations, the mediators persuaded Carbonneau to present his point of view directly to the Mohawks. Before meeting the men and women of the barricade, Carbonneau told the media that the town had set a Wednesday morning deadline for removal of the barricade. If the Mohawks defied the ultimatum, Carbonneau said, the town would bring in heavy equipment to remove the logs and stones. According to Carbonneau, officers of the Sûreté du Québec would accompany the municipal crews to prevent the Mohawks from interfering with the operation.

"Before we met Carbonneau we heard over the radio that the town was going to use the police to enforce the injunction," says Denise Tolley, of the Kanesatake Cultural Centre, "we wanted to be prepared.

"Everybody agreed that we should meet and continue talking to the mediators. There was always the hope that the people of Oka would have some sense that a golf course could go anywhere, but a cemetery has to stay put. And a few of us thought that we had to call the Warriors at Akwesasne and Kahnawake to get our barricades ready because the threat of attack was very, very real. The townspeople were getting mad. The mayor was getting mad. And we were just going to stay put."

Convinced that the injunction and golf-course expansion were part of a plan to divide and conquer the Mohawk nation, the protesters at Kanesatake considered a violent, if not armed, confrontation with the police. On the advice of Akwesasne Warriors, they fortified the barricades with thick logs and barbed wire. In Mohawk homes, the Warriors and a few Kanesatake activists hatched a makeshift plan to defend the territory: a handful of unarmed men in fatigues and bandanas would be stationed at the barricade as decoys; a half dozen others would be armed and take cover in the heavily forested grove. If the Sûreté du Québec charged the barricades and attacked, the hidden Warriors would use their assault rifles to drive them back.

"It's gone beyond the issue of the golf course," said 32-year-old Chrystal Nicholas, a member of the Kanesatake Longhouse who stood at the barricade but had little, if any, knowledge about the defense plan. "It's a question of the outside people having their way, and telling us what to do. We don't want to be in that position again. Not here, not anywhere. It started with the golf course and it probably could end with the golf-course expansion being stopped or diverted from the Pines.

"But if the town continues to insist that the Pines be taken, then this will be a fight that has very little to do with a golf course. No one should underestimate our resolve to fight."

Despite the prospect of an impending showdown, golfers seemed oblivious to the conflict unfolding just a few hundred yards away from their tees and fairways. "It's really an Indian problem; the trouble is not with us," said pro-shop manager Yvon Pilon. "It's time for us to expand and have the full 18 holes that are needed for a serious club—and, if it is possible, to use some of the land for condominiums or homes to enjoy the beauty of this setting. We know what we want and the politics will take care of itself."

"We are here to relax and forget about the problems of society," says a man identifying himself only as Robert. He grudgingly admits to following the newspaper and television accounts of the protest. "I love to play golf and I want to make sure I can play. If the Mohawks or any other native group wants to make their claim, that's fine for the courthouse or the parliament. But this is where I want to be in the summer."

21

THE SQ LOSES A STROKE

As the Warriors turned their attention toward Kanesatake in May and June, Kakwirakeron found himself increasingly isolated from the leadership: he wanted to concentrate on the negotiations chaired by Dr. Henrik Dullea, but his colleagues were clearly opposed.

"It was a political disagreement," says Minnie Garrow. "No more, no less. The majority of us could not consider any discussion with the state until the police were gone. It was a simple decision. And we knew that this belief caused the people of Kanesatake to reach out to us. They knew we would not compromise even if the police were right on top of us. But it's different for Kakwirakeron. He believes in dialogue. That's his style. We felt that a real dialogue could not take place. This was not a personal decision, but a tactical one."

With the Warriors concentrating their energy on Kanesatake, Kakwirakeron prepared for the next phase of his case: the sentencing and appeal. Unwilling to trust Seth Shapiro, he turned to Victor Aronow, a Massachusetts lawyer who had extensive experience with aboriginal cases. "There were two major problems," says Aronow. "The first was chemistry. Even before the prostitution incident, it took an enormous effort for them to communicate. Seth's arrest added to the strain. The second problem was Seth's relative inexperience as a trial lawyer. It's very hard alone, especially if you are not a seasoned practitioner."

Shortly after Aronow began to review the trial record, Kakwirakeron's mother died. In order to properly attend to her burial and fulfill
his traditional religious obligations, Kakwirakeron won a delay of sentencing until July 10, three months after the verdict. "We took that as
a very good sign," says Aronow. "It showed that the judge had respect
for Kakwirakeron, his beliefs, and his family. I guess it raised my ex-
pectations that he would not send him to jail."

When the sentencing date arrived, Kakwirakeron, his wife, Verna
Montour, their children, Aronow, and Mohawk supporters filled U.S.
District Court Judge Neal McCurn's court. After the lawyers spoke,
McCurn turned to the defendant, who rose and began his speech in a
calm, deliberate voice.

"I thank Judge Neal McCurn for giving me an opportunity to stand
up here and speak to you. I would like to give special greetings and
thanks to yourself and to all the supporters here. I would like to thank
the prosecutor, John Duncan, for elevating me within the community
to a position that perhaps will benefit him in sentencing. However, it
has no reality or benefit to me within the community or structure of
the Warriors Society.

"I would just like to restate some things for your consideration and
for everyone here. I do have respect for you and the way you conducted
the trial. There are some disagreements, of course, that I have had, but
for the most part what I am going to say does not reflect directly upon
yourself. However, I would like to state for the record that my name is
Kakwirakeron. I am of the Bear Clan and I am a proud citizen of the
Mohawk nation as a member of the Six Nations of the Iroquois Confederacy. I stand before you not in my mind or in the minds of my
people as a criminal, but I stand before you as a prisoner of an unde-
clared war against the Mohawk nation, against all native people who
still sincerely believe in our sovereignty.

"Our people have always been a proud people here on this continent. We were nations long before the Europeans came and discovered
our shores. And when they came, we shared with them. At that time,
we had an economic system that was consistent with the way all of us
have been put on this earth. Our people were hunters, our people were
fishermen, they gathered, we were agriculturalists. We planted and
supplemented our economy in many ways. Today, there is no game
left for us to hunt and support our people. Today, if you take the fish
out of the rivers, they're not edible—they're poisonous, they're toxic,
hazardous to our health and the health of anyone that attempts to

take them as food. In the territory we come from, if you try to plant food, crops, you will find that the land has been poisoned by pollution from nearby factories. You will find you cannot raise animals, beef, for you will not be able to eat it or you will not be able to sell it because of pollution. These are the traditional ways in which our people survive.

"Today, we live in what you call upstate New York, what we call sovereign territory, the Mohawk nation. You describe it as economically depressed because there is very little employment in that whole Northern District of New York, as you call it. And people in our community tried to find an economy to survive. You condemned it. You criminalized it. You made the people that participate in it criminals. You send in your forces, and you send in many, in conjunction with the Canadian government who sends in the army, who send in their federal police, who send in their provincial police from two provinces. They have closed down that community. There is no economy left in Akwesasne, except for those few that are on the payroll of the federal government of Canada or the federal government of the United States.

"Over a thousand people lost their jobs by that invasion and that occupation, and when you figure that those were adults and that most of them were married, you double that to 2,000. You figure that many of them have two to three children and you quickly bring up that figure to 4,000 to 5,000 people affected in an entire community with a population of only 8,500. That is the reality of what has happened to our community at Akwesasne. It's not written about, it's not talked about, but it's the reality.

"You may be able to arrest my physical body, which you have done; you may be able to cause physical injury to my body, which you have done; you may be able to incarcerate it, as you have done; you may even be able to terminate it, which you may or may not do. The spirit lives in me and the spirit lives in all native people that really, sincerely believe in our right to exist here as equals. You cannot arrest that spirit. You cannot injure it or incarcerate it. You cannot exterminate it even if you try. Our people are made from the clay of this Turtle Island and we were here long before the white man came and we lived proud. We stood up straight. We protected. We defended. We fed our people. We led good lives, happy lives. We had the same problems that exist anywhere in the world, but we dealt with them and we were not dictated to by anyone. We are still here with your presence and we will be here long after you are gone, for the Creator has put us here.

"The spirit of freedom, the spirit of sovereignty, the spirit of equality, the spirit of human dignity will not be quashed by this court. Before you came, there was the Great Law. It was the supreme law of the land. And when your people came and asked to share this land, we entered a two-row wampum, which said yes, we can travel side by side on this river of life, but we are equal—you in your vessel, we in our canoe. In our canoe, we carry all of our things—our language, our laws, our culture, our spirituality, our traditions. And you likewise have set the same in your vessel. But we will not legislate or make laws over each other. We will not dictate to each other. Our people lived up to that. But there has been a breakdown in the communication.

"What you have done to me as an individual, which matters nothing, which matters very little compared to what you are doing to the family, to the people, to the Indian nations, not bands or tribes or any other derogatory term, but Indian nations that still live on this continent, you cannot take that away. We are here forever. And one day we will stand here as equals once again in physical form, but in our spirituality we have always been equal and we will continue to be so.

"I do not beg this court for mercy. For I have taken a solemn oath to uphold the constitution, the Great Law of our people. Whatever sentence you wish to impose or you intend to impose, I realize that what my lawyer says and I realize that what I say will have no effect on that. So I stand here and accept what you wish to impose on me, but not as a criminal, for I am not a criminal. It is not criminal to stand up and defend the sovereignty of your people. You may downplay your role to what you have done to the Mohawk people and for that only the Creator and yourselves can straighten that out. We are not your subjects and we are not your slaves; we are equal. One day that will be realized. I stand here as a proud Mohawk citizen."

A few minutes later, McCurn sentenced Kakwirakeron to 10 months in jail to be served while his appeal was pending.

That night, Francis Boots walked the Mohawk barricade at Oka, checking the lines of barbed wire and sandbags, surveying the hidden sentry posts dug into the brush. Satisfied, he returned to the open encampment near the cemetery under the broad shade of the towering pines. "I went to sleep under the night sky," he says. "Over the radio we could speak with people from Akwesasne who told us about Kak-wirakeron, and we were saddened.

"A few of us had come to Kanesatake a few days earlier. We set up a base and a radio system, which could send a signal to the Warrior headquarters in Kahnawake. From there, they could relay it to Akwe-sasne or other native communities. Then came the barricade and other defenses. We worked hard and fast, but each night would come and there would be peace. We heard that Quebec Premier Robert Bour-assa and his minister for Native Affairs, John Ciaccia, had talked to the mayor and told him to wait before enforcing the injunction. I went to sleep believing there was time."

A handful of Mohawk women awakened with the break of daylight, after 5:00 a.m. Ellen Gabriel and Denise Tolley organized the tobacco-burning ceremony that marks the beginning of each day, the smoke carrying words of gratitude for the light. From their vantage point near the lacrosse box, the women noticed a jagged line of green-and-white Sûreté du Québec cars pulled over on the far side of Highway 344. As the prayers and chants continued past 6:00 a.m., a couple of un-marked vans arrived; a group of officers took out flak jackets, gas masks, bulletproof vests, and rifles.

"They started walking up the pavement to the path," recalls Ga-briel. "We wanted to continue our ceremonies, but couldn't. An offi-cer motioned for one of us to come down.

"When we got to the barricade, which was empty, they asked for a spokesman or leader. I told them they could talk to me or Denise and we asked them to put away their guns. We told them that women and children were present. There was no need for guns or violence.

"They didn't hear me and they asked again for a leader. I tried to explain to them that we work by consensus. You could see that more officers were creeping up—I'd say there were a dozen or so. And we stood there, Denise and myself, looking at the cops while the cops looked at us. Then someone told us about the injunction and that they were there to enforce it. I said, 'Look, there's no need for guns or violence. There are women and children here. We have men as well, but no need for violence.'

"Once again, the police wanted a spokesman or someone with au-thority. I went through the explanation about consensus and then started to walk away. I wasn't going to do anything and they knew that. Denise wasn't going to do anything and they knew that, too. But we heard the bang. I mean real loud, right behind our ears. Tear gas.

Bang! It came again. We couldn't believe this. I ran down to the barricade, yelling and swearing, 'Stop this fucking shit! You animals. We have women and children here. How do you expect us to negotiate with you when you're gassing us?' I was pissed off. They just wanted to intimidate us. We weren't going to let it work. I was shrieking at the top of my lungs."

The firing of the tear-gas canisters immediately aroused Boots and Johnny Cree, who came upon the women fleeing the gas, which had begun to blow back toward the police. "The women were scared and panicked," recounts Cree. "They asked me to go to the barricade and I did.

"'Are you the leader?' someone asked.

"'No,' I answered, telling them that we have no leader. You could see this frustrated them. A few spoke about the injunction and said they had to take down the barricade, whether we liked it or not. I tried to tell them about the Pines and the cemetery. I said it was like a church to us. One officer shook his head and tried to be polite, but he said he couldn't bend. Another just said he was a policeman following orders, doing his job.

"I told them about the women and children performing a ceremony when they fired. There was no need for tear gas and hurting young people. They went back to talking about the barricade, and I said I would go ask all of us to meet and talk about leaving. The officers nodded and said we had five minutes. I told them we need 90 minutes, that the decision has to be made with everybody. We went back and forth and they gave me 45 minutes."

With the policemen watching, Cree walked up the path to the lacrosse box, where the women and handful of men had gathered to finish the morning ceremony. Boots had withdrawn to the communications post that linked the Warriors at Kanesatake with their counterparts in Kahnawake and Akwesasne.

"Our people could see the Sûreté du Québec rolling up the road," says Boots. "There were riot police in gray, SWAT teams in black, and regular officers in green. It was a huge squad, maybe a hundred to 120 in all. Then the helicopter began to circle overhead. There was no question they wanted to scare the shit out of us.

"We gathered the people near the cemetery. The people were told that the police had guns and had fired tear gas. It was clear that a fight meant bloodshed. We told them and they did not want to leave, especially the women, who were angry that they had been gassed."

"They were attacking women and children. We would not leave. That would be a victory for them," says Ellen Gabriel. "We had to be stronger than them. The SQ had to reveal to the world that they would be willing to shoot at women and children."

Cree pleaded with the men and women. Stating his fear of violence, he asked the Mohawks to consider giving up the barricade.

"The answer was no," says Tolley. "Johnny saw that and went back."

At the barricade, Cree told the police that the Mohawks would not leave. An officer explained that they would not clear the land until the women and children had moved to safety on the police side of Highway 344. Though he doubted that the women would leave their men, Cree asked for time to approach them. The police agreed.

As Cree walked up the path, a contingent of Mohawks had gathered several hundred yards to the west of police lines. Pulling cars and spare tires across the highway, they set up a new barricade to prevent policemen from circling around the back of the Pines. Burning the rubber to create a plume of thick black smoke, the men pulled out a chain saw and cut one of the large trees that lined the road's shoulder. A squad of riot police approached and fired two tear-gas canisters, then retreated as the wind diverted the cloud from its target.

When Cree reached the lacrosse box, Gabriel led a group of women down the path, burning sweetgrass and chanting Mohawk prayers. More than two dozen officers gazed in amazement as the women walked within inches of their weapons and sprinkled the ash at their feet. "Why do you want to kill me and my children?" shouted one woman.

From behind the police lines, a yellow front-end loader rumbled toward the barricade. On either side marched a contingent of police protected by bulletproof vests, automatic rifles pointed forward. Tear-gas canisters exploded behind the barricade. Wheezing and crying, Gabriel, Tolley, and others took a few steps toward the police, then stopped. *Bang!* Another tear-gas canister.

"Somebody tried to pick a canister up and throw it back," says Gabriel. "The wind helped us, but you couldn't really see much, except for the outline of the bulldozer and silhouettes of the policemen coming forward. The machine was going to take down the barricade and the cops were going right up the path."

The women screamed and retreated. To their left came an explosion. In the woods, two Warriors who had served in the United States

Army recognized the sound as that of a concussion grenade. They informed the other sentries, and the walkie-talkies crackled through the forest. At the communications base, Boots got in contact with Warriors at Kahnawake, who relayed the sounds of yelling and explosions to Akwesasne.

"The whole Mohawk nation knew that an attack had begun," says Minnie Garrow.

As the wind dispersed the gas, the police fired another round of concussion grenades, covering the advance of the heavily armed riot squad. The officers moved around the barricade and its sign declaring "Mohawk Territory—No Trespassing." "Our men saw them come up the path," says Boots, "and the cops fanned out—a few officers trying to get in the trees, others sweeping wide to the east, trying to cut off our sides. Over the radio, I heard someone yell about a boy on his tricycle, and somebody grabbed him out of the way.

"As the police came up the path, another one of our men was hidden in the ditch and he could see them coming. He was armed and he waited, wondering if they were going to stop. They didn't. You could hear the tear gas and the grenades. The police were coming closer and he jumped up."

The advancing officers opened fire as the Mohawk radios crackled with instructions to shoot back over the heads of the policemen. After a furious 24-second exchange, 31-year-old SQ Cpl. Marcel Lemay lay beside a tree, his chest filling with blood from the slug that ripped through a crack along the side of his bulletproof vest. Within a minute an ambulance had sped into view; the paramedics rushed to Lemay's side, placed him on a stretcher, and raced down the path. Once inside the rig, he was rushed to the hospital.

Moments later, when the winds shifted and blew back the tear gas, the shocked SQ beat a disorganized retreat. Unsure if the Mohawks would shoot again, the police ran. The masked sentries moved forward. One Mohawk hopped into the driver's seat of a green-and-white SQ cruiser. A few moments later, another Mohawk captured a second cruiser, and a third hopped into the front-end loader.

"The police left the keys inside," continues Boots. "The stretch of road was empty, and we could control the hill that led up to our cemetery. We were scared that they would come back right away and attack. If they had retreated and regrouped and come again, we would have been lost. We only had enough ammunition for a minute."

To defend themselves, the Warriors pulled the captured cruisers across Highway 344, cut down a few more trees, and moved stones and earth with the front-end loader to shore up the barricades. "We knew it wasn't enough," continues Boots. "Our thinking was, the police lost one of theirs and they wanted to slaughter us. The helicopters kept buzzing over our heads."

In an effort to deceive the SQ, the Mohawks used a tactic that had worked successfully in Akwesasne. They sent out false and misleading radio transmissions implying that there were close to a hundred Warriors defending the cemetery. "We wanted the SQ to think that we were crawling with guns everywhere," Boots points out. "We wanted to scare them as much as they scared us. It was our only hope until we could get our defense settled and establish regular contact with Mohawks in other communities."

At the bottom of the hill, on Highway 344, the police commanders desperately tried to regroup their men, still stunned by the shooting and worried by the Mohawk radio chatter. As reporters and towns-people streamed to the scene, the front-end loader pushed a cruiser across the road. Then a masked Warrior climbed on top of the crunched vehicle and proudly waved his assault rifle over his head.

"The police didn't believe our strength," recounts Denise Tolley, "and until that moment I don't think we did either. When the men started to build the new barricades and push around the cruisers, we understood that we had control of our land. By running away and trying to figure out what to do next, the SQ let us hold the land. From that point, I knew it would be different. They could use their guns or their helicopters or their gas, but that could not change the feeling that we stood on the land we were fighting for. It was no longer a dispute, it was a victory."

As the front-end loader and captured police cars fortified barricades at approaches to the Pines, Mohawk cars and fallen trees created road-blocks at the northern entrance on Centre Road and farther west on Highway 344, near the junction of St. Germain Road. "We didn't have very many people," says Boots, "less than two dozen men with weapons, but everybody knew what had to be done after the police pulled back. We saw that the police kept coming and stopping at the bottom of the hill. It was clear that the SQ were going to surround us. We thought that once they cut us off, they would come in. So we had to protect all the entrances. To fool them we wanted to show that we had enough people with guns to be on the barricades. We had to act fast."

Shortly after 9:30 a.m., the men and women of Kanesatake received unexpected help: 18 miles to the southeast on the southern shore of the St. Lawrence, a dozen Mohawk militants from the Kahnawake reserve, including several veterans of the United States Army, gathered their weapons and bags of sand and cement. They drove four minutes on Highway 138 to the Mercier Bridge, a major commuter link. Dressed in camouflage fatigues and caps, boots, and bandanas, the Mohawks jumped out of their pickups and brandished their .30 calibre rifles, M-16s, and AK-47s. Stopping traffic and chasing away repair crews, they built a wall of sandbags supported by construction material at the junction of Highways 132 and 138.

"We did it on our own," says Cookie McComber, one of the Mohawks who organized the bold move without informing the Kahnawake Warriors Society or the band council. "We figured on taking the bridge to protest the SQ attacks and tell them that they had to deal with us as well as the Mohawks at Kanesatake."

22

BOURASSA PLAYS
THE BUNKER

Kahnawake Grand Chief Joseph Norton, members of the band council, and the Kahnawake Warriors Society were puzzled if not outraged by the men who took it upon themselves to seize the bridge. Unlike others at Kanesatake and Akwesasne, the Mohawk factions at Kahnawake had worked out a loose but reliable system of coordinating protests and political activity. In 1988, after the Royal Canadian Mounted Police staged a massive raid against the territory's smoke shops, Norton and the band council endorsed the Warriors' occupation of the bridge's southern span. As the Warriors pulled an 18-wheeler across Highway 132 and dumped gravel on the road, Norton pressured the federal government to discuss plans for self-government. From those talks, starting in January 1990, Norton and Quebec's minister for Native Affairs, John Ciaccia, were engaged in serious negotiations to grant Kahnawake jurisdiction over its own legal and commercial affairs, including the lucrative tobacco business.

"We had been making progress," explains Norton. "Ciaccia was eager to reach an agreement that would give us our own judicial system. We took that to mean a big step toward legalizing the cigarette trade on our land, and bingo if we wanted it here. We believed that if the Mohawks could get a self-government plan at Kahnawake, then they could get one at Kanesatake and Akwesasne. Sure, I was against the expansion of the golf course and the use of the police, but I did not want our plans to be tied to the golf course."

"The seizure of the Mercier Bridge happened so fast," says Kahna-wake Warriors Society spokesman Kenneth Deer. "There was no plan, no coordination. We were thinking of ways to help the Mohawks at Kanesatake, and all of a sudden we hear that members of our community are on the bridge with guns. We had to stand behind them, but we didn't have any idea what it would mean."

The immediate result was two dozen Warriors driving from the center of Kahnawake: the first group headed two miles southwest to set up a barricade on Highway 138 near the town of Châteauguay; the second traveled three miles due south to block Highway 221; the third moved about a mile and a half east to cut off Highway 132. The traffic jams stretched for miles.

Around 10:00 a.m., the communications base at Kanesatake received a radio message that Mohawks had seized the Mercier Bridge and vowed to blow it up if the Sûreté du Québec launched another attack on the Pines. "When we passed the word around, you could hear the yells and screams across the woods," Boots says. "The police now had to fight us on two fronts. They could not isolate us as a group of militants in the woods. They had to see us as a major political problem, not a bunch of thugs or criminals."

Fifteen minutes later, Cpl. Marcel Lemay was pronounced dead in the emergency room of a hospital in St. Eustache.

"In the beginning, we really didn't know if it was our bullets that killed him, and we were very nervous about it," says Boots. "The thought that one of us was responsible for the killing and would be arrested was very much on our minds. The possibility of arrests or prosecutions was there, but we were worried for our safety. We were fighting for our lives. We had to think about self-preservation, not the legal system and which bullet killed Corporal Lemay."

"It was an armed insurrection," says a top-level aide to Bourassa. "We didn't know what was next. Our police had been defeated and all we heard about was roaming Mohawks with guns. We thought this could be our version of hell—the city shut down, the police in retreat and the Mohawks standing on top of police cars with their AK-47s held high over their heads."

Throughout the morning, frantic phone calls between provincial and federal officials made it clear that the crisis would remain in Bour-assa's hands. In Ottawa, aides to Prime Minister Mulroney and his minister for Indian and Northern Affairs, Tom Siddon, deliberately sidestepped the crisis. Siddon was on vacation in British Columbia and refused to order his staff to take any action other than keeping an eye on events as they developed. "It's nothing we can get involved in," he reportedly told a member of his staff. In relaying that message to Bourassa's office, federal officials claimed they lacked jurisdiction because a provincial policeman had been shot in an action designed to enforce an injunction issued by a provincial court. Among themselves, aides to Mulroney and Siddon agreed that the Mohawk success was a political embarrassment that should not be allowed to spread to Ottawa.

Without federal help, Bourassa had to rely on his then minister of Public Safety, Sam Elkas, to hold the line. After the humiliating defeat at Oka and the closure of the Mercier Bridge, Elkas's first job was to organize and execute a massive display of force to create the illusion of control at the barricades. Next, he ordered an intensive inquiry into the circumstances surrounding the attack that climaxed in Lemay's death. As he spoke with regional commanders, Elkas came to the startling realization that no one in the Sûreté du Québec's upper echelon had formally authorized the assault, or submitted any tactical plan to oust the Mohawks.

"The whole operation broke almost every rule in our book," says the aide to Bourassa. "What a mess! More than a hundred policemen were told to attack, and no one knew who gave the order, when they gave the order, and what the attack plan was."

As Elkas and Bourassa scrambled to exercise their authority, another complication arose at the hospital in St. Eustache: doctors and forensic pathologists indicated that the police might have fired the bullet that killed Lemay. They believed the shot came from beside or behind the advancing officer, not from the front. Provincial officials reeled at the magnitude of the mistakes made in one morning.

"By noon," says the aide to Bourassa, "it felt like we had lost all of Montreal."

Despite near panic, Bourassa projected a calm confidence in his support for the Sûreté du Québec. He insisted that the police had not invaded Mohawk territory. Rather, the premier said, the SQ had assembled to enforce the law and arrest defiant Mohawks on the barricade in front of the Pines. Calling the shooting of Lemay "revolting and intolerable," Bourassa never gave any hint of the forensic findings, let alone the high-level confusion over who ordered and organized the Sûreté du Québec presence. He described the officers as men of peace who resisted the temptation to seek vengeance and retreated in an effort to spare Mohawk women and children from getting caught in a violent shootout. Insisting that he would not bend to Mohawks with guns, Bourassa vowed to reject any demands as long as traffic remained blocked on any road, whether Highway 344 or the Mercier Bridge.

"For a few hours in the late morning and early afternoon, it was hard for us to really get to the work that had to be done," explains Francis Boots. "It didn't seem real, that a few of us could push back what really was an army of policemen. Some of the men ran into the clubhouse, where they helped themselves to drinks, food, glasses, and what they called souvenirs. They were happy and they wanted to rub it in to the townspeople who hated us.

"At some point, the front-end loader rolled down the grass and the greens. The men took carts and clubs, motoring around from one tee to the next, supposedly playing a round of golf, joking about the Oka open. Then it kind of hit each of us that our success had more to do with ourselves and our own people. We showed ourselves that we had the power and the strength to stand on our feet. We showed other Mohawks that we are a strong nation when we work together. That is what really made us happy. And we started to get some work done."

The Mohawks surmised that the police would counterattack right after sunset to cut off any opportunity for Warriors to use the cover of darkness to sneak in with weapons and supplies. Then, they assumed, the police would use heavy equipment to dismantle one of the barricades, as helicopters shone lights from above. At the same time, the Warriors worried, officers would use flares and begin a march through the Pines.

Working with the front-end loader, the Mohawks dug trenches and foxholes throughout the encampment and across several fairways. Near the roads and paths, they took down trees and dragged them into positions that would block an advancing column. Men and women also used shovels and pickaxes to construct obstacles and traps designed to trip up police if they broke through. "It didn't make sense for them to wait," adds Boots. "We thought they would understand that the longer they took, the stronger we would become."

But the Warriors did not know of the confusion in the leadership of the SQ and other provincial authorities. Though Bourassa's performance gave the impression of a coordinated approach to the crisis, his office was flooded by competing requests and reports. Oka Mayor Jean Ouellette went into hiding and was not available to clarify his role in requesting the Sûreté du Québec raid; but South Shore Mayor Jean

Bosco Bourcier of Châteauguay demanded prompt police action to re-move the Mercier Bridge barricades that left his town clogged with commuters and their cars. Montreal officials arranged alternative routes to the city as employers faced the possibility of workers' need-ing two to three hours to journey to their jobs. In Quebec City, person-nel and finance officials saw the massive deployment of manpower and equipment draining the provincial coffers. And then there was the need to investigate serious crimes: the killing of a policeman; the sei-zure of police property that included cars, radios, guns and tear gas; and the defiance of a court injunction.

While Bourassa talked tough and led the Mohawks to believe that another attack was on the way, Minister of Public Safety Elkas re-ported that Lemay's death was the result of poor planning by the SQ, their failure to study the terrain, and their spotty knowledge of their adversary. To organize another assault would require several days of study and coordination. Counseling a de facto state of siege to show the Mohawks they were surrounded by superior firepower, Elkas pointed out that authorities had still to gain access to evidence at the scene of Lemay's shooting. With the Mohawks clearly unwilling to trust the Sûreté du Québec, Deputy Justice Minister Jacques Beau-doin ordered the Montreal Urban Community Police Force to handle the probe. To give the MUC detectives any chance of examining the crime scene, Beaudoin and others reasoned, the provincial govern-ment had to send a non-police negotiator to strike a deal with the Mohawks: a moratorium on Sûreté du Québec raids in exchange for access to the scene of the Lemay shooting. As evening approached, Bourassa settled on his course of action to begin on the next day. He would send Native Affairs Minister Ciaccia to mediate, while the po-lice waited it out and wore the Mohawks down.

Throughout the first day and night of the standoff, the militants on the bridge, led by Cookie McComber, spent a great deal of time talk-ing to Allan and Paul Delaronde of the Kahnawake Warriors, trying to straighten out the chain of command. McComber argued that their group took the risk and therefore were entitled to set the terms for relinquishing the bridge. The Delaronde brothers, however, refused to accept a secondary role, claiming the traditional jurisdiction of the Kahnawake Warriors Society gave it the power to make military and political decisions concerning the defense of Mohawk territory at

Kahnawake. Recognizing that their dispute had to be resolved before the police could exploit their differences, both sides came to a compromise: the men on the bridge agreed to work under the jurisdiction of the Kahnawake Warriors provided that the society included the militants in all negotiating sessions. Though their tenuous alliance underscored the divisions within the Mohawk community, both sides agreed to stand by their barricades until the police had backed off.

After a tense night of watching the SQ's red and white Mars lights flash from the northern portion of the span, several masked militants stepped out on the empty pavement of the bridge and approached the span's superstructure. Hundreds of feet above the river, they attached what appeared to be dynamite charges to the girders, to back up their threat of blowing up the bridge if officers attacked any Mohawk community.

The daring move was an elaborate charade, in the hope that the police would not call their bluff, for the militants had no explosives. They gathered cylindrical flares, taped them together, and attached string to look like fuse wire. The ruse worked—everyone believed the bridge was wired to blow from the opening moments of the standoff.

While the remarkable stunt illustrated the flair and cunning of these men, it also highlighted their unpredictability. Unlike the Warrior leaders, they were not driven by the formal demands of tradition and obedience to the Great Law; their motive was to dramatically show their defiance and independence of authority. Among the group were sons of former Kahnawake ironworkers who grew up in the United States and served in Vietnam or the U.S. Army's Special Forces. They reentered Mohawk life in the late 1970s or early 1980s, walking high steel until the building boom flattened. No longer able to find construction work, the men returned to the St. Lawrence. Accustomed to enormous physical risks, they saw themselves as working-class heroes and Mohawk freedom fighters who had learned more from the Viet Cong than from any hunters who stalked the forests for bear and deer.

On the morning after the shooting, the men on the bridge shared the headlines with the long-simmering protest over the Oka golf course. From Scandinavia to Asia, television stations received footage of armed, masked Mohawks holding the bridge or standing on top of police cruisers, defiantly staring down intimidated police officers. Newspapers carried accounts of Cpl. Marcel Lemay's death and the seizure of the Mercier Bridge.

The flood of publicity was yet another element Premier Robert Bourassa could not control. Reporters cast the Mohawks as innocent victims of shortsighted or foolish bullies determined to use their political might to expand a golf course. As a last resort, Quebec officials hoped to contain the damage by villifying the Mohawks as renegades who had eagerly killed Lemay. But Lise Proulx, a spokeswoman for the Montreal Urban Community Police, immediately discredited that claim. "We can't say for sure from which side the bullet was fired," Proulx said, "whether from the Sûreté du Québec or the Mohawks."

To make matters worse for the Quebec leaders, dozens of Canadian politicians and interest groups openly questioned the actions of the SQ and Bourassa. The leader of the Crees, Matthew Coon-Come, predicted that the provincial government's handling of the standoff would stiffen native resistance to expansion of the vast power project at James Bay. George Erasmus, then national chief of the Assembly of First Nations, warned that another attack on the Mohawks might ignite violent demonstrations on reserves across Canada. Mayors and municipal councilors of the suburban towns close to Oka and the Mercier Bridge urged the premier to crack down on the Mohawks. Led by Châteauguay's Mayor Jean Bosco Bourcier, they threatened to take the law into their own hands if the roads were not cleared.

But the biggest blow to Bourassa's credibility came from the ranks of the SQ. Jocelyn Turcotte, president of the 4,500-member provincial police union, pointed out that the officers who attacked the Mohawks still didn't know who ordered and approved the raid.

"The officers were placed in a very dangerous situation and no one wants to take responsibility for it," says Turcotte. "Everybody agrees that the mayor of Oka asked for the police, but he can't order them to attack. The truth is either being hidden or nobody really does know because of the confusion. How did this happen? How did one of our men die in an attack that wasn't planned or authorized? Where were the regional commanders? The minister of Public Safety?"

The tumultuous reactions overshadowed the difficulties experienced by residents of Oka and Kanesatake not directly involved in the standoff. Besides the police roadblocks and checkpoints that monitored all traffic in and out of the village, the water-treatment plant, behind Mohawk lines, malfunctioned. Establishing a strip of Highway 344 as a no-man's-land, Mohawks and police agreed to allow technicians to repair the plant and restore water service.

Over their radio system, the Warriors had arranged for caravans of cars and trucks to drive into Oka, approach the barricades, and seek permission to resupply the encampment and those Mohawks afraid to leave their homes. As each driver pulled up, the police searched the car and questioned passengers about their ethnicity and their destination. "If the drivers were natives or Mohawks, or just sympathetic whites with groceries," says Ellen Gabriel, "the police would not let them get through. It was that simple."

Across the river at Kahnawake, a similar policy went into effect. If a Mohawk left the reserve, even to go shopping or tend to an errand, he or she was not allowed to return. Although Mohawks in both territories eluded police by sneaking through the woods or using boats, they could not meet the demand for necessities. "We had several thousand people surrounded by the police," says Francis Boots. "To get food, water, and take care of what our children need—this is a basic human right."

When Quebec's minister of Native Affairs, John Ciaccia, arrived on July 12 at 6:00 p.m., the police escorted him into no-man's-land, where he met Ellen Gabriel accompanied by two masked women. Immediately agreeing to meet with Warriors behind the Mohawk barricade, Ciaccia walked up the hill and took a seat at the camping table set up for negotiations. In a formal but cordial manner, both sides stated their demands: the Mohawks wanted no arrests for the shooting and the seizure of the Mercier Bridge, a complete withdrawal of the police at Kanesatake and Kahnawake, and a guarantee that the golf course would not expand into the Pines. Ciaccia ruled out amnesty, but sought Mohawk cooperation with the MUC inquiry into Lemay's death. He promised the police would not attack and pressed the Mohawks to remove the barricades, especially on the Mercier Bridge. Eager for at least one area of agreement, Ciaccia asked Mohawks for a gesture of good faith by cooperating with the MUC. Warriors agreed to accompany MUC investigators to the scene if the Sûreté du Québec refrained from further attacks. Ciaccia tentatively agreed.

Since the discussions were being held on their territory, Mohawks insisted on following their tradition of limiting important negotiations to daylight hours. At 8:30, they broke off talks, pledging to resume shortly after sunrise. Ciaccia agreed to keep the details of their discussions private, and he faced reporters with Ellen Gabriel. "There will be no hostilities on either side," Ciaccia said of the overnight truce.

Gabriel gave a hint of optimism: "We want to take the message we received from Mr. Ciaccia about the agreements the government wants to make with us back to our people. We need some time to do that and we need a good night's rest."

During the next three days, the Mohawks had to make the difficult transition from confrontation to negotiation. Moving into the basement of a single-family house previously converted into a drug and alcohol treatment center, the Warriors organized what would become the backbone of a negotiating committee. Guided by Boots and the recently arrived Akwesasne faithkeeper, Loran Thompson, the committee initially included Ellen Gabriel, Denise Tolley, and Mavis Etienne from Kanesatake; and Joe Deom, Laura Norton, and Dale Dionne from Kahnawake. Dubbing their headquarters "the pit," the committee had a telephone, telecopier, copying machine, and word processor at its disposal. As they settled in to draft a proposal for negotiations, the committee agreed to work according to the Great Law's rule of consensus, not majority rule. "We had to talk out our positions until everyone could agree," says Loran Thompson. "Among ourselves, people would argue and compromise, but then we could present a unified position to our adversaries."

On Friday, July 13, Ciaccia told the Mohawks that Bourassa had loosened police restrictions on shipments of food and other necessities. While the Mohawks accepted this as a move toward reconciliation, they told Ciaccia that they could not offer any serious concessions until police left Mohawk lands.

At first, Ciaccia countered that the SQ could not leave unless the Mohawks agreed to surrender their weapons. Immediately rejecting this approach, the Mohawks pressed for a resolution of land-claim issues once the occupation ended. When the minister asked if a withdrawal would lead to the re-opening of the Mercier Bridge, the Mohawks answered yes. For hours, Ciaccia probed for any sign of internal division or weakness that would allow him to immediately end the blockade that was rerouting more than 60,000 cars each day. Again and again, the Mohawks responded that a police withdrawal was the only way to clear the roads.

On Highway 138, just outside Kahnawake, an angry mob of 300 South Shore residents gathered on the police side of the Mohawk barricade, shouting obscenities and demanding that officers use force to clear the road. They began to shove against the police line, sparking a fight with the SQ. Pushed off the road, the mob regrouped in the parking lot of a nearby shopping center, where they saw two young men in camouflage fatigues enter a supermarket. The crowd attacked the pair, who were beaten so badly that they required hospital treatment. The victims turned out to be young whites in army-style pants.

The ugly confrontation increased the pressure on Ciaccia to strike a deal that would clear the bridge. He told the premier that the Mohawks would not move unless the police pulled back. As the negotiations continued on Saturday, the premier's staff suggested a compromise: if the police begin a step-by-step withdrawal, his aides asked, would the Mohawks begin to vacate the bridge and dismantle their barricades?

The Mohawks said they would consider this plan if it included an amnesty for fighting the police at Kanesatake and taking the bridge. Though the government agreed not to press charges for seizing the bridge—which occurred without violence—officials insisted on prosecutions for shooting at police. "We didn't know what to do," says Francis Boots, "because it was obvious that Ciaccia wanted a quick resolution. He wouldn't budge about the shooting of Lemay and we knew that. So we had to decide to continue to get the most out of him and take our chances about prosecution or stand firm."

Late Saturday afternoon, Ciaccia saw the outline of a deal: a religious order, acceptable to both parties, would monitor the gradual withdrawal of the police. Once enough officers had left Mohawk territory, the barricades would be taken down; this would trigger the second phase of police withdrawal. Mohawks would not be arrested or prosecuted for taking the bridge or damaging police property, but they were to cooperate with MUC inquiry into Lemay's death.

When Ciaccia returned on Sunday morning, he was accompanied by several clergymen, including Bishop Charles Valois of St. Jérôme, who asked if he was acceptable as monitor of the police withdrawal. Within minutes, the Mohawks approved, raising hopes that a deal could be finalized by sundown. Turning to their outstanding demands, the Mohawks asked Ciaccia to support a federal initiative that would grant Mohawks rights to the burial ground in the Pines and address a land claim for territory given to the Sulpician monks in the eighteenth century. Without hesitation, Ciaccia agreed. Second, the Mohawks sought a public inquiry into provincial and federal government delays in addressing the Mohawk claims in and around Oka. Concerned that this investigation would influence the criminal probe and expose the confused policies and procedures that led to the fatal raid, Ciaccia rejected this condition, but counterproposed a provincial inquiry on federal policies and Indian Affairs Minister Tom Siddon's refusal to join the negotiations. When Ciaccia promised native representation on the panel, the Mohawks accepted.

"We have the agreement," Ciaccia told reporters as he left the encampment on Sunday evening, "it's just a question of working out the details for putting it into effect."

23

THE POLS PUTT
FOR PAR

On Monday morning, July 16, it took less than four hours to undo four days of negotiations: the Mohawks and Ciaccia could not agree on how many policemen had to be withdrawn before the barricades would come down. Under pressure from Sûreté du Québec commanders, Ciaccia refused to disclose how many officers had left Oka on Sunday night and how many remained. Insisting on this information, the Mohawks vowed to hold their lines until Ciaccia or the SQ complied. According to several policemen at the barricades, fewer than 100 of the more than 1,000 officers were to be reassigned; but commanders would neither confirm nor deny these claims.

As word of the impasse reached reporters, several called SQ headquarters. Spokeswoman Ghislaine Blanchette acknowledged the withdrawal of some officers but would not offer any details. "We substantially reduced the number of officers as a demonstration of goodwill and willingness to support the negotiating efforts," Blanchette said, adding that the provincial police had asked federal authorities to send in the Mounties as replacements. The Mohawks became enraged when they heard the news on the radio.

"It was a double-cross, an absolute violation of any agreement that we made," charges Ellen Gabriel. "Our point was to get the police out of our land. It didn't matter whether the cops were federal or provincial. They had to leave for the barricades to come down."

As the agreement collapsed, an exasperated Ciaccia walked into no-man's-land, where his staff cleared a path through the crowd of reporters. For the second time in a week, his plans with the Mohawks had been undercut by the police, who were supposed to be on his side. On July 9, two days before the death of Cpl. Marcel Lemay, he had personally appealed to Oka Mayor Jean Ouellette to refrain from calling in the SQ. Then the police further embarrassed the government by blocking food shipments. And now, after his hard work had won him some limited trust, the provincial cops made a secret deal to call in the Mounties, a move that would offset any reduction of SQ officers.

"For the first days, we tried to work with Ciaccia and the government. We saw that they wanted a deal as a political settlement and we were eager for that," says Francis Boots. "We tried to trust them, and look what happened. They never wanted to remove the police. They just wanted to replace one police force with another. The provincial government wanted a police settlement, not a political one.

"That was one problem. Another was keeping ourselves together. Though the world saw us as Mohawks united in the barricades, we had a number of divisions and factions that had different ideas. First, there was the negotiating committee in the treatment center basement. We were supposedly in charge, and we had to do everything— meet reporters, draft proposals, arrange for supplies and people to be smuggled in and out. Across the river, there were the men and women of Kahnawake working hard to control their own differences between the band council, the Warriors, and the people on the bridge.

"Ciaccia could have gone across the river and started talking to people at Kahnawake and we would have had no means of coordinating our efforts. We were making one decision after another without any real focus or sense of purpose. We didn't have a central negotiating committee that represented Kanesatake and Kahnawake. Then we realized that people from Akwesasne were here and they should be represented because we are one Mohawk nation and the government was occupying our land at all three places. So getting all of our factions and communities represented was a real big problem.

"The next problem was finding one or two people to present our case to the public and to embarrass the provincial government. We had made Bourassa and the police look foolish and we had to keep that up. We had to get our message out to our people and those who could see between the lines."

By Monday afternoon, the Mohawks were molding a negotiating

committee with representation from different territories and factions. In Kanesatake, Ellen Gabriel, Denise Tolley, and Johnny Cree supported the barricades and the militant tactics, while band council members led by Grand Chief George Martin disapproved of confrontation. In Kahnawake, the men on the bridge led by Cookie McComber had kept their fragile alliance with Warriors Society leaders Allan Delaronde, Kenneth Deer, and others. Though Kahnawake Grand Chief Joseph Norton initially opposed taking the bridge, he started to come around as band councilors and other influential members of the community backed the militant stand. The Akwesasne group—Boots, Loran Thompson, and a handful of Warriors—openly supported the confrontation and pledged the support of hundreds in their community.

"We had to put all of these factions together and that was very, very difficult because we all had different concerns," continues Boots. "The people of Kanesatake were worried that outsiders were taking over the community. George Martin was worried that the people from Kahnawake and Akwesasne would make the battle much bigger than it had to be. He wanted the golf course stopped, the police removed, and the land claim addressed. That was enough.

"But the men on the bridge had to get amnesty. And once you were talking about amnesty in Kahnawake, other people in that community had questions about the cigarette trade. 'If we could get amnesty for the bridge, does that mean we have amnesty for our businesses?' Or they wanted to know, did the standoff affect what started in 1988 when they took the bridge to protest the raid of cigarette dealers? They felt they had to protect these gains.

"And from Akwesasne, we had our own agenda. We wanted to show the governments of the United States and Canada that the white border would not prevent the Mohawks from acting together. We wanted the Canadian government to formally recognize us as a nation, to deal with us as a country, not a band or tribe."

Instead of forging a committee that would place one faction over the other, the Mohawks developed a multi-tiered compromise that gave each territory the right to select representatives to a balanced negotiating committee: the Warriors continued to oversee the barricades, while Mohawk band-council leaders reached out for political support. On July 17, Norton announced his desire to convene a gathering of all Canadian band-council chiefs at Kahnawake. Other Mohawks contacted the Quebec Human Rights Commission, which was denied transport through police lines. In Ottawa, more than 400 na-tives marched in front of Parliament, while leaders of the New Dem-ocratic and Liberal parties denounced the federal Conservative government's refusal to join negotiations.

After consulting with the Department of National Defence, Que-bec Premier Bourassa, Public Safety Minister Sam Elkas and Sûreté du Québec Commandant Robert Lavigne announced that army "admin-istrative and support staff" had moved from their base at Valcartier near Quebec City to Longue Pointe on the eastern edge of Montreal. "We are making preparations to intervene," said Canadian Forces spokesman Capt. Alain François. "It would be inappropriate to say more or how many people are involved because we do not want to imperil the operation."

That night, more than 4,000 South Shore residents gathered on Highway 138 to burn a Mohawk in effigy. Face-to-face with riot police with shields, helmets, and nightsticks, the crowd jeered the armed and masked Mohawks who manned the barricade a few hundred yards away, chanting, "Savages, savages."

The next morning, Bourassa mildly rebuked the Québécois protes-ters, insisting his government was working hard to protect their inter-ests. "The people we are thinking of are those who are prevented from working, from making a living in a normal fashion for the past week," he said, pointing out that the provincial government had arranged for transportation to help suburban residents cope with the extended commute into Montreal. "We have to appeal to natives that violence is not the way to help their cause, to cause prejudice among thousands and thousands of workers."

But Bourassa's refusal to denounce the Mohawks angered thou-sands of South Shore residents who again gathered in Châteauguay and broke through the Sûreté du Québec lines. This time, the protes-ters were pushed back by more than 300 Mounties, who were bused to the scene. After several skirmishes, the demonstrators regrouped on Highway 138 and burned an effigy labeled "Bourassa."

"It was one royal fucking mess," says Stanley Cohen. "The police were everywhere and they were not letting any people or any food come in. The Mohawks were holed up in the woods, trying to keep together a very shaky set of alliances. Federal officials were fighting with the pro-vincial officials, and the provincial officials were tripping all over themselves. Ciaccia had said one thing, but the SQ did another. Siddon said the federals wouldn't get involved, but the army was meeting with the police. You couldn't believe anybody.

"I was asked to be legal adviser to the Akwesasne part of the negotiating team. The Warriors from Akwesasne were scared that something was going to happen—a raid, an army attack, or even just a bad deal that would give the police a chance to arrest Mohawks once they left the territory. So they asked me to come up, and I walked into this incredible mess."

The Kahnawake Warriors asked for William Kunstler, who arrived with Cohen on July 17. Though the two lawyers had worked together on several cases in New York, they differed on tactics. "Kunstler wanted us to cut a deal to get the police out of there and prevent our people from getting arrested," says Ellen Gabriel. "He figured the government would jump at an arrangement that would let them negotiate the specifics one at a time. Stanley wanted to dig in, take hold, and force recognition of the Mohawk nation. There were advantages to both sides, but it had to be talked over and thought out."

While the Mohawks convened their loosely structured negotiating committee on July 19, Siddon and then Canadian solicitor general Pierre Cadieux praised Ciaccia, but implied that provincial officials had rejected in the spring a federal initiative to buy the Pines and preserve the Mohawk burial grounds. "We recognize the inadequacy of the land base at Oka as a problem that would be resolved," Siddon insisted, "and we are prepared to address the social and economic development needs of Kanesatake. But we won't talk while there are barricades and we won't talk in circumstances where firearms are used to provoke negotiations."

Quebec Minister of Municipal Affairs Yvon Picotte labeled Siddon "Deaf, dumb and blind. He is ill-informed about the situation and disconnected from reality." As Mohawks watched the provincial and federal governments trade insults, they closed ranks and hardened their resolve to resist any short-term deal, believing neither Ottawa nor Quebec. "They couldn't trust each other, so how could we trust them?" asks Denise Tolley. "Earlier they tried to trick us by saying the SQ would withdraw, but they didn't tell us about the plans to send in the Mounties. Now, Bourassa was talking about the troops and Siddon was telling us to put down our guns. He's got to be nuts."

Led by the Warriors from Akwesasne and Kahnawake, the negotiating team chose to hold the bridge and the Pines until the provincial and federal governments specifically consented to five conditions: 1) that all negotiations be carried out on the basis that the Mohawks are a sovereign nation; 2) that title to the disputed land at Oka be turned over to the Kanesatake band; 3) that police completely withdraw from the entrances to Kanesatake and Kahnawake before the barricades could be removed; 4) that after the police backed off and barricades were taken down, officers would not interfere with Mohawks leaving the territories, for a period of 48 hours; 5) that all other issues, including criminal prosecution, be brought before the World Court in The Hague. Seeing that the Mohawks felt more comfortable with Cohen, Kunstler left while the new proposals were being issued to the press.

Bourassa immediately rejected the proposal; Ciaccia told reporters that the Mohawks had shown they no longer wanted to negotiate in good faith.

More than 150 native chiefs met at Kahnawake on Friday, July 20. Though Kahnawake Grand Chief Joseph Norton had criticized the seizure of the Mercier Bridge and the barricades in Kanesatake, he quickly turned the conference into an outpouring of support for the militants. Warrior Dan Martin was showered with applause when he suggested that Canada's native communities form their own Warriors Societies to be linked in an ad hoc force to defend their territories across Canada. The chiefs also applauded Martin's suggestion that native people block roads through their own communities. "You should nationalize all highways and toll them," he said.

The chiefs adopted a set of sweeping resolutions demanding that Prime Minister Brian Mulroney's government order the withdrawal of the police, extend amnesty, and recall Parliament from its summer recess. If the government failed to take these steps, the chiefs promised to call on the world community to impose economic sanctions on Canada until the Mohawk dispute was settled. The chiefs also vowed to take "appropriate and reasonable actions" if another attack on Mohawks were ordered.

"When the army moves in, we will consider that to be an official declaration of war," said Cree Grand Chief George Wapatchee, whose band council represents men and women living in the vicinity of the James Bay hydroelectric projects. "We will act accordingly."

As the chiefs raised the ante, so did federal politicians who opposed Mulroney. New Democratic Party leader Audrey McLaughlin made a highly publicized visit to Oka, where she met with several Warriors and endorsed their demand that Mulroney's government enter the talks. "This is a national crisis," McLaughlin said. "Where is the prime minister?"

Mulroney sent Siddon out to reply. In a letter released to the press and printed in *The Globe and Mail*, Siddon claimed that he and Ciaccia had agreed that "the public security aspect was a provincial responsibility." Though Siddon said the federal government remained ready to render assistance, "at no time have I received any request to intervene."

While the politicians chipped away at one another, the SQ blocked shipments of food into Kanesatake. They turned away a caravan of 200 residents from nearby Laval trying to deliver a donation of canned goods. The police blocked a delegation from the International Red Cross and a column of Trappist monks, who live at a nearby monastery and are renowned for their specialty cheeses. When then Quebec Education minister Claude Ryan visited the site, he donned a bulletproof vest to show his support for the police and told reporters that the halting of food shipments had become provincial government policy.

The use of food as a weapon drew an outcry from the Quebec human rights commission and the Montreal-based Canadian Centre for Human Rights, which harshly denounced Bourassa and his men. On the basis of these statements and an impassioned letter from members of the Mohawk negotiating team, Nadia Younes, spokeswoman for United Nations Secretary General Javier Perez de Cuellar, told reporters that her boss had "urgently referred the matter to the U.N. Human Rights Center in Geneva." The Mohawks then announced that they would send Kenneth Deer to address the diplomats. Deer's mission got a boost from the Quebec provincial ombudsman, Daniel Jacoby, who condemned the food blockade. "How can we have reached this point," Jacoby asked, "in a society which is supposedly democratic?"

Amid the backlash from the SQ's harsh tactics, Ciaccia called a press conference on Monday, July 23, announcing his desire to resume face-to-face discussions providing two conditions were met: first, he wanted to meet Mohawks on neutral ground, as the Pines were "an armed camp"; second, he insisted that Mohawk negotiators come only from Kanesatake and Kahnawake, in effect banning Akwesasne from the talks.

Less than an hour later, Harry Swain, the federal deputy minister for Indian Affairs, agreed, providing his comments were unattributed, to speak freely with *Globe and Mail* reporter Geoffrey York, author of *The Dispossessed,* a thought-provoking study of Canada's policy toward native communities. In a rambling discussion, Swain claimed that Warriors from Akwesasne had "hijacked" the dispute. "The Warriors," he said, "are a criminal organization" consisting of many Vietnam veterans or former members of the U.S. Army who are looking for action. "In effect," Swain said, "it is a potent combination of guns, cash, and ideology. They are pretty successful in cloaking themselves in the guise of Indian rights."

The next day, *The Globe and Mail* published Swain's broadsides in a story that pointed out, "Mr. Swain, accompanied by other senior officials from the department, spoke to reporters on the condition that none of them be identified. Because of the serious nature of the allegations, *The Globe and Mail* has chosen to attribute the comments at the briefing.

"Later yesterday, Indian Affairs Minister Thomas Siddon contradicted his own deputy minister and denied several of Mr. Swain's allegations. He denied that the Mohawk Warriors were a criminal organization and that they hijacked the Oka talks. 'I don't subscribe to rumors myself,' he said."

Though the Mohawks could laugh at the politicos' blunders, they also detected a danger signal. "This was their first attempt to manipulate the divisions in our nation," says Francis Boots. "It was clumsy and funny, but they had an idea that we were not pulled together. Divide and conquer has always been the best tactic of white governments."

The Mohawks desperately tried to form a cohesive negotiating strategy. Since Corporal Lemay's death, they had relied on holding the provincial police at bay while manipulating the tensions between Ottawa and Quebec; but now they had to convert their military success into a political program. Their immediate need was to tighten their organization and to work efficiently. For the first two weeks of the standoff, the Mohawks on both sides of Montreal communicated via radio, telephone, and the nightly boat rides that smuggled food, people, and equipment back and forth. The loose arrangement allowed each group to exercise autonomy and balance the other; but the lengthy, overcrowded meetings in the treatment center prevented the Mohawks from hammering out a plan for negotiations.

"We were all over each other, mixing and matching chores, making it impossible to focus on each particular concern," says Joe Deom, a soft-spoken, white-haired Kahnawake Mohawk who supported the barricades and repeatedly pressed the Warriors to formalize a negotiating team. "We had the power to win something, but we didn't have any division of labor or real organization."

Adds Francis Boots, "Everything was getting overloaded and blocked up. We needed a place to deal with reporters and logistics, and we needed a separate place to meet and think the negotiation strategy out. It was time to establish a political command post outside of Kanesatake so we could have better contacts with the outside world."

This need became more urgent as Quebec Public Safety Minister Elkas told reporters that any second raid would combine policemen and soldiers. A spokesman for the Department of National Defence denied that there had been any formal request for troops, but acknowledged that federal Indian Affairs Minister Tom Siddon met with Defence Minister William McKnight and Solicitor General Pierre Cadieux to discuss the possibility of a military deployment. This added support to the earlier statement by Jocelyn Turcotte, the president of the provincial police union, indicating that officers recalled from the barricades would be replaced by soldiers.

"There was so much going on and we couldn't keep track of it," says Boots. "Every day we had reporters in Kanesatake bringing word of this development or that development. We would spend hours and hours tracking down rumors and pieces of information to make sure that we were in step with our people in Kahnawake.

"It was time for some of us to be under a different roof, and we figured that Kahnawake was the right place because the bridge was the key to our success—we could convince the army or the police that their second attack would force us to blow up the bridge. And more than anything else, the government wanted the bridge back."

Working their radios and telephones, the Warriors of Akwesasne hatched a plan: to protect Francis Boots, their war chief, and make use of his talents to organize supplies and communications, he would be smuggled from Kanesatake to Kahnawake, where a group of Mohawk leaders would try to coordinate the efforts of the Kahnawake and Kanesatake band councils, the Warriors, and the militants on the bridge. Boots would work in what would be called the Mohawk Nation Office, as official liaison between the Akwesasne Warriors in the Pines, the militants on the bridge, and the Kahnawake Warriors. "We had to find a way to set the agenda. Some of the biggest problems were the splits within our nation," says Boots. "I had to get out of Kanesa-take, where there were people who were only interested in talking about the police and the barricades. That was talking in the government's language. We had to turn the tables on the whole situation. We had to back away from the military and the fighting and put this into the context of our nation demanding sovereignty."

The Warriors' political efforts received help from the Quebec Ligue des Droits et des Libertés, which arranged for Jean Claude Foque, the secretary general of the Paris-based International Human Rights Federation, to visit the Mohawks and investigate claims that provincial authorities systematically violated their rights. His arrival was followed by an announcement by the Canadian Human Rights Commission, the first federal agency to recommend the direct participation of Prime Minister Mulroney. "It would be tragic if the confrontation deteriorated further and violence erupted again," wrote Deputy Commissioner Michelle Falardeau-Ramsay. "This must not be allowed to happen."

Such high-profile criticism prompted federal Indian and Northern Affairs Minister Tom Siddon to convene a July 26 meeting with his provincial counterpart, Quebec's minister of Native Affairs, John Ciaccia. Siddon raised the possibility of amnesty for some Mohawks and committed the federal government to buying the Pines from the town and adjoining landowner Maxime Rousseau. Once the federal government held the title, Siddon said, it would turn the parcel over to the Kanesatake band council. After the session, Siddon told reporters, "The country cannot wait. That was the message we took most firmly to Mr. Ciaccia. Time is of the essence. Significant steps are now required to break the impasse."

Though this position showed signs of conciliation and flexibility, the Warriors were extremely wary of claims that Siddon's statement represented a softening of the government's position. Their suspicions proved correct later that afternoon, when John McKenna, chief of staff to Quebec's minister of Public Safety, Sam Elkas, claimed SQ ballistics tests indicated Mohawks fired the bullet that killed Lemay. Asked to elaborate on the specific results, McKenna declined.

"They were trying to play the good guy–bad guy routine," says Boots. "First, Siddon says something nice. Then a policeman accuses us of murder."

The final attempt at manipulation arrived in the early evening when Ciaccia sent a letter expressing his desire to resume negotiations outside the barricades provided that the Mohawks laid down their weapons. "As soon as we were starting to make progress in showing that our situation was political—a matter of human rights violations and something that needed to be addressed as the Mohawk nation to the Canadian nation—the federal and provincial authorities wanted to talk about guns and make us look like killers and criminals," says Boots.

The next day, after the Mohawks dismissed Ciaccia's proposal, Boots was smuggled out of Kanesatake and taken into Kahnawake. "It was time to press our advantage and set the agenda for serious negotiations," he says. "We needed to talk about our issues, not theirs."

24

MOHAWK GOLF: ALL
CHIEFS, NO INDIANS

Despite the efforts of the negotiating committee, the Mohawks could not overcome the many splits in their communities. Picking at the festering sores of bingo and gaming, the anti-gambling faction from Akwesasne traveled to Montreal, where they met with provincial officials and issued a statement reflecting the concerns of the traditionalist Grand Council of Chiefs from the Iroquois Confederacy. "The existence of a paramilitary group calling itself the Warriors will only hamper matters and destroy real efforts at a settlement," said Barbara Barnes, representing the antis. "The Warriors are a gang of criminals. They are dictating what is going on, and the people of the Kanesatake community are not having their say."

The statement immediately encouraged other Mohawks to speak up, especially George Martin and Clarence Simon, who had bitterly contested the position of grand chief of the Kanesatake band council. "The Warriors just came here and took it upon themselves to put the barricades up," said Simon. "At the beginning, we had some people who practiced our traditional religion who wanted to protest by putting up a little barricade on a dirt path. And it stayed that way until the town got the injunction. Then the Warriors came and cut down some trees and moved some stones. The next thing we knew, they brought guns. We didn't see that until it was too late."

Added Martin, "The federal and provincial governments recognize the band council as the only legitimate representatives of the people on our territory and we are not even on the negotiating committee. Because I am on the band council, part of what they call the 'puppet' government, the Warriors from Akwesasne and Kahnawake don't see me as a legitimate representative. At least they see me as a Mohawk, but they don't want my perspective on the committee."

Though the Kahnawake band council voted to support the Warrior barricades on the bridge and highways, some councilors, notably Grand Chief Joseph Norton, expressed ambivalence about committing to armed resistance. "Sometimes I wonder if the Warriors are going down the right path, but then you cannot underestimate our determination to protect our heritage. The Warriors may make the wrong move, or I may disagree with them, but they are Mohawks standing up for all of our rights. I will support that even though I disagree with some of the particular tactics. After all, I have a 16-year-old son who is behind the barricades. Is he a criminal? No. Do I disagree with him? Sometimes. Is he a heartless killer? Absolutely not."

With the Mohawks showing signs of dissension, the federal and provincial governments pressed for an advantage. At the July 27 cabinet meeting, Prime Minister Brian Mulroney announced that he would meet the press and make a conciliatory statement, then let Siddon and Ciaccia tend to the details of resuming talks. Claiming that federal officials urged Quebec to back away from a second attack, Mulroney and his aides wanted to isolate the Warriors and help a different faction—perhaps the elected band council leaders—maneuver into a leadership position. Appealing for negotiation rather than confrontation, the prime minister said, "I believe our native people over decades and centuries have not been well treated by Canada and Canadians."

After Mulroney's statement, an eager Siddon announced that the federal government had spent $1.4 million to purchase 12 hectares from a part of the Pines owned by Maxime Rousseau and sought to spend another $3 million on the portion sold to the town. Repeating his pledge to convey the land to the Kanesatake band council, Siddon said the federal government would settle land claims to expand the Mohawks' territorial base. From Quebec City, Ciaccia promised provincial support for Mohawk title to more land if the barricades were dismantled and discussions begun again.

While the Mohawks studied the proposal, the residents of Oka immediately took to the streets to denounce it. An overflow crowd forced the village council to hold its Saturday, July 28, meeting in a small park beside the municipal building. To the cheers of the crowd bearing placards that read "Savages Go Home!" and "What about Rights for Whites?", Mayor Jean Ouellette said he would demand government compensation for 31 families evicted from their homes to accommodate the police barricades. Then he addressed the federal proposal to buy about 12 hectares of the Pines from the town and turn it over to the Mohawks. "It's ours," he said to another round of cheers. "If we want to sell, we can sell it for whatever we want."

Three days later, more than 400 people jammed the council meeting held to formally consider the federal government's offer of more than $3.8 million for land that had cost the town $90,000. Speaker after speaker rose to criticize the deal and urge the council to reject any amount of money. Mayor Ouellette drew a raucous round of cheers when he announced that he would refuse to accept the federal government's money. "We will not sign anything until those barricades come down," he said in a firm voice.

About an hour later, Jean Pierre Marcellin took the microphone. An emigre from France, he cautioned his fellow townspeople about the perils of seeking revenge, and he began to speak about negotiating with the Mohawks. Boos and jeers hounded him from the stage. "I was trying to say to the crowd, 'You're Québécois and proud,'" Marcellin recalls. "So I wanted the people to think about the Indians saying, 'We're Mohawks and proud.' But no one wanted to listen. They don't seem to understand that if French Canada wants to be a distinct society, then the Indians have the same rights."

After Marcellin left the meeting, he went to his neighbor's house on Oka's main street. Sitting in the living room, he heard a rock crash through the window of his antique store located on the ground floor of the adjacent building. The next day, August 1, more than 12,000 residents of the South Shore marched through the town of Châteauguay, yelling and chanting, "We want our bridge!" and "Bring in the army!"

While residents marched, the Mohawk negotiating committee traded facsimile messages with Ciaccia. Insisting that they would not lay down their arms or dismantle the barricades, the Mohawks demanded that the federal and provincial governments agree to three pre-conditions before "serious negotiations" could begin: 1) the police would allow passage of shipments of food and medicine; 2) the Mohawks could have unlimited access to spiritual and legal advisers; and 3) the Canadians would accept the presence of international observers to monitor the talks and the conduct of the police.

"He kept telling us that in his letters he had agreed in principle to the pre-conditions," says Deom. "Well, that was not good enough. We wanted a formal declaration. Something that the provincial and federal governments could not renege on." Under pressure from residents of suburban Montreal, Quebec Premier Bourassa had to give the appearance of a hard line, while Ottawa had the luxury of being able to give the impression of flexibility.

"This was a critical period for Bourassa," says Stanley Cohen. "He was in the middle of all three parties and he couldn't find a way out. To give in to the crowds and order a police raid would have been a bloodbath and an immediate political disaster. He couldn't trust Ottawa because Mulroney and Siddon would not become directly involved in the talks—they wanted Bourassa to take the heat. And he couldn't give in to us.

"He came up with a very good ploy. He invited a representative of the Assembly of First Nations and Joe Norton to direct discussions. This put us in a bind. If we let them go, then we were sending a message that the province could walk around the Kanesatake negotiating committee to conduct discussions. If we didn't let them go, we gave Bourassa the opportunity to say that the Mohawks were not interested in face-to-face discussions at the highest level of the provincial government."

After hours of discussion, the Mohawk negotiating committee remained divided on Bourassa's invitation to Norton. "I wanted to go," Norton says. "There was no way I could be stopped. The Warriors knew that I supported the blockades and the demands that we have a written agreement on the three pre-conditions. They had to trust me."

On the morning of August 2, Norton and Konrad Siuoi, the French-speaking leader of the Assembly of First Nations of Quebec and Labrador, took their seats across the table from the premier and Ciaccia. In a meeting that would later be described as candid and cordial, Bourassa and Ciaccia began by proclaiming their support for the three Mohawk demands. By the afternoon, Norton and Sioui stood beside the premier as he announced the accord.

"We have no objection to the application of those pre-conditions," Bourassa said. "I pointed out the considerable inconvenience for the populations of the South Shore and Oka, and the Mohawk leaders are conscious of this. Imagine the reactions of the citizens if the George Washington Bridge in New York or the Pont Neuf in Paris were shut down for four weeks. The government is taking all possible steps to obtain a peaceful solution. I don't think anyone has anything to gain from a violent confrontation."

Though Norton cautioned that "some very important technical points remain to be cleared up," he joined Siuoi, Bourassa, and Ciaccia in a conciliatory posture. Ciaccia said a written draft would be ready within a few hours; Norton nodded and smiled.

This announcement, however, further divided Mohawks who wanted negotiations from Warriors who wanted confrontation. In Kanesatake, Grand Chief George Martin denounced the negotiating committee members from Akwesasne and Kahnawake as outside agitators. "This is not their territory, not their reserve," Martin said. "They should get the hell out."

By way of reply, six Warriors beat Martin up and fired guns at his house in an effort to silence him. Vowing to press charges, Martin said that Warriors also assaulted and shot at his political ally, Gerry Etienne. Both men escaped serious injury.

"The whole situation was being taken away from us; it wasn't good," says Francis Boots. "First, Bourassa beat us by going around the negotiating committee. Standing there with Joe Norton, he sent the message that many Mohawks do not agree with the Warriors and that negotiations could take place without the committee at Kanesatake. He divided us.

"Second, George Martin saw that Joe Norton from Kahnawake was getting a chance to speak directly to the premier. This was a humiliation to him. He figured the whole crisis started over the golf course that threatened his people." Boots said the attacks on Martin and Etienne began when they smuggled liquor past the police checkpoint, a move that mixed heated politics with the explosive quality of alcohol. "In the excitement, some shots were fired," Boots deadpans. "It got to be a little bit too much."

Acutely aware that Martin and Norton offered Bourassa an alternative to the Warriors, the negotiating committee spent several days trying to resolve differences within the Mohawk communities. Everybody agreed that representatives of the provincial and federal governments had to sign a formal agreement to abide by the three preconditions; however, the Mohawk factions bitterly argued over the next step. Band councilors from Kanesatake and Kahnawake proposed a partial dismantling of the barricades; the militants insisted that the fortifications had to stay. The Warriors wanted to solidify the critical alliance between their men on the barricades and the militants on the Mercier Bridge. "We always kept coming back to that," says Joe Deom. "As long as we controlled the bridge, we had a lot of power."

The Warriors believed that Bourassa was attempting two sets of negotiations—one for the golf course, another for the bridge. To show the premier that divide-and-conquer tactics would only harden the Warriors' resolve, they insisted that the roads would not be cleared until the police withdrew and negotiations began to address the Mohawks' territorial demands.

"Totally unacceptable," replied John Ciaccia, who immediately won the support of his federal counterpart, Tom Siddon. "The Mohawks want the government of Quebec to accept in advance and in writing that it will negotiate over Mohawk territory, including Akwesasne—part of which covers land in New York State and Ontario, beyond our jurisdiction. We have said many times, and so has the federal government, that we will not negotiate territorial questions as long as the barricades are in place."

When word of the demands became public, several hundred South Shore residents launched sit-ins that further obstructed traffic in and out of Montreal. During the morning rush hour on Friday, August 3, a group of protesters including Ricardo Lopez, the Conservative Member of Parliament for Châteauguay, closed the Champlain Bridge for 45 minutes. Other protests targeted Highway 15 leading to the United States and Highway 132 along the St. Lawrence River. In the afternoon, demonstrators hit the Monseigneur Langlois Bridge near Valleyfield.

"We are demanding action by the army," said Lopez, who frequently joined his constituents in marches calling for a military attack on the Mohawk barricades. "The longer the government waits, the harder it will be for the soldiers to take control."

Two days later, Bourassa issued a terse statement designed to divide the Mohawks and bolster his support among the white residents of suburban Montreal. "The government has made every effort to arrive at a negotiated settlement," he said. "No one can reproach us for our efforts. So I say to the Mohawks, you have 48 hours to accept a negotiated solution and it is in your interest to do so. If, within 48 hours, you have not accepted to negotiate, you leave us no choice but to draw the necessary conclusions and take the appropriate measures to deal with this situation."

At first, Bourassa's ploy had mixed results. Martin continued his open attacks on the Warriors, but Norton joined with the militants to defy the premier. "One day we are working to reach out and talk, the next day the door gets slammed in our face," Norton says. "This is not productive. Either the government of Quebec agrees to the pre-conditions and negotiates without a time limit or the premier calls in the troops. It can't go on both ways."

"We will not be bullied by the power and arrogance of Quebec," added Ellen Gabriel, announcing that the negotiating committee at the treatment center would deliberately let the deadline pass. "We will wait for the moment and see what kind of response we will get."

To Gabriel and others working out of the center, Bourassa's statement was a symbol of weakness and frustration. They saw him as unable to endure a lengthy standoff and desperate to involve the federal government. "He wants to divide us so he can show his voters and the country a success like clearing the bridge," said Deom. "If we keep that from him, he continues to appear weak and indecisive. The more we embarrass him, the more respect we will have in Ottawa.

"The Canadians can try to divide us and play off our factions. Well, we can try to divide them. We see the ultimatum as a clear threat to our safety and security. They are telling us to make an agreement within 48 hours or else—does that sound like negotiating in good faith? No. Our presence here has shown the Canadians, the Americans, and the world that we will stand up and stare down these threats. We are not afraid. You can use your imagination as to what we might do, but we are prepared for the worst."

As the 48 hours ticked by, the Warriors remained remarkably calm, now that they considered an attack inevitable. In Kanesatake, thousands of rounds of ammunition and Molotov cocktails were brought to the barricades; trenches and booby traps were dug into the woods. At the territory's community center, storage space became a food bank, and recreation and meeting rooms served as an emergency shelter for more than 150 men, women, and children escaping the expected crossfire. At the roadblocks in Kahnawake, ironworkers welded scraps of metal into the shape of a mounted machine gun and painted it black. They posted it 30 yards behind one of the barricades to give the misleading show of firepower. On the Mercier Bridge, Mohawks drilled into the concrete roadway and placed small amounts of plastic explosives.

"This time it was going to go with a big ka-boom," said one of the masked men on the bridge.

25

MULRONEY SWINGS THE BIG STICK

The attack never came.

After setting a deadline backed by the implicit use of force, Bourassa let it lapse without a police charge. On the advice of Sûreté du Québec commanders who believed that a battle might kill officers and civilians, the premier recognized that Quebec did not have the weaponry or political will to endure the losses that would force the Mohawks out of their barricades. As one provincial politician summed it up, "It's time for the army."

In telephone calls and meetings throughout August 7 and 8, Bourassa and Ciaccia presented their plan to federal officials: troops would replace the more than 1,500 officers of the SQ and the 500 Royal Canadian Mounted Police. Prime Minister Brian Mulroney's government made a simple deal—Ottawa would send in the troops if Bourassa requested help and agreed that federal officials play a leading role in subsequent negotiations. Although the terms required Quebec politicians to support Mulroney and publicly admit failure, Bourassa accepted.

On Wednesday, August 8, Mulroney returned from an emergency visit to U.S. President George Bush, who was gathering support for an international military response to Iraq's invasion of Kuwait. After telling the American leader that Canada would add its forces to the international defense of Saudi Arabia, Mulroney had to consider dispatching more than 4,000 troops to crush a rebellion outside Montreal. Though the prime minister dismissed any comparison, the irony was obvious: at the time he committed Canadians to a foreign military intervention, the prime minister invoked the National Defence Act to use the same troops to protect Quebec from the aspirations of the country's aboriginal population. After last-minute consultations, Mulroney and Bourassa agreed that the mobilization against the Mohawks should be tempered by the appointment of an intermediary, former Quebec Superior Court chief justice Alan Gold, a labor law specialist who had successfully resolved thorny collective-bargaining disputes.

The decision to dispatch troops was the first internal deployment of the armed forces since the federal government had used the harsher terms of the War Measures Act to suspend civil liberties and round up suspected Quebec separatist militants in 1970. Though Bourassa had also been provincial premier at the time of the earlier crisis, the historical overtones remained unspoken as Mulroney explained that the Quebec government was now requesting troops because the standoffs were deemed a threat to security. By this request, the prime minister said, authority for the crisis had been transferred from the province to the federal government.

"The object of the troops is to replace the Sûreté du Québec officers who, after a month or so, are presumably fatigued," said Mulroney, indicating that the troops would not take offensive action as long as the Mohawks showed a desire to negotiate with government officials or Judge Gold. "The mediation process must work. It can work. We must make every effort to settle our differences without violence."

Shortly after Mulroney made his announcement, Mayor Jean Ouellette and the town council of Oka met to reconsider the federal offer to buy its lands in the Pines. Without the anti-Mohawk rhetoric characteristic of earlier sessions, the council reversed its opposition and agreed to sell the parcel—in effect blocking expansion of the golf course into the Mohawk burial grounds. "That's what started this dispute in the first place," says Luc Carbonneau, the lawyer for the council. "This is our part to bring about a meaningful resolution."

The next morning, the masked men on the barricades expected to see troops, but the SQ remained. As explained by Lt. Gen. Kent Foster, commander of the Canadian Forces Mobile Command—a unit described as "an army SWAT team"—approximately 4,400 troops were placed on alert, but quartered on the eastern edge of Montreal. Instead of squaring off with the army, the Warriors received a call from Judge Gold, who expressed his desire to come behind the barricades. Though the Mohawks consented, they were frightened, wondering whether the visit was a ruse to distract their attention from a possible armed forces attack. Emboldened by their victory on July 11, many of the Warriors believed they could fight the police to a standstill, but they knew that their automatic weapons and beer-bottle firebombs would not stand up to armored personnel carriers, tanks, and helicopters.

The Mohawk militants understood that the ability to intimidate was their best weapon. Having carefully cultivated the image of fierce men willing to die for their cause, they knew that it was relatively easy to scare the police, who were not trained to fight wars. As former military men themselves, many of the Warriors recognized the subtle but important distinction between cops cracking down on outlaws and troops besieging an enemy. "The Canadians made an irreversible choice," says Boots. "They told us, their own people, and the world that they were willing to use the military to solve a political problem. The tables were turned. *They* made the decision to use the threat of bloodshed to force a solution.

"The government made it clear that we had to negotiate or face the overwhelming power of the army. Their strategy toward us was simple and straightforward—talk with us on our terms or get slaughtered. Our choice was also very simple. Obedience or defiance.

"In Kanesatake, most of the negotiators in the treatment center wanted defiance, while moderates on the band council were furiously trying to cut a deal. But the men at the barricades held firm and the people in the treatment center were in control. There were divisions, but the negotiating committee still had the hard face. In Kahnawake, the feeling was a little bit different. You could hear people say that we had made our point, and it was time to talk, and cut this out before the army came in."

Kahnawake Grand Chief Norton privately told Mohawks that he wanted an end to the standoff that had shut down his territory. Frustrated with the tactics that had led to the presence of troops, Norton claimed to be "optimistic and confident" that the Mercier Bridge could be opened in two weeks.

In the treatment center, Mohawk negotiators saw this as a dangerous development that might undermine their standing with Gold. He sought to allay fears of an attack, describing his immediate task as

getting Mohawks and federal officials to begin face-to-face negotiations. When asked if the government negotiating team would report
directly to Mulroney, Gold replied that the prime minister would select the representatives. Impressed, the Mohawks repeated their commitment to binding negotiations to remove the barricades and settle
the land claims once their pre-conditions were met. Agreeing to present this position to Mulroney, Gold left, asking the Mohawks to refrain from speaking with reporters about their talks.

Gold's visit gave the Mohawks some reason to trust the federal government, but Bourassa almost destroyed it the very next day, when it
became known that he was holding a secret meeting with military
and police commanders. The Mohawks perceived the session as
symptomatic of the ongoing duplicity orchestrated by the provincial
and federal governments: every time the feds made a friendly gesture,
provincial officials struck a menacing pose.

"More than any other time, we were convinced that Bourassa
couldn't let us talk and walk our way out of this," says Boots. "We had
embarrassed him and we believed he had to strike back to satisfy the
racist crowds demonstrating against us and to show Quebec that he
would not let Ottawa call the shots in the Québécois homeland."

While the premier conducted his meeting, Gold persuaded Siddon
and Ciaccia to re-examine the pre-conditions and sign an agreement
to get serious talks started. "You had to give the Mohawks something
to get them to the negotiating table," says a federal official who
worked with the mediator. "Whether the government liked it or
not, that was the plain and simple reality. The judge told it to Siddon straight up 'Make the first move.' And if you look at the pre-
conditions, you could see that the government wasn't giving anything
up by signing them. The government had already said it wasn't going
to starve the Mohawks. So Gold urged Siddon to give the Mohawks
the satisfaction of putting it on paper."

On Sunday afternoon, August 12, Siddon and his provincial counterpart, Ciaccia, went behind the barricades less than 20 yards from
the site of Lemay's death. Surrounded by masked Warriors in camouflage fatigues, they signed agreements that guaranteed the Mohawks
access to food, medicine, clothing, spiritual advisers, legal advisers,
and international observers.

"It was a tremendous victory," says Joe Deom. "We held our ground
and forced the Canadians to come to us and recognize us as a nation,
not a band or disruptive ethnic group. The governments of Canada

and Quebec have been forced to admit that they cannot push us around without paying a price."

Hours after the signing ceremony, more than 3,000 South Shore residents marched on the Sûreté du Québec barricades in Châteauguay, chanting anti-government and anti-Mohawk slogans. Supported by the RCMP, SQ officers pushed into the column of demonstrators, hoping to disperse them before they reached the aluminum-and-wire roadblocks used to cut off traffic. In response, many of the protesters hurled stones and beer bottles, bloodying at least eight Mounties. As the confrontation erupted, a flanking column of SQ riot police fired tear-gas canisters. The crowd panicked and ran back down Highway 138.

At the Petro-Canada station beside the police barricade, André Lauzin believed his lungs were going to explode. "It was horrible," he said, wiping his eyes and wheezing. "I could see women and children caught in the crowd. They were running and falling. I was afraid someone was going to get trampled."

The Châteauguay riot came on the heels of a violent anti-Mohawk protest in St. Louis de Gonzague, where 100 provincial officers attacked 150 demonstrators blocking a drawbridge over the St. Lawrence Seaway. In clearing the narrow span, the police viciously clubbed the protesters, dented the cars blocking the roadway, and arrested their leader, Yvon Poitras, a retired provincial policeman who lives on the South Shore.

As the gassed and beaten demonstrators regrouped near the middle of Châteauguay, they marched on the nearby police station at Ste. Martine, where Poitras and others were being held. The 200 demonstrators went on a rampage, breaking windows and destroying two squad cars. The police forced the protesters back with yet another wave of gassings and beatings.

"It is outrageous," Poitras said after his release. "The police do not act against the outlaws who kill one of their own and take control of a bridge; but they beat and gas us, respectable citizens who have a right to protest in our own towns."

On the night of August 13, more than 400 people pelted the police lines with rocks and metal objects, and brandished tire irons and baseball bats. The RCMP and SQ riot squads lobbed tear-gas canisters and pushed the crowd back to the town's main street. The retreating protesters continued their chant, "We want the army!" Nearby hospitals reported more than 75 people requiring treatment for injuries.

The chief of the SQ, Robert Lavigne, went on camera to make his first public comment since the 34-day standoff began. "We are incapable of maintaining peace and order and to enforce the law with the resources we have," Lavigne said.

His candid assessment and the possibility of more violence forced the federal government to respond. On Tuesday afternoon, August 14, Prime Minister Brian Mulroney appointed his former principal secretary and close friend, Montreal lawyer Bernard Roy, as chief federal negotiator. The prime minister's intention to give negotiations top priority was undercut by military officials who held press conferences in Ottawa and Quebec City. Gen. John de Chastelain, chief of the Defence Staff, said that more than 4,400 soldiers from the Fifth Mechanized Brigade would be placed on alert, ready to take over for the police at any time. In Valcartier, the brigade's commander, Brig. Gen. Armand Roy, announced that he was sending 2,629 soldiers, 874 jeeps, 270 armored personnel carriers, and 12 helicopters into the Montreal area under the direction of Lt. Gen. Kent Foster. The troops would initially set up at four locations: Blainville and St. Benoit near Oka, St. Remi and Farnham near Kahnawake.

That night, Châteauguay and South Shore demonstrators encountered police clustered in groups of three and four among the crowd instead of giving the protesters a fixed line to aim rocks and bottles at. The marchers chanted their slogans and dispersed without serious incident. A few hours later, the troops left their barracks for suburban Montreal.

At dawn on August 16, tractor trailers carrying the armored personnel carriers, known as Grizzlies, rolled into the middle of St. Benoit, followed by school buses carrying more than 500 soldiers. The deployment rumbled down Dumouchel Street to an open field, where soldiers pitched their tents and organized camp.

During the nights of rioting at Châteauguay, the Mohawks kept an uncharacteristically low profile, trying to patch internal divisions. For weeks, ideological and territorial splits had threatened to throw the entire Mohawk leadership into disarray, but each time the Warriors and militants prevailed by citing the need for unity in the face of an invasion. "Once the agreement was signed in the Pines, the government became more credible in the eyes of some of our people," says Francis Boots.

"By coming to us and sitting on our land and saying we recognize your rights, the government took away one of our biggest arguments. Siddon and Ciaccia showed signs of good faith. They came to us personally and put their names on a document that basically said negotiation is the way. Though the Warriors were afraid of the troops and not the police, the moderates were afraid of the police, not the troops. And every night of rioting in Châteauguay softened some of our people's beliefs toward the army, when Mohawks saw the police beat their own."

After stormy discussions and heated arguments, Mohawk negotiators clustered in the treatment center in Kanesatake and the nation office in Kahnawake came to the conclusion that their negotiating strategy had to combine the concerns of people from all territories, including Akwesasne. "There was just no other way around this," says Joe Deom. "For five weeks, we had all worked together despite big, big differences. We could not cut this guy out and that guy in. We had to come as one nation and present ourselves as people from different areas that had specific needs and concerns."

Citing the Great Law's tradition of consensus, the Mohawk factions agreed that the committee would be a large group that came to an agreement on each issue, not simple majority rule. The Mohawks organized themselves by territory and allowed each community to decide how many negotiators and observers it wanted. The Mohawks said they were ready to begin once a team of 24 observers from the International Federation of Human Rights took their positions along the barricades.

On August 16, Bernard Roy was joined by Marc Lafrenière, Monique Courchesne, Roger Gagnon, and Fred Drummie of the federal ministry of Indian and Northern Affairs to await the Mohawks at the Dorval Hilton. Quebec's negotiating team comprised Alex Paterson, the chancellor of McGill University, Georges Beauchemin, the provincial deputy minister for Native Affairs, and Marie Rinfret, a lawyer from the Justice ministry. When the 54 Mohawk negotiators arrived in a special bus provided by the federal government, both Roy and Paterson voiced their objections, saying they expected no more than three Mohawks to be official negotiators. After several hours of bickering, a compromise gave the Mohawk committee five official spokespersons at the bargaining table; the others could observe the sessions.

"In many ways, we had to start at the beginning," says Minnie Garrow, who was an observer to the talks. "The federals were interested in separating the issue of the barricades from the land and amnesty. To them, this was about clearing the bridge, stopping the golf course, finding a few more acres for Mohawks, and how to get through some prosecutions. The Quebec team said something about the murder of their policeman, but that was glossed over for a while. The feds wanted us to cut a deal so everything could go back to normal.

"Well, we told them that we didn't want normal. To us, normal meant oppression. The band councils and the welfare grants and the economic development programs did not work. The leadership of the Mohawk nation had nothing to do with the system set up by Canada.

"If they wanted the barricades to go, then normal had to go. If they wanted the bridge cleared, then changes had to take place. We didn't have to turn the entire system upside down in a day. We told them our goal was to set out a framework so they could take time and make a plan and we could take time and make a plan. When we talked like this, they thought we were threatening to keep the bridge blocked forever.

"We had to keep telling them that we wanted the barricades down, too. We wanted the police and the army gone, but the first step was a framework for real change, not new grants or different agencies. Real, fundamental changes—the people on our land dealing with the people on their land."

As the dialogue entered its second day, the provincial police formally requested that the troops replace them on the barricades surrounding Kahnawake and Kanesatake. On Friday, August 17, Lieutenant General Foster announced that he had completed a deployment plan for his soldiers and they needed two days to make their final preparations. Insisting that the mission would not involve an armed attack on the barricades, Foster said all troop positions would be made public and went to great lengths to assure the Mohawks that he did not want to disrupt negotiations. Despite concern over the possibility of surprise attack, the Mohawks decided to continue the discussions through Saturday, August 18.

"For us, it always kept coming back to sovereignty," says Garrow. "For them, it kept coming back to the bridge and the barricades, traffic and the police. By Saturday, we figured that if we could come back with a written position, something for them to study, that might help. Both sides decided it would be a good idea to take a break on Sunday, and that's when we figured we could work on our position paper. It would outline our thoughts and show them that we were committed to negotiation. And that's when we really turned to Stanley Cohen. The Akwesasne delegation said that he should put this paper together. He knew how to write and negotiate with a lawyer like Bernard Roy."

On Monday morning, as the Mohawks put the finishing touches on their position paper, the first column of troops in armored personnel carriers rolled into Kanesatake and Kahnawake. Dozens of Mohawks came to the barricades to watch the soldiers come up to the police lines and methodically replace officers who had spent 40 days working 12-hour shifts. Along Highway 138 in Châteauguay, the troops were cheered by townspeople as they replaced the aluminum crowd-control barriers with concrete blocks and concertina razor wire.

In order to avoid mistakes that could spark a battle outside Châteauguay, two soldiers walked toward the Mohawk lines and asked for representatives to meet them on a strip of highway. Two masked Warriors with AK-47s agreed and the four men stood alone for 10 minutes, exchanging information about their positions. The soldiers said they would not advance and would keep part of Highway 138 a neutral zone. If the troops held their ground, the Warriors said, the Mohawks would not fire. But any sudden unannounced movement toward the barricade would be seen as a provocation. The soldiers said they understood, and the four men shook hands before returning to their lines.

On Highway 344, however, the troops kept coming forward. Having replaced the police at the bottom of the hill, troop commanders refused to accept a one-kilometer neutral zone. If they stopped at this position, commanders reasoned, the troops could not get a full view of the Mohawk defenses and they would be clear targets for hidden snipers firing downhill. To improve their position, the troops moved up the hill.

Alarmed, the Warriors cleared the Kanesatake barricades of women and children and set up their ammunition supplies for battle. The Warriors ordered their men into the hidden traps and bunkers, urging restraint until the troops fired the first shot. They watched the triangular formation of loud, clanking armor approach, expecting the machine guns to open fire once they hit the midpoint of the hill. But the personnel carriers stopped and a jagged line of soldiers kept walking, C-7 semi-automatic rifles and C-8 machine guns slung over their shoulders. They stretched coils of barbed wire across the road at 400 meters past the old police line.

The scare made the Mohawks furious, and they registered their anger by boycotting the negotiating session scheduled for 10:00 a.m. inside the Trappist monastery at Oka. Bernard Roy, Alex Paterson, and their teams waited for two hours, but the Mohawks refused to call. If the talks were to continue, the Canadians had to come to them.

Shortly after noon, the Canadian negotiators met the Mohawks in the middle of the new neutral zone. For an hour, the federal and provincial officials worked to calm the Mohawks, who demanded a pledge from Roy as personal representative of the prime minister. When Roy guaranteed that the troops would not move closer, the Mohawks agreed to resume face-to-face negotiations the next morning after they sent the Canadians their position paper on sovereignty. The typed, single-spaced, six-page report quotes the Great Law, colonial-era treaties, and the United Nations Universal Declaration on Human Rights, and states that these pacts have unequivocally given Mohawks "the rights accorded every people in the world—the right to our nationality, the right of our nation and confederacy to exist and the right to an area of government and society. Ours is the strongest natural legal right known to humans—the aboriginal right. . . . If Canada fails in its wisdom to grow, and answers with its police or military, we will and must defend our homeland and our people. That is required under our law. This must be understood by Canada and the Canadian people."

26
SOLDIERS SHOW
THEIR IRON

When the negotiations resumed beneath the rounded arches of the Romanesque-style monastery in Oka, the Mohawks made a surprising show of unity behind a three-point proposal put forward by the Akwesasne Warriors: first, the disputed Pines were to be given to the Mohawks for preservation as a burial ground; second, the Canadian government would recognize the creation of a legitimate Mohawk Nation, known as Kanienkehaka, which would consist of six territories—Kanesatake, Kahnawake, Akwesasne, Ganienkeh, Tyiendenago, and portions of the Six Nations reserve; third, the provincial and federal governments would allow an international probe of two alleged sets of criminal offenses—the shooting of Cpl. Marcel Lemay, the seizure of the bridge, and the standoffs; and the illegal sale of tobacco and the operation of the high-stakes bingo hall in Kahnawake.

Furious with this proposal, Roy and Paterson pointed out that they could not make any settlement that included those parts of Akwesasne and Ganienkeh covered by New York and United States jurisdictions. The Quebec negotiators could not handle discussions concerning Tyiendenago or Six Nations, as these were located in the Province of Ontario. As to criminal charges, federal and provincial negotiators said that Quebec Premier Robert Bourassa would insist prosecutions were needed to bolster his sagging political profile.

As the angry negotiations continued, the army wheeled more than

1,400 soldiers into position around Kanesatake and Kahnawake. The increasing show of force pleased the townspeople, but it also gave the Warriors renewed credibility. The army's high profile allowed the Warriors to argue successfully that unity was needed in the face of a threatened invasion. Even moderates such as Kahnawake Grand Chief Joseph Norton joined in denouncing the government's obvious efforts at intimidation. "If this isn't negotiating at the point of a gun," Norton told reporters, "I'd like to know what is."

Several federal officials admitted that the negotiators found themselves stuck between conflicting political realities. To satisfy Bourassa and the residents of the South Shore, they had to accept a continuous display of military strength. To satisfy Prime Minister Mulroney's desire to upstage Quebec and bring peace through talks that he had started, they had to continue chipping away at Mohawk proposals, getting them to focus on removal of the barricades.

On the night of August 11, the residents of LaSalle blocked the roadway on the northern span of the Mercier Bridge to keep Mohawks from Kahnawake from attending the negotiating session in the monastery. Using cars, sticks, and branches, threatening to stone Mohawk vehicles and smash their windows, a small crowd stood guard. At the same time, a group of residents of nearby Dorval realized that Mohawks were planning to ferry supplies across the river to Kahnawake from a wooden dock built near property owned by Quebec's Native Affairs Minister John Ciaccia. While the LaSalle residents were able to hold the bridge, police broke up the crowd at Dorval the next day.

At the negotiating table, the Mohawks told the government that the barricades could be taken down if Ottawa and Quebec agreed to a specific schedule for discussing land claims and sovereignty. To show their sincerity, the Mohawks produced a proposed agreement in principle and a draft master agreement. The first two items of the four-point agreement in principle stated the Mohawks would dismantle the barricades and replace each with a checkpoint designed to ensure and secure the safety of Kahnawake and Kanesatake. They also agreed to open the Mercier Bridge and all other routes to emergency vehicles. In exchange, the Canadians were to drop all projected prosecutions and agree to develop a framework for negotiating the territorial claims of the Mohawk Nation.

The draft master agreement asked for the immediate transfer of 67 acres, including the Pines and surrounding areas; a one-year time frame for resolving claims for other lands near Kanesatake; a binding commitment to define lands to be recognized as part of the Mohawk Nation or Kanienkehaka; and, a binding commitment to start a nation-to-nation relationship between Canadian governments and Kanienkehaka once the territorial disputes had been resolved.

"We knew we were asking for Canada to rework its entire approach to native affairs," says Francis Boots, "but we had time to do all this. To get the barricades down, we could work on the agreement in principle and then work on the master agreement. To us, it was simple. Get an agreement about the big goal, take down the barricades, and then work on the larger issues. Right across the table, we told the government that we wanted the barricades down, but our safety and our future had to be guaranteed. We didn't want this to happen again."

On the morning of Thursday, August 23, the army moved forward again. At the barricade on Highway 344 in Kanesatake, Warriors, amassing their ammunition, huddled behind the felled trees and overturned cars. A flurry of radio messages alerted the men on the Mercier Bridge who, through the static, heard the growl of the Grizzlies coming up the hill. For an endless minute or two, the men on the bridge wondered if they should detonate a small charge as a warning or wait for a specific communication. In Kanesatake, where the armored personnel carriers were less than 100 yards from the barricade, Warriors cocked their AK-47s and flicked off the safeties. Along the ridge, hidden by brush and tree cover, others drew a bead on the soldiers marching with weapons in their hands. The advance stopped within 10 yards of the barricade and soldiers rolled out their barbed wire, pushing another five yards forward to set up their perimeter.

The Mohawk walkie-talkies crackled with orders to lower weapons; the men on the bridge relaxed. As the soldiers unraveled their wire, a masked man stood on top of the barricade, his gun slung behind his back, waving the Warrior flag, a blue-eyed, bronzed Mohawk imposed on a flash of yellow on a bright red field.

"What the hell were we going to do?" says Cohen. "This was the pattern. Make a little progress, the army comes closer. Now there was nowhere for the army to go in Kanesatake. They hadn't moved yet in Kahnawake, but everybody knew that was just a matter of time. Shooting soldiers would be suicide, and immediately going back to the table would be giving in."

After a few hours' discussion, the Mohawks agreed to resume negotiations on Friday, August 24. "The army did a very good job in narrowing the options," continues Cohen. "What choice was there? Only talking. On the barricades, we were surrounded, and that meant the government could demand more and more. My job was to review their demands and draft new proposals. Everybody had the feeling that time was starting to run out. This was going on for 44 days and the government had to get some results. It was more than a gun to our heads. The tanks were about to roll over our backs."

When the negotiations reconvened the government teams concentrated on the agreement in principle, seeking to ensure that the Mohawks understood that their signatures would lead to an immediate dismantling of the barricade. "Traffic, traffic, traffic," said Ellen Gabriel. "That was their biggest concern. How many times did we have to say that we don't like traffic jams either, that this was about our rights? Recognize our rights and the bridge is open again. It seemed really simple." Throughout the day, Gabriel and other Mohawks told officials that setting up a framework for long-term negotiations over land and jurisdiction would be the key to unlocking the immediate dispute over the roads and Mercier Bridge. "Finally it started to sink in," adds Gabriel. "Everyone could give up the guns and the barricades in a day or two if we agreed to take the time to solve the long-term problems."

When the discussions adjourned that afternoon, Alex Paterson, the chief negotiator, was optimistic. "We're so close," he said. "I don't want to say that tomorrow is the crucial day, but it will be very important."

The next day, Saturday, August 25, the Mohawks brought to the table a three-page document calling for the immediate removal of the barricades in exchange for provincial and federal agreement to negotiate land claims, and formal recognition of Kanienkehaka. As detailed in the proposal, each side would maintain a checkpoint and armed forces to guarantee security at the Mercier Bridge and the entrances to Kanesatake and Kahnawake.

This proposal marked the first time that the Mohawks agreed to dismantle the roadblocks before police or military personnel left the area. Nonetheless, chief federal negotiator Bernard Roy and his Quebec counterpart, Alex Paterson, broke off the talks, insisting they could not accept this form of sovereignty or the continued presence of armed Warriors.

"I thought we made a major concession," says Cohen. "We said that the barricades would come down before the army left."

In his first extended comment on the negotiations, a frustrated and visibly shaken Roy told reporters that any further negotiations had to include a Mohawk offer to remove all barricades on the highways and the bridge. "Given the sensitivity of the situation, given the firepower of both sides," he said, "it doesn't take a hell of a lot to have a situation that could be serious." Mohawks and soldiers, said Roy, were "eyeball to eyeball, seeing who is going to blink first." Any false move could "quickly deteriorate to a catastrophe."

To the anti-Mohawk demonstrators of LaSalle and Châteauguay, a worried Paterson added, "For God's sake, cool it! The things that are going on around us aren't helping the situation. But I'm afraid that if the position of the Mohawks remains the same, I don't at the moment see the solution by way of negotiation."

That evening the prime minister undertook a blatant move to ingratiate himself with the elected band council chiefs, describing them as "peace-loving" and promising to negotiate with them if they broke away from the militants. "I'm ready to go the extra mile to avoid a confrontation," he said, "but the laws of Canada are going to be applied in the same way across the nation. We are not going to accede to requests from Warriors, some of whom are not even Canadian citizens, whose actions have been, to understate the case, illegal for some period of time. They don't seem to realize that they are in Canada and that we can't have two different approaches to the law. I and the government will not accept that this situation will persist interminably. We will take the necessary measures."

Fearing an invasion, Mohawk moderates at Kahnawake convened a community meeting attended by 600 people. Convinced that continued defiance of the government would provoke a battle and result in an army occupation, the assembled Kahnawake Mohawks implored their band council to strike a separate deal and present a sign of good faith to the Canadians. In a series of conversations, federal and provincial negotiators and representatives spoke with band councilor Walter Goodleaf, Grand Chief Norton and traditional Chief Billy Two Rivers and succeeded in establishing a second channel for negotiations.

"With the machine guns and bayonets pointed at our women and children, tanks ready to roll right over us, we had to think of saving lives," says Francis Boots. "And that tore us apart. Our differences could not be overcome when one mistake could mean a terrible battle."

For the first time in seven weeks, Bourassa and his aides felt they could force the Mohawks into a humiliating defeat. With an ever-widening split between Mohawk factions, Bourassa understood that military force would further isolate the Warriors. On Monday, August 27, federal and provincial officials formally asked the armed forces to remove the barricades.

The first step depended on chief negotiators Roy and Paterson, and Quebec's Deputy Native Affairs Minister Georges Beauchemin calling a news conference. While Roy voiced his frustration at the Akwesasne Warriors for repeatedly issuing demands that went far beyond the scope of a golf course at Oka and the Mercier Bridge, Paterson singled out Cohen and his "interesting speeches" that deliberately skirted the issue of the barricades. Beauchemin described the land disputes as a ruse for Mohawks trying to gain ownership of a large part of the town of Oka, all of the island of Montreal, vast portions of Quebec along the St. Lawrence River, a slice of southeastern Ontario, and pieces of New York and Vermont.

An hour after these remarks, Bourassa accused the Mohawks of making "unacceptable demands." Claiming that negotiations with the Warriors were no longer possible, the premier requested that the troops take control and remove the barricades. "We've been negotiating for 10 days. It's enough. In the last weeks since the army was called, everything was done to avoid a bloodbath and that's still the government's policy," Bourassa declared. Turning his attention to the Warriors, he said, "I don't think there is any precedent in the Western world of a large city living with hundreds of armed people. I don't think anyone in Canada or Quebec can blame the government for lack of prudence."

After Bourassa's statement, the action cut to Ottawa, where Minister of Indian and Northern Affairs Tom Siddon told reporters, "Law and order must now prevail. The governments of Canada and Quebec cannot agree to a balkanization of Canada, which would see First Nations become independent sovereign states."

The final salvo came from Gen. John de Chastelain, chief of the Defence Staff: "Mohawk people can just leave the barricades alone, or better still, take them down for us. And all we'll do is come in and take the pieces away and fill in the holes. But if somebody wants to shoot at us with heavy weapons, which are in their possession, or with machine guns, which are in their possession, or hand grenades, which we believe are in their possession, then we have to respond."

The orchestrated sequence of press conferences added to the confusion behind Mohawk lines. In Kahnawake, band council officials announced plans to evacuate residents who wished to leave. Dozens immediately jumped into small boats that motored across the river, docking in Dorval at the jetty abutting property owned by John Ciaccia. Seeing the exodus, more than 150 others signed up for a convoy of cars to be arranged through Alwyn Morris, a Kahnawake resident who won a gold and a bronze medal for Canada during the 1984 Olympics. Considered a national hero for his performance in the single and pairs kayak events, Morris won international attention at the awards ceremony when he accepted his medal by raising an eagle feather to honor his Mohawk heritage.

As Morris contacted the provincial police in the evening, Grand Chief Norton and traditional Chief Billy Two Rivers resumed discussions with provincial and federal officials; other band councilors urged direct discussions with the army. Completely breaking ranks with the Mohawks in Kanesatake, Norton flew to Ottawa to conduct negotiations with Siddon. "I think there is a way to salvage this," he told reporters before leaving for the airport.

On the Mercier Bridge and inside the headquarters of the Kahnawake Warriors Society, the militants pondered the shambles that they had hoped to be a united Mohawk leadership. Recognizing that clearing the bridge was the army's first objective, the Kahnawake Warriors held their own meeting to decide on a plan to abandon their roadblocks and escape the military advance. In this secret session, several Kahnawake Warriors and the men on the bridge opted for their own plan without telling other Mohawks—direct telephone discussions with the army to arrange a face-saving scenario. They would not resist an armored advance if the army allowed them to filter back into the community without arrest.

Their proposal received a lukewarm response. Though the commanders could not give any guarantees, they indicated that an advance was at least 36 hours away and discussions could continue. A second, secret, informal proposal was made: if the Kahnawake Warriors were allowed to land a small plane to airlift men and women out of the territory before the attack, the men on the bridge would not shoot at troops dismantling the barricades on the bridge and highways. The military never replied; the men of Kahnawake figured it was worth the risk to proceed.

At Kanesatake, in a voice choked with anger and fear, Ellen Gabriel pleaded for negotiations to resume in the monastery. "We are asking for peace," she said to the Canadian people. "Can you live with blood on your hands? Are you willing to defer this most important decision to your elected leaders alone or will you stand with us and demand that your leaders return to the bargaining table?

"We have women and children here, and we are not armed. What can we do against an army? There are not just Warriors here. A lot of you don't realize that there are not just Warriors here."

A few yards away stood Joe Deom, speaking in a calm, gentle voice: "Mohawks are waiting for the violent assault with peaceful hearts and tranquil minds," he said. "Ours is the just and honorable position. It flows from our laws and our way. Our enemies have no such honor."

27

LEOPARDS AND GRIZZLIES
APPROACH

On Tuesday, August 28, the federal and provincial governments knew they were on the verge of dividing their Mohawk adversaries and reopening the Mercier Bridge. In Ottawa, Prime Minister Mulroney scheduled a special cabinet meeting, after which Tom Siddon would continue discussions with Kahnawake Grand Chief Norton. In Montreal, Premier Bourassa authorized his Native Affairs Minister, John Ciaccia, Public Security Minister Sam Elkas and chief negotiator Alex Paterson to discuss a possible settlement with moderates.

"It was a three-ring circus," says Francis Boots. "On one side were the talks in Ottawa with Siddon and Joe Norton. On the other side were talks at the Dorval Hilton, where Ciaccia and a few other band councilors were getting together. And in the middle you had the prime minister and the generals saying the troops were on their way. The Mohawk leadership really didn't exist anymore. At the barricades at Kanesatake and on the Mercier Bridge, Warriors and militants were alone."

The politicians, bureaucrats, and generals set up yet another series of press conferences to sway public opinion and send their messages to all Mohawk factions. First, Mulroney issued an appeal for Mohawks to surrender before the military moved in. "To the Warriors, I say, 'Do not put the innocent people of Kanesatake and Kahnawake and the surrounding communities at risk. Take down the barricades yourselves, now. If you persist in your illegal activities, you will bring both danger and dishonor to your people. Let reason prevail, and assist us in creating a climate that will create real progress and justice for all members of the Mohawk people.'" Questioned about the attack plan, the prime minister said the army "will not fire the first shot."

To back up Mulroney, the military released a slick, high-tech video that described the Mohawk fortifications in a collage of aerial photographs, television news footage, and still photos. The video showed suspected bunkers, booby traps, anti-tank trenches, roadblocks, and snipers' nests constructed by the Warriors during the 49 days of standoff. Designed to fill television's need for exciting pictures and pithy soundbites, the presentation cast the Warriors as a formidable foe equipped with armor-piercing shells, Uzis, AK-47s, possibly a .50 caliber machine gun and an M-72 tank gun that could pierce the armored personnel carriers.

Noting that many Warriors had fought for United States armed forces in Korea and Vietnam, the soundtrack issued an ominous warning: "Even a handful of combat-ready Warriors could be a difficult challenge . . . if a large number of Warriors are committed to armed resistance, casualties on both sides will inevitably be serious."

The video then showed soldiers on patrol. Behind them were small howitzers to cover the advance, Grizzly armored personnel carriers, and Leopard tanks. Described as the army's strongest and most modern, the German-manufactured tanks were seen outfitted with special bulldozer attachments to tear into the barricades. The voiceover made the point that the tanks were not carrying ammunition for their large guns.

After the video screen went dark, Department of National Defence spokesman Col. Alain Forand said he expected a battle of several days. Pointing to a detailed map of trenches, barricades, and encampment at Kahnawake, Forand said of his adversary, "Either he is a new Napoleon and thought it up himself, or he has had military experience, or he has read a lot of books and knows how to apply the principles."

In the headquarters of the mobile command at St. Hubert, Lt. Gen. Kent Foster told reporters he planned a gradual assault that would grind away at the resistance. He sketched a plan relying on the troops' overwhelming superiority in numbers and matériel: Leopard tanks would lead the advance and dismantle the barricades before soldiers entered Mohawk territory in armored personnel carriers. "No one out there should be expecting an attack by 5,000 soldiers," Foster said. "That is not the way to address this problem."

Shortly after 2:00 p.m., negotiations between Mohawks and provincial authorities at the Dorval Hilton produced what moderates believed to be an encouraging sign. With the approval of Public Safety Minister Elkas and Premier Bourassa, a convoy of 75 cars was allowed to leave Kahnawake via the Mercier Bridge. Organized by Alwyn Morris, the line of cars drove around the Kahnawake barricade and stopped at a police checkpoint on the outskirts of LaSalle.

As a Sûreté du Québec team meticulously searched each car, more than 30 demonstrators gathered to watch and chant anti-Mohawk slogans from the side of the road. Two hours later, the crowd had swelled into an angry mob of 500, urging the cops to arrest the motorists and their passengers, mostly older men, women, and children. Unnerved by the racist taunts and threats, the Mohawks appealed to the police for protection and a quicker pace for the searches; but the officers insisted on thoroughly checking each Mohawk vehicle. When the police finally waved on the cars, a deluge of rocks and construction debris rained on the convoy, denting cars and shattering more than a dozen windows or windshields. Nine people were hurt, including a paraplegic struck on the back of the head with a rock and a baby sprayed with broken glass.

Three hours later, traditional Chief Billy Two Rivers emerged from talks with provincial officials and army commanders. "The way things look, we are very optimistic that within 24 hours an agreement will be concluded," he said. Though Quebec Minister of Public Security Elkas shared some of his enthusiasm, he pointed out that the army had yet to sign off on the accord. "Right now," Elkas said, "it's between the army and the Mohawks. I'm hoping they can work out a deal." When asked by reporters for his version of the talks, Brig. Gen. Armand Roy, commander of the Fifth Mechanized Brigade, said discussions would continue the next day, but troops would not slow down or halt preparations to remove barricades.

As Roy spoke, heavy cloud cover blew in over Montreal and its South Shore, giving a small Cessna aircraft an opportunity to fly unnoticed above the treeline at Kahnawake and dip into a clearing around 8:15 p.m. After a quick stop to pick up several passengers, the plane flew southeast, crossing into the United States. Fifteen minutes later, another Cessna arrived, again hugging the treeline before landing and taking off again. Around 9:00 p.m., a third plane appeared, took on passengers and returned to the skies. The Kahnawake Warriors had completed their airlift; the men remaining on the bridge were ready to give up.

. . .

The growl of armored personnel carriers came with the morning's first light on Highway 138. The Grizzlies and the M113s stopped several yards from the barricades, their engines idling; soldiers huddled to the side of the road. Behind the barricade of cars, construction debris, and a white camping trailer, the masked Mohawks kept low, trying to communicate with the handful of militants left on the Mercier Bridge and at a command post in the center of Kahnawake. Though the troops were poised for an attack, the Warriors were told not to shoot unless the army opened fire.

At the Dorval Hilton, army negotiators greeted the day by resuming discussions with Grand Chief Norton and Chief Two Rivers. The negotiators were to keep in constant contact with an officer at the military base in Farnham, where troops, personnel carriers, and three Leopard tanks were awaiting dispatch to the bridge. By the time negotiations started, supply troops in Farnham had loaded the tanks onto flatbed trucks. There they sat, awaiting the order to move on.

Told of the activity on Highway 138 and the plan to move on the bridge later in the day, platoons of television, newspaper, and radio reporters converged on the line between Châteauguay and Kahnawake. Their up-to-the-minute broadcasts drew crowds to witness what many believed would be a historic occasion. The gathering cheered the soldiers and many people offered to fetch food and soft drinks from pizzerias and fast-food restaurants down the road. "It's so very strange," said one soldier, crouching beside a concrete block. "Don't these people realize that shooting and killing could start at any moment?"

Receiving the order to pull out from Lt. Col. Greg Mitchell, stationed near Kahnawake, the troops at Farnham formed a column that rolled down Highway 104. Clanking and clamoring past Fort Chambly National Park, the armor needed more than two hours to rumble into La Prairie and turn onto the Boulevard Tachereau, which led straight into Highway 132 and the blocked bridge.

As the troops came into view, the Mohawks on the bridge held their fire, while the Leopards and Grizzlies wheeled into place. At about 5:00 p.m., the troops came to a halt well within range of Mohawk weapons. Sticking to the unspoken agreement that had allowed the airlift on the previous night, three men in camouflage fatigues and T-shirts walked out of the barricade unarmed. A khaki-clad officer led a group of soldiers to meet them halfway. Before the Canadians stopped walking, the Mohawks placed a peace pipe on the bridge's cracked pavement. In a conversation that took less than five minutes, the Mohawks agreed to help the soldiers remove the barricades at Kahnawake and open the bridge. By 5:30, a Mohawk had driven his bulldozer through the first line of the roadblocks. The troops cheered. Less than an hour later, the troops on Highway 138 joined Mohawks in taking down the Châteauguay roadblock.

That evening, Norton stepped into the lobby of the Dorval Hilton and announced a deal had been reached: the provincial and federal governments would transfer the disputed golf course land to the Kanesatake band council; and the army would forgo further military action if the Warriors laid down their arms and took down the barricades across Highway 344. "As far as I'm concerned we've reached a very historical period," Norton said, "and we can look forward to a peaceful, calm settling of this situation from here on in."

On August 30, the day after the masked Mohawks joined Canadian forces in clearing the Mercier Bridge, military and provincial officials sought to widen the ever-growing splits among their native adversaries. Army commanders and representatives of Quebec Premier Robert Bourassa opened talks at the Dorval Hilton to a delegation led by Leon Shenandoah, the fiercely anti-gaming and anti-Warrior chief of the Iroquois Confederacy. An Onondaga leader who claims to be the spiritual and political leader of all Iroquois who follow the traditions of the Longhouse, the quiet, soft-spoken Shenandoah is a close ally of Mike Mitchell, Jake Swamp, and Tom Porter, the Akwesasne Mohawks passionately opposed to the Warriors. Throughout the tussle over casinos and the months of tension between New York State Police and Akwesasne Warriors, Shenandoah had repeatedly denounced the Warriors and refused to recognize them as Iroquois who followed the Great Law.

For most of the summer, militant Mohawks had virtually banned Shenandoah from Kanesatake. But the deal to open the bridge offered him an opportunity to play the role of an Iroquois leader strong enough to stand up to Warriors. Shenandoah told Canadian authorities that he would not support a blanket amnesty for Mohawks carrying weapons or blocking the bridge or highways. Not surprisingly, his position immediately drew harsh criticism from the Mohawks still holding out, but it also prompted a rebuke from Kahnawake Grand Chief Norton and traditional Chief Two Rivers, who felt they needed an amnesty to protect their people from reprisals.

"We need a guarantee that the SQ or the troops will not come storming in here and take away half of our people who they claim participated in a roadblock one way or another," said Norton, who had joined the negotiations. "This is a point that cannot be bargained away. We need to protect ourselves and so do the people of Kanesatake. Without some kind of accord with the police and the troops, what's to prevent officers and soldiers from storming through and beating people up? Nothing. The government has to understand that and so do all of the negotiators from our side. We have to make a stand for this."

Shenandoah and his delegation walked away from the table, refusing to make any plea that would benefit the Warriors. Provincial negotiators and army officials used his departure to claim that Mohawks and their representatives broke off the talks; they unleashed a torrent of criticism at Norton and Two Rivers. At one point, SQ spokesman Constable Richard Bourdon denounced Norton.

The Canadian political assault succeeded in splintering the Mohawks into at least four groups: the Warriors still holding the Kanesatake barricades, who did not have a place at the bargaining table; the Kanesatake moderates such as band council Chief George Martin, who wanted a deal for the Pines in exchange for dismantling the remaining roadblocks; the Kahnawake Mohawks such as Norton and Two Rivers, who held out for some form of protection from the police; and the Warriors outside the barricades, mostly from Akwesasne, who claimed they spoke for their brethren behind the armed roadblocks.

"We were all fighting and competing with each other," says Akwesasne activist Diane Lazore. "One Mohawk faction against another Mohawk faction. We had so many different stories and so many different points of view. There were so many rumors and so many untruths. We were running around and around and the government was watching us crumble. They could see it was only a matter of time before the Warriors in Kanesatake gave up or got so frustrated with the pressure that they would do something so outrageous that the army would have good reason to attack.

"Minnie, Francis, and I were in the hotel and at Kahnawake trying to get direct talks between the government and our people in Kanesatake. Ever since the negotiations at the monastery had broken down, every other Mohawk faction was trying to cut its own deal, and the government would not talk to the Warriors. So I tried to get into the negotiations through Joe Norton or Billy Two Rivers. Francis and Minnie tried other ways. We had to do something to get the government to see us so we could tell them to talk with the people in Kanesatake.

"The Quebec officials and the army didn't listen to me because they didn't have to. Once we lost the bridge, we lost our power. After Leon Shenandoah left, the Canadians were sure they could find other Iroquois who didn't like the Warriors. So we tried to find someone in the confederacy who was supportive and get them up here."

The Warriors did not have to look very hard: Shenandoah's decision alienated the Oneida chiefs, who sent a dissenting delegation to Dorval. "This isn't the time to fight about our disagreements or one faction's thirst for power over the other," said Oneida traditional Chief Terry Doxtator, in a veiled reference to Shenandoah. "This is a time to stand together and show that members of the Iroquois Confederacy cannot be bullied into betraying each other. This is a time for honor, not dishonor."

Besides Doxtator, the Oneida delegation included spiritual healer Bruce Elijah, Bob Antone, and Mike Myers, a man who had extensive dealings with Kahnawake Mohawks through the cigarette trade. Myers served as a behind-the-scenes adviser working out of the Mohawk Nation Office, while Doxtator, Harper, and Antone took center stage, presenting themselves to the Canadians as people who could get negotiations started again.

"The trap was closing tighter and tighter and tighter," recalls Stanley Cohen, "and we knew it. The Warriors understood that holding the barricade would lead them face-to-face with troops, tanks, and armored personnel carriers. Absolutely no one wanted that. As soon as the bridge went and all the factions started going at each other, the Warriors inside Kanesatake knew three things: they could no longer threaten their way out; they could not fight their way out; and they could not negotiate their way out. There was only one possibility— tricking their way out or using their mobility and their superior knowledge of the woods to get to safety."

The men at Kanesatake started to work on an escape for women and children: first, they would call on several of the older and middle-aged men to create a diversion that would allow their younger counterparts to slip through the trees; then they would launch phony radio dispatches, bursts of gunfire discharged in the wrong direction, and a fake offer to negotiate. The goal was to tie up troops throughout an afternoon and night.

"We wanted to create a crisis that would draw the army's attention in the late afternoon or early evening," says one Warrior. "We would send people to negotiate and they would buy time as we would slip out into the northwestern hills or hook up with people on the river.

When morning came, the negotiators would come back and talk for a bit, then let the army come in. And no one would be here."

"We knew they were going to come," says another Warrior. "And we did not want to surrender. Nor did we want all of us to die, when we believed there was a chance to prevail and we wanted to take it."

But the bitter divisions between the militants and the Kanesatake band council forced the Warriors into action before they were ready. On Saturday morning, September 1, several Warriors attacked and beat up band councilor Francis Jacobs and his son Corey, who had threatened to tell the SQ the names of several masked Mohawks who had burgled a nearby home. Unwilling to be intimidated, Jacobs and other moderates telephoned the provincial authorities, asking them to get the Warriors out of Kanesatake.

The military commanders used the beating as a pretext to flex the army's muscle. The surveillance photos produced by low-flying helicopters and reconnaissance jets showed that the Warriors had virtually abandoned two of their three barricades: one on the western side of Highway 344 and the second, on the northern perimeter at Ste. Germaine Road. Troops and Grizzly armored personnel carriers could easily maneuver the wooded roadbed and make a rear-end advance to the main Warrior barricade.

After 1:00 p.m., several dozen camouflaged soldiers with faces painted green skirted the undefended barricades. Backed by armored personnel carriers and directed by low-flying helicopters, they spread out among the pines and approached the Warriors' lines from behind in a wide arc around the cemetery and remaining barricade. Coming out of the woods above the lacrosse box, the troops came face-to-face with "Bolt Pin," a masked, unarmed Warrior on a golf cart.

In order to buy time and allow others to escape, Bolt Pin cursed the soldiers and commanders as a Grizzly inched up to his cart. At one point, he broke out into hyena-like laughter at the absurdity of an unarmed Mohawk holding up a column of well-equipped soldiers and their fancy machine. To prolong the diversion, the Warriors sent forward a dozen men who remained hidden in the woods. Then they dispatched their prized piece of armor, the front-end loader captured on the day Cpl. Marcel Lemay had been shot. As the machine groaned and grunted forward, the masked men added to the taunts and jeers. For a few minutes more, Bolt Pin stood his ground before diving over to a line of bushes.

The soldiers followed until they noticed the jagged line of Mohawks planted in the brush. On orders, the troops brought their C–7 semi-automatic assault rifles up into firing position. Several could have blown Bolt Pin's head to pieces. Without flinching, he watched the soldiers take aim.

"We won't fire the first shot," said Bolt Pin, "and we will not move."

A minute later, a yell followed by a war whoop came from the woods, but it did not rattle the soldiers. Then a Warrior loudly said he planned to "slug that fuckin' arrogant asshole" in a reference to the commanding officer. Another Warrior taunted the soldiers. "Shoot, you fuckers, shoot!" he said louder and louder.

It appeared that the Warriors had frozen the soldiers and laid the groundwork for their diversion. But then they heard the metallic hum of an all-terrain motorcycle coming from the rear.

"Get the fuck out of the way," came the woman's voice. "Move back. This is what they want you to do."

Unaware of the plan to hold the soldiers at bay until darkness, Jenny Jack, a Mohawk supporter who had come to the barricade as a representative of the Tlingit people of British Columbia, rumbled into the middle of the showdown. Surprised and confused, the Warriors lost their concentration as Jack wailed away with threats "to kick your fuckin' ass if you don't pull back and get out of the way of these fuckin' soldiers." Jack went into the bushes and dragged out a Warrior. The men gathered in a small circle down the dirt path, almost at the edge of the highway. The soldiers did not move.

"What could we have done?" says one of the men. "Stand there and argue with her as the soldiers stand ready to blow our brains out? It was just fuckin' amazing. Goddamn unbelievable."

After a short caucus, the Warriors and the army opened negotiations, each representative holding a semi-automatic rifle at his side. Knowing that they had nowhere to go but down toward the river, the Warriors agreed to retreat, letting the soldiers take the main barricade without firing a shot.

By sundown, the Warriors were preparing their defense of a 100-by-200-yard patch of land surrounding the two-story treatment center. Home to the Warrior-led negotiating committee for most of the summer, the five-bedroom house had become the last outpost for 40 to 50 Mohawks, mostly women and children, including a dozen armed Warriors. Ten to 15 reporters and photographers camped in tents beside a clogged septic tank in the back yard. Across Highway 344, more than

400 members of the highly decorated Royal 22nd Regiment, the Vingt-Deuxième or the Van Doos, built a barbed-wire-and-sandbag fence backed by a line of Grizzlies equipped with .50 caliber machine guns and high-powered searchlights.

The next morning, combat engineers spent hours combing the logs, stones, and overturned Sûreté du Québec cars for explosive booby traps on the main barricade across Highway 344. Then a bulldozer shoved the debris aside within a half hour. On the side of the road, two Canadian soldiers quietly took down the official flag of the Vietnam veterans, respectfully folding it into a triangle and handing it over to a Warrior representative.

The war of attrition had begun. As the media focused on the standoff at the treatment center, soldiers moved into Kahnawake, surrounding the longhouse and Mohawk Nation office on the afternoon of September 3. The SQ had obtained a judge's warrant to raid the longhouse in search of weapons. With several dozen troops serving as an escort, cops struck at the center of Kahnawake without encountering any serious resistance. After cops scuffled with a crowd of 30 Mohawk women, they seized a .50 caliber armor-piercing gun, three AK–47s, and a Ruger Mini-14 rifle.

Kahnawake Grand Chief Joseph Norton had been humiliated. "He told his people and the world that giving up the bridge would avoid the possibility of a military attack," says Joe Deom, a Mohawk negotiator who supported the Warriors. "The army and the police rammed it down his throat."

Norton told reporters that the weapons were planted by troops and claimed he was a victim of the army's double-cross. His rhetoric won headlines and stiffened resistance among the Warriors in the treatment center: They now had proof that only a written guarantee could protect them from such an attack. The Canadians, of course, rejected any deal in writing and repeated demands that Warriors lay down their guns. In yet another effort to divide the Mohawks, the provincial officials offered to helicopter a renowned Montreal criminal lawyer into the treatment center so he could confer with Mohawks and advise them about their rights when they were ready to give up.

"The Canadians were jerking us around left and right," says Robert Skidders, known as Mad Jap, a Warrior who came to the treatment center from Akwesasne. "Talk here, see him, do this, try that. But when they offered the lawyer to come in and discuss surrender, Stanley got the idea of telling them, 'Yeah, we'll think about surrender but we don't need a lawyer to arrange it. We need some of our own people to come here and help us think this through.'

"When we told them that we'd consider walking out, the army creamed their pants and said, 'Sure, we can give you a couple of your own people.' They asked, 'Who?' And we had to be real slick. We knew they wouldn't give us a Warrior and we didn't want anybody from the band council. So we thought about it and we figured we could live with Oneidas—Bob Antone, Terry Doxtator, and their healer, Bruce Elijah."

The three Oneidas received an army escort to the Warrior lines. "For the first time in several weeks," says Cohen, "we could see at least a few of the people who were negotiating for us. Through the Oneidas, we thought we had a direct channel to the government."

On September 5, Minister of Indian and Northern Affairs Tom Siddon gave the Oneidas a warm reception and praised their efforts. "Much of the discussion today was about generating trust," he said, after the three-hour session with Doxtator, Antone, and native leaders from across Canada. Siddon said the Oneidas' information about the siege at Kanesatake "helped make it clear that we must do something to relieve that stress." Did that mean acceding to Doxtator's demand that troops pull back? Siddon said that could not be done without provincial approval.

The next day, as Quebec's government proudly re-opened the Mercier Bridge to traffic, the army offered to protect surrendering Warriors from the Sûreté du Québec. Canada's Chief of the National Defence Staff, Gen. John de Chastelain, said troops would disarm the Mohawks, escort them to a military location, and house them to ensure "a dignified and nonviolent end to this crisis." Though the Mohawks rejected the offer, de Chastelain's conciliatory rhetoric alarmed Quebec Premier Robert Bourassa, who labeled the Warriors "criminals" and vowed to prosecute them. The premier denounced his critics in Ottawa and claimed that his government was "defending democracy against people armed with weapons like an M-50." He said that provincial officials were discussing the possibility of an army attack.

That night, the Warriors raised plastic sheets to block the glare of searchlights; soldiers used their bayonets to shred the material. Verbal taunts were followed by both sides hurling stones and daring the other to open fire. "If you want to fuck around," yelled one soldier, "then we'll fuck around!" As the rocks flew, one Warrior ran up to the fence, wildly swinging a baseball bat. Soldiers sighted him in their rifles. In response, the Warriors raised their weapons and each side stared at the other. Less than a minute later, Skidders came charging up to the Warrior line and barked at his men to lower their guns. "We can't do it this way," he said. "It's not gonna work out like this."

At 4:00 the next morning, September 8, the army made their next move, sending four soldiers through the razor wire to scout the Warrior defenses and fortifications. Moving through the brush, the soldiers found Warrior Randy Horne asleep in his trench. The 42-year-old ironworker, known as "Spudwrench," woke up as the soldiers surrounded him and took his gun. Fearing for his life, he desperately reached for his knife and inflicted minor cuts as the four soldiers beat his face, then ran.

"I started yelling and they started beating me with something on my head about 25 times," Spudwrench said, as he was carried back to the treatment center, his face oozing blood. "There were three guys holding me down."

The infuriated Mohawks raced to the wire and yelled for immediate medical attention. The army agreed only if one Mohawk stepped outside the Warrior lines to prevent hostage taking. The Warriors immediately agreed, knowing that Dr. David Gorman, who tends to the Mohawks at Akwesasne, was in the area. Gorman was led blindfolded through army lines and left for the Mohawks. He recommended that Spudwrench be hospitalized. Commanders finally gave permission but only after 10 hours of intense negotiations.

28
THE GENERALS
WIN A TROPHY

"The day after the soldiers beat Spudwrench, they expected us to retaliate but we didn't," said Mad Jap. "You could see the soldiers were
really worried, looking at every movement, and wondering when were
we going to come over and get them.

"During the day, we looked at them and they looked at us. But at
night, it got really fucked up and crazy. The army would shine lights
and have its helicopters go up and down and swirling around. There
were flares shot up and the sky would get this big reddish glow like a
neon light over it all.

"You could see the barbed-wire outlines and you could hear the
radios and the motors of their personnel carriers. We tried to use mir-
rors and the plastic sheets and yell war whoops or curse. No one really
knew who was what and what was where, but you were watching and
feeling that something terrible could happen at any moment."

Despite provocations and taunts, the armed men on both sides of
the barricades held their fire for different reasons. The Mohawks
knew that any sign of aggression would trigger a deadly response; the
soldiers knew they could not be seen as trigger-happy cowboys.
Though the Canadian officials saw the Mohawks' militancy as the
beginnings of an armed aboriginal insurrection, they refused to negotiate the underlying political and economic issues of land claims, sovereignty, taxation, and control over natural resources. The standoffs

simply had to be contained to prevent similar uprisings across Canada. For federal officials, the standoff became a test of national will; for Quebec, it became a challenge to the provincial government's perceived ability to control its own destiny and solve its own problems. As a result of these conflicting agendas, the army, equipped to fight a war, had only the mandate to serve as a high-tech police force: the troops were to place a perimeter around the dangerous politics and keep the peace.

While the Canadians wrangled over provincial and federal differences, factions among the Mohawks made their last grabs for power. Outside the barricades, leaders of the Iroquois Confederacy exploited television images of masked, heavily armed Mohawks to support their view of the Warriors as violent and irresponsible people who gamble, smuggle tobacco, and play with guns. Leon Shenandoah, Tom Porter, and others presented themselves, by way of contrast, as smoking peace pipes, attending sweat lodges and living in harmony with the natural order. Moderates such as Kahnawake Grand Chief Joe Norton and traditionalist Billy Two Rivers compared the Warriors' militancy with their own ability as leaders to reason with government officials while protecting the Mohawks' government grants and social programs. Militants such as Francis Boots, Minnie Garrow, and Diane Lazore pleaded with their fellow Mohawks to recognize that the Warriors' hard line was the people's only chance for real change, by strengthening their political identity and weakening the hold of white authority.

These divisions in the Mohawk community poured into the treatment center where, day after day, night after night, surreal confrontations threatened to become deadly violence. Cramped living conditions and restricted access to food, water, medicine, and clothes only exacerbated the tension.

"We were constantly pulling ourselves back from the edge," recalls one of the Warriors. "Each day we took one step closer and closer."

Hoping to buy time for a resolution more honorable than surrender and less bloody than a fight, the men patrolled the razor-wire line that marked their boundary. The women took over communications and organized the shifts of duty and tasks: they did most of the cooking, the men tending to repairs or construction, especially those of the overflowing septic system, dubbed "the monster." Though the men and women together considered negotiating positions and strategies concerning the military or the press, it became clear that they saw their predicament in different terms. The priority of the heavily armed men was to protect themselves from major criminal charges and long prison terms by insisting on a formal commitment to extensive negotiations about land claims and sovereignty. The women understood these concerns, but pressed for a deal that preserved the Pines and prevented bloodshed.

"No one was right or wrong, but there were some big disagreements," says Lorraine Montour, who had traveled from Akwesasne only to be barricaded into the treatment center. "A lot of it came down to the question of guns and weapons. Many of us knew that the Warriors had to have their guns and had to walk the line for protection, but we were looking for a way out of violence and we were worried that many of the men boxed themselves into a position where the shooting could start at any moment.

"On the other hand, we knew we just couldn't walk out of the treatment center without a guarantee that the men would not be hauled off or beaten. So there was this constant tugging and pulling, the men thinking they had to hold on to their weapons until an amnesty, and many of the women wanting to get this nightmare over with. We told the men that we had won the golf club, we had shown Canada and the world the justice of our cause, and now it was time to go out. We've established our honor."

To the men, those victories were not enough. "If we are going to do all of this, risk our lives and then end up in jail for years," said one Warrior, "then the Canadian government will at least have to recognize that the Mohawks are a legitimate nation with legitimate claims to the land. If they don't recognize that and make a commitment to resolve these claims, the men feel we should hold out."

With moderate Mohawks telling officials of these divisions, the Canadian government hardened its position, to further weaken the holdouts. Provincial and federal negotiators refused any possibility of amnesty or immunity, and federal Justice Minister Kim Campbell sternly warned that police and prosecutors would not be deterred from making arrests. "We must not confuse the highly legitimate concerns of the Indian people with the resistance of the armed Warriors at Oka," she said. "The situation that we see at Oka today is a law-enforcement situation. The Warriors at Oka do not represent legitimate native grievances legitimately advanced. They carry guns, they are resisting the enforcement of the law, and we will not negotiate with them. We will discuss the terms of their surrender of their firearms.

"The Canadian Forces offered to provide the Mohawk Warriors with safe custody if they laid down their weapons and came from behind their barricades peacefully. They were, of course, not offered immunity from prosecution for illegal acts committed during the crisis. If the Warriors accepted it, their safety would be guaranteed. Once they were identified, decisions could be made as to whether they could be charged with criminal offenses. If not charged, they would go free. If charged, they would have a fair trial with all the protection that the Charter of Rights and Freedoms, the law, and the courts provide.

"The army's offer has been turned down by the Warriors, who continue, it would appear, to seek a total amnesty. The government cannot and will not accept that the Warriors are not governed by the laws of this country, including the Criminal Code."

Unwilling to be intimidated by Campbell's tough rhetoric, the Warriors and their legal adviser, Stanley Cohen, insisted the next day that any agreement contain a provision to protect Mohawks from prosecution. "As a lawyer representing people who were seen with and videotaped with weapons, and observed in confrontations with the army, I could not recommend or endorse my clients' walking out into the arms of the police," Cohen says. "My job is to keep people out of jail."

Throughout the stormy discussions, Bob Antone, the Oneida leader negotiating for the Mohawk holdouts, repeatedly asked Cohen and the armed men to soften their position.

"Bob was telling us that our positions had to take into consideration other Mohawks across the river, that the Warriors just couldn't think of themselves," says Cohen. "But the armed men were the people who were going to jail. They had to think of themselves. They didn't want to be divisive. They wanted to be protected, and I think Bob got the message because he helped put together a very good proposal that outlined our broad political concerns and expressed our willingness to leave and go into military custody if two conditions were met: 1) an international tribunal would investigate criminal charges; and 2) the Canadians would sign a long-term commitment to negotiate issues such as land claims, sovereignty, taxes, and rights to natural resources."

Less than an hour after Antone announced the proposal on September 11, Quebec Premier Robert Bourassa rejected it, saying the Mohawks would not receive any special exemption from provincial laws. To highlight that point, the Sûreté du Québec arrested Spudwrench, who had been released from the hospital and was being kept in military custody at the Farnham barracks. When Spudwrench was presented to the court at St. Jerome, prosecutors charged him with wearing a disguise with the intent of committing a crime, criminal mischief, obstructing justice, participating in a riot, and possession of a dangerous weapon. Standing before the judge, his stitched-up face swollen and bruised, Spudwrench tried to straighten his back and stand tall when the clerk asked in French for his plea. "Not guilty," came his response, in English.

With more than a dozen reporters inside the encampment, the Canadian public was treated to a barrage of pictures of combat-ready soldiers and heavily armed Mohawks nicknamed "Beekeeper," "Blackjack," "Noriega," "Freddy Krueger," "Christmas," "Beaver," "Hunter," "The General," "Blondie," and "Lasagna," perhaps the most infamous of them all.

A burly 32-year-old man whose black handlebar mustache hinted at his mixed Mohawk and Italian heritage, Ronald "Lasagna" Cross or Casalpro, grew up in the small but vocal Mohawk community of ironworkers who settled in New York City. Nicknamed for his favorite dish, he carried himself with the working-class swagger of neighborhoods like Flatbush and Greenpoint, where a fast mouth is as important to self-defense as fast hands.

When the troops first encircled the treatment center on September 1, Lasagna and others positioned themselves within inches of the pale, young soldiers who stood ramrod straight, their weapons slung over their shoulders. With television cameras catching every blink, one Warrior moved right into the face of Pvt. Patrick Cloutier and whispered, "Boo." When Cloutier snapped to attention and returned the stare, the Warrior taunted him with "motherfucker" and "Are you ready to die?"

Cloutier remained silent and the Warrior eventually walked away, but Lasagna soon took over the spotlight, directing another profane diatribe at the soldiers. For the media and the Canadian public, these tense, verbal barrages became the quintessential scenes of the treatment center standoff. As the negotiations sputtered in one false start after another, such vignettes gave the public their image of the Warriors, masked, rough-and-tumble men making obscene or militant gestures, eagerly playing the role of a defiant and fierce cadre of freedom fighters. Each day, the men would play macho for the camera or bait the soldiers; each night, men and women would entertain themselves, gathering around the television in the treatment center to watch their antics.

After two weeks of this spectacle, on September 13, the army clamped down on reporters and photographers, jamming their cellular phones and interrupting their couriers for film and videotape. Troops also cut the telephone line into the treatment center, leaving open only a direct link to the army command post. According to Maj. John Paul MacDonald, the army's press liaison officer, the decision to cut all telephone communications was designed to force the Warriors "to concentrate attention on the negotiations via the hot line." Mac-Donald dismissed suggestions that the army or other government officials were deliberately censoring the Warriors in an attempt to control public opinion.

The media retaliated by declaring the army afraid of the Warriors' ability to capture the imagination of television viewers and newspaper readers. "All of a sudden Canadian bureaucrats, commentators, politicians, or reporters are talking about how both sides had turned this into a media war," says Stanley Cohen, "that we had an elaborate media strategy to manipulate the news. Well, it was the army and the government that cut off the reporters' phones. It was the army and the government that prepared this extra-fancy video of weapons and toys and the great Mohawk danger.

"Look, we had a strategy about when we should release information. We had a strategy about selecting spokespeople to read our formal statements; but we did not have any plan to tow a particular political line.

"All kinds of Mohawks were talking and saying all kinds of things. Some Mohawks called us thugs, other Mohawks called us heroes. Some Mohawks announced they were the only ones who should negotiate with the government. Others said the Warriors had to be at the table. We were a reporters' paradise because every faction had something to say and a lot of individuals got a kick out of being on camera. A lot of people were sitting on those barricades for more than two months and they clowned around to break the tension.

"But a media war? Are you kidding? When armored personnel carriers are surrounding you, the battlefield is not a television set."

With the Kanesatake Mohawks cut off from the outside world, the army pumped up the pressure. For three tense days, discussions took place at the Dorval Hilton, Pointe Claire, and on the hot line; but progress was nonexistent. The bureaucrats, politicians, and generals sensed the Mohawk despair and pressed for victory. Knowing the fate of Spudwrench, the armed men would not bend on their demand for amnesty or an international tribunal to consider detention and criminal charges.

On September 16, Brig. Gen. Armand Roy, commander of the Fifth Mechanized Brigade, announced that the military was now controlling the negotiations. Though Roy would not reveal the terms of any deal or proposal, his remarks gave all factions the strong impression that a deadline had been set for a surrender: if the deadline lapsed, the troops would advance. In the treatment center, the women continued to express their concerns over the Warriors' inflexibility, but they were overpowered by the men's stoicism. "We could not back down and we were not sure that we had won something," said one Warrior. "We weren't sure that we had accomplished anything."

While the situation stabilized at Kanesatake, violence erupted at Kahnawake on September 18, when the army joined the Sûreté du Québec in a raid on Tekakwitha Island. Located in the shadow of the Mercier Bridge, the island served as the Mohawk's marina and is connected to the southern shore of the St. Lawrence by a small bridge. Arriving by boat and helicopter at 2:30 p.m., fewer than 50 soldiers and cops hit the western edge of the island and moved east toward the bridge, where a crowd of several hundred angry men, women, and children had gathered behind Grand Chief Joseph Norton.

Despite pleas for calm, the crowd taunted the invaders, and rocks sailed through the air. Under strict orders to refrain from firing, the soldiers retreated and the Mohawk men surged forward, punching and kicking their uniformed adversaries. To protect themselves, the police fired tear gas and maneuvered a truck to block the Mohawk retreat. Fighting off the gas, the Mohawks charged again.

To the army's chagrin, the riot unfolded before television crews, which broadcast live footage of the battle. As the bloody confrontation was displayed coast to coast, the besieged Mohawks at Kanesatake huddled around the television and cheered whenever the soldiers took a punch.

After several hours of retreats and advances, the brawl for Tekakwitha Island came to an end when the soldiers were authorized to fire in the air while moving backward. The Mohawk men stopped in their tracks, allowing the troops to retreat. More than 75 Mohawks required hospital treatment for cuts, bruises, and broken bones. The army said 19 soldiers required medical attention, including one who had been beaten semi-conscious and another who had to have part of his ear surgically re-attached.

29
THE WARRIORS
HIT THE FLAG

"The riot at Tekakwitha Island was just another sign of confusion and disorganization. We weren't holding it together and the Canadians were just doing everything they could to keep us fighting and scared and confused," says Diane Lazore.

"Those of us on the outside who were sympathetic to the Warriors knew we had to do something for the men. We always figured we could get the women and children out, but we were worried about the men. Sometime after the riot, the army restored some kind of phone communications so the people in the treatment center could talk to the Mohawk Nation Office. We figured that the army was listening to everything, so we spoke in Mohawk and a kind of coded shorthand.

"The men wanted us to buy time so they could plan a possible escape. Their idea was to have a surrender and create some kind of diversion so they could make a run for it through the woods. To the Warriors and to people who thought like I did, the riot made it clear that it didn't make a difference if people walked out to the troops or the cops. The men were going to get clubbed, while the women and children would, hopefully, be released."

Fearing that political or territorial infighting within the Mohawk community would prompt a betrayal or inadvertent leak, the Warriors kept their plans to themselves. The easiest route would take them through the woods, across Highway 344, up the ridge, and into the hills.

"The government would not meet with any of our representatives, would not talk with us about anything except surrender and laying down weapons," adds Stanley Cohen. "So it was a basic choice—fight or run.

"The men understood that the military or police attack was inevitable. People like Lasagna and Blackjack and Noriega and Beekeeper would be forced to shoot if anyone crossed the line. They did not want to be in that position.

"So they started to plan among themselves. The men became increasingly aloof from the women and the Oneida negotiators, Bob Antone and Terry Doxtator. The Warrior men faced a different set of risks. You could feel the encampment pulling itself apart, but the men did not want to do anything that could start the shooting unless the army attacked."

The day after the Tekakwitha Island brawl, army commanders sent a letter to all Mohawk factions, rejecting any discussion of amnesty, land claims, sovereignty, or other Mohawk concerns. "The army will not get involved in political matters," Brig. Gen. Armand Roy said. "There will be no discussions of Oka land claims by anyone until the Warriors have disengaged and placed themselves in military custody."

Roy's statement left very little time for the armed men to organize their escape. The Warriors asked sympathetic Mohawks on the outside to continue discussions with the government even though Antone had rejected the army's terms. But the government rebuffed any attempt to bring the Warriors to the bargaining table, and federal and provincial officials reached out to moderates or members of the confederacy to increase divisions within the Mohawk ranks.

"The government knew that the Warriors didn't want anyone else to speak for them, so they deliberately spoke to all the other factions instead of Minnie, Francis, or myself," says Lazore. "This plan worked really well because we had to spend most of our time trying to figure out who was speaking and who they were speaking for. There was no real direct communication with the Warriors at all, which is exactly what the government wanted."

The army commanders then raised the possibility of SQ officers replacing the troops. Such a move would guarantee the arrest of all Mohawks in the treatment center; it would also end military assurances that there would be no police brutality. Hoping to raise the specter of fierce police-Mohawk confrontation, the province ordered the SQ to shut down a peace camp erected to dramatize sympathy with the besieged Mohawks. For 17 days, the encampment on the outskirts

of Oka attracted crowds that peaked at more than 700, before dwin-
dling to fewer than 50. Around 6:00 p.m. on September 21, riot police
moved through the field of tents and flagpoles, telling the campers to
leave. When a dozen refused, they dragged them across the field and
into the police vehicles. As the peace campers were taken away, the
cops tore down the tents and flagpoles. The next morning, Robert Lavigne, director-general of the SQ, arrived at Kanesatake and toured the
army positions, in order to plan a police deployment.

That night Kahnawake Grand Chief Joseph Norton convened a special meeting in the Mohawk Nation Office. It brought together representatives of virtually every faction, several Canadian lawyers, and a
United States TV crew. Brandishing a sheaf of papers, Norton announced that Quebec's minister of Native Affairs, John Ciaccia, had
submitted extensive proposals for negotiations to begin once the Warriors laid down their weapons. As described by Norton, land, taxation,
rights to natural resources, sovereignty, and jurisdiction would each
be negotiated by separate committees.

"Sitting there and listening to what was going on," recalls Minnie
Garrow, "I saw that all kinds of informal discussions were taking
place. The government wanted to get this deal going and so did many
of the people in Kahnawake, who spoke about how Ciaccia was willing to work out the issue of tax-free cigarettes being sold on Mohawk
land.

"All of a sudden, with the tanks ready to roll, we are having a big
meeting and the Warriors' safety is being discussed at the same time
as the cigarette business. Then I notice something else. Sitting at the
table and talking about his discussions with the prosecutor's office is
Phil Schneider, the lawyer who represents Doug George on murder
charges for killing Harry Edwards, Jr., in Akwesasne. I get up and say
'Wait a minute. He's telling the meeting about the arrests of Mohawks
still holding out. The Akwesasne delegation has to leave for a minute
and discuss whether or not we should participate in this.'

"So we go outside of the room, a few of us—Diane, Francis and
John Boots, myself—and we don't know what to do. We really don't
know who to trust anymore."

But Norton and the Kahnawake delegation chose to support Ciaccia's proposals even if it meant backing the Warriors' surrender. He
also called for the creation of a Mohawk Nation executive committee
that would coordinate negotiations on the provincial plan and legal
efforts on behalf of men and women who would give themselves up at
Kanesatake.

"The Warrior men expected that other people were going to speak with the government and carry on informal discussions, but they did not know that proposals hinged on their surrender," says Cohen. "I'm sure that some of them suspected that this was going on, but when they heard that others had talked with Ciaccia and never told them, they were really pissed—their own people were arranging for their arrest.

"At the same time, inside the treatment center it was getting very, very tense. All of the pressure, all of the deprivation, all of our differences were coming out. The men had their position, the women had theirs, and both sides were on edge. I was getting forced out.

"Bob Antone and one of the women inside the treatment center told me that the nation office had talked to the army and secured a promise that I would not be arrested if I left. I shook my head and told them the people from Akwesasne—the people who retained me as their lawyer—did not say get out. Also, the men wanted me to stay, and they included Warriors from Akwesasne who were my clients. Well, I was told the people in the nation office had made these arrangements and a lot of the women agreed. So I knew I had to go.

"The decisions were being made way beyond the treatment center and the people under siege were now just there to be moved about for other political purposes."

On Sunday, September 23, just hours after the Rev. Jesse Jackson stood before the razor wire in a dapper trench coat and double-breasted suit to film a television spot, Cohen told the army that he was ready to walk out and meet his lawyer. As he stepped beyond the wire, he was arrested and jailed by the Sûreté du Québec.

As the moderates in the Mohawk Nation Office attended to what the military called "disengagement," the Warriors played for time to escape. On Tuesday night, September 25, Blackjack tested the army's tripwires. With a hook at the end of a long stick, he crawled around the perimeter, howling and shrieking as he set off flares. With each reddish-pink burst, the soldiers braced for a breakout that never came.

Instead, Warriors hid in the low brush on their side of the wire, hooting at the unnerved troops. To flush them out, frustrated soldiers hooked up a fire hose and sprayed into the compound, but they could not get the water to penetrate the heavy cover. The Warriors stashed their weapons and climbed up into the trees, mocking the soldiers with requests for a shower, shampoo, and towels. A second group of Warriors hurled stones over the wire.

At one point, several Mohawk women stepped out of the house with water-filled condoms, the latex bulging into phallic caricatures that were heaved over the wire. Watching their missiles arch into spotlight beams tinted by the neon flares, the women burst into loud, deep laughter. When the condoms hit the ground and splattered, even the soldiers laughed.

But an officer put a halt to the frivolity by ordering his troops to lock and load, then fix, bayonets. Stunned by the command, the Mohawks retreated, slowly walking into the house. There the giggles struck them again. Several emerged with more water-filled condoms. This time, the soldiers did not respond.

Though the water fight released weeks of tensions, Blackjack's daring crawl neutralized the flares that would have exploded as the men made their dash for freedom. When morning broke on September 26, the Mohawk Nation Office finished the deal that called on the besieged men and women to walk out in a line, submit to a weapons search, and then board buses that would take them to the military base at Farnham. There they would be processed for detention or release. By mid-afternoon, Beekeeper and Hunter took down the Warrior flag. Each man holding one side, they ran to the yard behind the house, where the men and women had started two fires—one burning weapons, tapes, papers, and other evidence, the second burning tobacco and sweet grass. Handguns and bullets were dumped into the septic system's cesspool amid jokes and wisecracks.

Waving the Warrior flag, a banner of the Iroquois Confederacy, and the Vietnam veterans' flag, the men joined the women for traditional chants and songs in a festive atmosphere that overcame the bitter differences about tactics and ideology. A soldier in a low-flying helicopter videotaped the entire afternoon.

The ceremonies and the destruction of anything that might be construed as evidence of a crime continued until early evening. Then the Mohawks gathered for the last time inside the house, forming a line with women and children in the front, men at the rear, holding flags that distracted from the body boards taken from the treatment center's first-aid supplies. The column marched forward, heading for the barbed wire and the soldiers near Highway 344, where more than a hundred supporters had gathered. As the Mohawks approached the wire, the women took a sudden right into the forest. The men ran for the perimeter, laying down the body boards over the razor wire. Surprised, the soldiers called for help. The Mohawks darted for the highway, but they ran right into the reinforcements. Others made it past the hill only to come upon the Sûreté du Québec. Within 20 minutes, the army and the police rounded up the crowd, using rifle butts and billy clubs to shove handcuffed Mohawks onto buses with barred windows. By 8:00 p.m., the Mohawks were on their way to military detention and arrest.

"We never got anybody out," says Minnie Garrow, who had come to Highway 344 and was arrested after she jumped on a soldier hitting a Mohawk woman. "A few slipped through, but it was a disaster. The army was shining those blinding lights, and I can still hear the screams when the soldiers swung their rifles or knocked people to the ground. It was horrible.

"We stood up for our land, for our rights, and our history and then we had to walk out to this. We can't forget and we won't. Remembering what happened is what we have left for ourselves and our children."

Sitting at his kitchen table overlooking the Friendship Bridge on Cornwall Island, Francis Boots shakes his head. "It's been two years since the antis attacked Tony's," he says, flashing an uneasy smile and then letting it go, "and life has gone from bad to worse.

"Now, the casinos are closed and people don't have jobs in Akwesasne. The police are still hovering about our land. There is very little trust between our community and Kahnawake, let alone Kahnawake and Kanesatake. Everyone is suspicious about who's talking to whom. Many of us worry that some Mohawks are going to ask the police to stay forever."

Boots acknowledges that casinos, police, elections, and government grants are important issues—but he insists that the real struggle is about Mohawk identity and who is best suited to interpret the latest round of resistance to white authority and to re-establish the Mohawk nation. "We have to figure out who is going to tell the next generation what it means to have stood up the way we did," he says, "to have seen ourselves as sovereign and independent despite our divisions, defeats, and betrayals."

Since the dismal end to the standoff in September 1990, Boots and the Warriors have had their own struggles and disputes. In Akwesasne, bitterness surrounding the arrest, conviction, and jailing of Kakwirakeron isolated Rowena General and Verna Montour, who believe that Boots and Minnie Garrow took advantage of Kakwirakeron's absence to strengthen their position and become leaders. Diane Lazore became estranged from Garrow because of rumors concerning the collection of money earmarked for the group's expenses. Although whispered allegations have circulated for months, nothing tangible has appeared.

"It's tense and uneasy," says Garrow. "I think many of us want to come together, but we can't. Too much has happened. While we have faced enemies outside our community, we have not faced each other."

"People have just drifted apart," says Lazore, whose brother Gordon was one of five Warriors detained without bail by Quebec authorities for more than six months. "There are so many different agendas and issues. No one trusts anybody else."

Stanley Cohen is the only non-Mohawk among the more than 40 men and women facing criminal charges in Quebec. Garrow and Boots stand by him, as do many of the men accused of crimes in New York State and Canada; but several Warriors from Kahnawake see him as just another white man who won the trust of Mohawks and then sold them out. The attacks on Cohen are also tainted by a streak of anti-Semitism as Mohawks on both sides of the border refer to him and Seth Shapiro by making disparaging comments about "Jewish lawyers."

"There is nothing I want to say about this," says Cohen. "I still represent clients in the Mohawk nation." (Cohen's efforts led a New York judge to dismiss charges against Warriors accused of attacking the anti-gaming barricades in April 1990.)

While the Warriors pull themselves apart, tribal council Chief L. David Jacobs, and band council leaders Joseph Norton, Mike Mitchell, and George Martin have identified their constituencies and actively pursued relations with government officials. These men believe they can reform the governments' approaches and thereby improve Mohawk life within the framework of existing laws and regulations.

In Akwesasne, anti- and pro-gaming factions continue their bitter feud. Though the violence appears to have stopped, distinct and antagonistic communities have developed within the territory. The United States federal courts have rejected appeals and ordered jail terms of two to three years for Tony Laughing, Eli Tarbell, and others arrested on July 20, 1989. The pro-gaming faction has control of the New York–chartered tribal council. Harold Tarbell has lost his seat as head chief and been replaced by Jacobs. Under his leadership, the council continues to press Gov. Mario Cuomo to negotiate a federally mandated "gaming compact." The discussions have been deadlocked for months.

On the Canadian side, Mike Mitchell continues his stewardship of the anti-gaming faction. Mitchell has brought millions into the community and strengthened his hand as a politician and a source of employment by negotiating provincial and federal grants and subsidies. Earlier this year, he came under an internal attack. Mitchell beat back the challenge and went on to run, unsuccessfully, for leader of Canada's national organization of aboriginal chiefs, the Assembly of First Nations.

In Kahnawake, months of muted dissension broke into the open in June 1991 when a renegade faction of Warriors traveled to Tripoli to receive a portion of $250,000 from Col. Moammar Qaddafi. The donation served several purposes: first, to help the Mohawk "freedom fighters" pay for the expense of building a nation; second, to thumb their noses at Canadian authorities; third, to highlight the accommodationist position taken by Grand Chief Joseph Norton; and fourth, to sneer at the established Kahnawake Warrior leadership, which has yet to recover from the taking of the Mercier Bridge.

At Kanesatake, the Mohawks are still overwhelmed by the siege. Though the golf course will not expand into the Pines, the territory's residents are unsure how to proceed. While a recent referendum changed the system of selecting chiefs, voter turnout was extremely low, as supporters of both the Warriors and the traditionalists refused to take part. Despite its formal power, the band council has lost the respect of the men and women it is supposed to serve.

Quebec Premier Robert Bourassa's government has yet to answer questions concerning the death of Cpl. Marcel Lemay. When federal officials held their inquiry, Bourassa and his ministers were unwilling to cooperate. Provincial officials have yet to offer a detailed, public explanation as to who ordered the Sûreté du Québec to fire tear gas and march up the hill on July 11.

At the end of May 1991, the provincial authorities announced that they will hold disciplinary hearings for 39 Sûreté du Québec officers accused of violating police rules on the use of force. Most of the charges stem from the police clubbing white demonstrators on the drawbridge at St. Louis de Gonzagues. Other charges relate to the officers' failure to protect the convoy of Mohawks seeking to leave Kahnawake the day before militants gave up the Mercier Bridge.

When provincial authorities announced the inquiry, they also re-leased a report from Quebec's assistant chief coroner, Dr. Paul Dionne. He could not make a final determination concerning Corporal Lemay's death, saying there were too many unanswered questions to draw any conclusions.

"The governments have always tried to come up with an official story," says Boots, "but they cannot tell us what happened or why. Whether it's New York or Quebec, Ottawa or Washington, the government wants to bury us in a mountain of paper.

"But we don't have to accept it. That's one power we still have, and we showed the whole world that we will exercise our right to the land and our right to protect ourselves from those who choose not to see us as a nation."

CHRONOLOGY

December 16, 1987: More than 200 New York State Police officers raid Akwesasne and remove 293 slot machines.

June 2, 1988: *Kahnawake Mohawks occupy the Mercier Bridge after more than 200 police raid the reserve and shut down smoke shops selling tax-free cigarettes. Grand Chief Joseph Norton begins self-rule discussions with Quebec Native Affairs Minister John Ciaccia.*

September 16, 1988: New York State Police raid the Bear's Den and seize slot machines. Owner Eli Tarbell unsuccessfully appeals to the office of Gov. Mario Cuomo for negotiations to legalize gaming on Mohawk land.

April–May 1989: Pro-gaming slate of L. David Jacobs and Lincoln White run for two of the three seats on the St. Regis Mohawk Tribal Council. Traditional members of the Akwesasne National Council join anti-gaming faction in formally requesting an FBI or state police raid on casinos.

June 3, 1989: Jacobs and White win the election. Head Chief Harold Tarbell is the only anti-gaming member on the elected council.

June 6, 1989: A barroom dispute leads to a riot at Tony's Vegas International casino. After the New York State Police arrest owner Tony Laughing on a misdemeanor gambling charge, the anti-gaming group ransacks the casino. The police cart away 200 slot machines from Tony's and the Bear's Den.

June 7, 1989: The New York State Police return to Akwesasne and remove slot machines from five other casinos.

June 10–11, 1989: Akwesasne Grand Chief Mike Mitchell and New York Head Chief Harold Tarbell organize anti-gaming group DRUMS and stage a protest march of 100 people. The pro-gaming faction responds with its own march of 600 people.

June–July 1989: New York State Police and FBI plan an elaborate raid to arrest casino owners on federal gambling charges.

July 20, 1989: More than 400 FBI agents and New York State Police officers meet armed resistance from two dozen Warriors in front of Tony's. While most of the raiding party avoids the confrontation, a standoff takes hold as the police begin negotiations with Kakwirakeron. Eleven Mohawks are arrested on gaming charges, while the police mount their own roadblocks to control traffic in and out of Akwesasne. Tony Laughing says he'll keep his casino open and remain a fugitive.

July 24, 1989: The Warriors seek to explain their position to the press by marching to the Route 37 traffic circle. State police in riot gear meet the column of 40 Mohawks and a melee erupts when the police and FBI arrest Kakwirakeron.

July 28, 1989: Cindy Herne organizes a demonstration of 85 unaffiliated people to protest the continued police blockade. Federal mediator Fletcher Graves arrives in Akwesasne and begins negotiations.

July 31, 1989: After 11 days of roadblocks, the state police withdraw as Gov. Mario Cuomo meets with the three elected chiefs in Albany. Cuomo hints that he'll begin negotiations to legalize gambling if Mohawks approve it in a referendum.

August 8, 1989: Mohawks vote nine to one in favor of casino gambling.

August 1989: U.S. Magistrate Gustave DeBianco holds a lengthy bail hearing for Kakwirakeron and denies prosecutor's request to detain him before trial.

August 26–27, 1989: The anti-gaming faction marches to the Warriors' headquarters. After a series of scuffles, they proceed to Tony's Vegas International, where security guards turn them back. They move down Route 37 to the Lucky Knight and set it on fire.

September 21, 1989: New York State Police arrest Tony Laughing after a high-speed chase off the reservation.

September–October 1989: *Kanesatake band council announces its objections to expansion of a private golf course that could uproot a Mohawk burial ground. Provincial and federal officials begin discussions with Mohawks, representatives of the Oka Golf Club, and Oka Mayor Jean Ouellette.*

October 11, 1989: Pro-gaming Chiefs L. David Jacobs and Lincoln White meet New York officials to discuss legalized gaming.

October 30–November 3, 1989: After the chase of Art Montour, Jr., shots are fired at the St. Regis Akwesasne Mohawk Police station. The Warriors, the anti-gaming faction, and local police are involved in car rammings.

November 13, 1989: Cindy Terrance discovers bullet holes in the windows of *The People's Voice.*

November 16, 1989: At the request of Akwesasne Grand Chief Mike Mitchell, the Sûreté du Québec dispatches several cars and officers to Akwesasne.

November 17, 1989: After meeting with the Warriors and dissident band councilor David Benedict, the Sûreté du Québec withdraws.

December 12, 1989: The Warriors damage a car belonging to Grand Chief Mike Mitchell's nephew, Mark. The anti-gaming faction chases the Warriors and discovers 70 rounds of ammunition.

January 1990: *Kahnawake Grand Chief Joseph Norton and Quebec Native Affairs Minister John Ciaccia begin negotiations to grant Kahnawake jurisdiction over its own legal and commercial affairs, including the cigarette business.*

January 13, 1990: Gerald McDonald shoots up Tony's Vegas International.

January 23, 1990: *Kanesatake band council splits as clan mothers oust Clarence Simon and replace him with George Martin. Fifty Mohawks march on the Caisse Populaire to freeze the band council funds.*

February 2, 1990: St. Regis Akwesasne Mohawk Police arrest three Warriors and seize automatic weapons.

February 1990: Akwesasne Grand Chief Mike Mitchell negotiates $30 million worth of grants for construction of a new community center, police station, arena, and other facilities.

March 1–4, 1990: St. Regis Akwesasne Mohawk Police seize automatic weapons after reports of shots fired at a teenage party. Shotgun blasts are reported at the home of a Mohawk constable, while another burst is fired at the police station.

March 6, 1990: Akwesasne Grand Chief Mike Mitchell calls a press conference to display weapons seized from the Warriors. He mentions plans for a blockade.

March 10–11, 1990: *After consulting with the Akwesasne Warriors, residents of Kanesatake protest golf course expansion by mounting a barricade on a dirt path leading to the burial ground.*

March 13, 1990: New York Head Chief Harold Tarbell releases U.S. Senate report calling Akwesasne "the worst situation in Indian country."

March 23, 1990: With the financial support of Canadian band council, Grand Chief Mike Mitchell and New York Head Chief Harold Tarbell, the anti-gaming faction sets up 24-hour roadblocks on Route 37.

March 26, 1990: Because of the skirmishes at the roadblocks, school officials suspend bus service to the reservation.

March 29, 1990: Kakwirakeron's lawyer, Seth Shapiro, arrested on the eve of trial.

March 30, 1990: An off-course National Guard medical helicopter is shot down during a snowstorm. After the pilot makes an emergency landing near Ganienkeh, armed Mohawks deny state police access to their land, commencing an 11-day standoff.

March 31, 1990: A few hours after 300 Mohawks clear the barricade at the Twin Bridges, the anti-gaming faction builds a new one.

April 2, 1990: U.S. Bureau of Indian Affairs agrees to appoint a mediator for the gambling dispute at Akwesasne.

April 3, 1990: The Mohawk Bingo Palace lays off more than 180 employees.

April 6, 1990: *The Kanesatake faction loyal to former grand chief George Martin occupies the band council office.*

April 10, 1990: The Ganienkeh standoff ends with the police searching a few homes and many of the armed Mohawks fleeing into the woods. Federal authorities issue arrest warrants for 14 Mohawks.

April 18–19, 1990: After Minnie Garrow witnesses the beating of pro-gaming Mohawk Richard Adams, the Warriors clear the barricade at the Twin Bridges. The anti-gaming faction rebuilds it.

April 21, 1990: David Terrance and family are burned out of their house.

April 23–24, 1990: Fire destroys the North American Indian Travelling College and the Warriors set up their own barricades within the reservation. The anti-gaming faction beats Tommy Square and the Warriors march on their barricades. Cars are burned and at least 200 rounds are shot in the air.

April 25, 1990: U.S. Sen. Daniel Inouye writes Gov. Mario Cuomo, urging him to dispatch National Guard troops. Cuomo refuses.

April 26, 1990: Anti-gaming activist Brian Cole is beaten while trying to re-establish barricades near Hogansburg. *A Quebec Superior Court judge at St. Jérôme grants an injunction barring Kanesatake Mohawks from continuing their protest of golf course expansion.*

April 27, 1990: Akwesasne Grand Chief Mike Mitchell announces plans to evacuate women and children. Canadian authorities place troops on alert near Cornwall, Ontario.

April 28–May 1,1990: Diane Lazore's house is attacked, then the anti-gaming faction gathers at Davey George's. Sporadic shooting turns into a furious exchange that kills Matthew Pyke. Before authorities discover the body of Harry Edwards, Jr., Lazore's house is burned and anti-gamblers block the fire trucks. The New York State Police, the Sûreté du Québec, the Ontario Provincial Police and the Royal Canadian Mounted Police dispatch hundreds of officers to Akwesasne.

May 2, 1990: *Kanesatake Mohawks ask the Akwesasne Warriors for help in maintaining the barricade protesting golf course expansion.*

May 3, 1990: *Canada's deputy minister for Indian and Northern Affairs, Harry Swain, says the government is willing to dispatch troops to restore order in Mohawk territory. New York officials refuse.*

May 8, 1990: *Regroupement des citoyens d'Oka demands municipality take title to forest land and begin golf course expansion.*

May 11–13, 1990: Quebec provincial prosecutor at Valleyfield files second-degree murder charges against Doug George, who surrenders.

June 7, 1990: *Quebec Superior Court judge at St. Jérôme denies injunction forcing Kanesatake Mohawks to end their protest.*

June 9–23, 1990: *Canadian first ministers scramble to meet the deadline for the Meech Lake accord, but Elijah Harper of the Red Sucker Lake Ojibway-Cree uses Manitoba's provincial legislature to defeat the initiative. Quebec Premier Robert Bourassa pledges to champion aboriginal rights if Harper and others reconsider.*

June 30, 1990: *The town of Oka wins an injunction ordering Mohawks to remove their barricade at Kanesatake. Town lawyer Luc Carbonneau threatens to use the police and heavy equipment if the Mohawks to do not comply.*

July 9, 1990: *Quebec's Minister of Native Affairs John Ciaccia requests Oka Mayor Jean Ouellette refrain from asking the police to attack the Mohawk barricade.*

July 10, 1990: Kakwirakeron is sentenced to 10 months in jail.

July 11, 1990: *More than 100 Sûreté du Québec officers attack the Kanesatake barricade. Armed Warriors open fire and the police shoot back. As Cpl. Marcel Lemay dies on the way to the hospital, unaffiliated Mohawk militants seize the Mercier Bridge and threaten to blow it up if the police launch another attack on Mohawks. To protect themselves, the Mohawks barricade Highway 3 in Oka and 138, 221, and 132 in Kahnawake. Federal Minister of Indian and Northern Affairs Tom Siddon declines to get involved.*

July 12–16, 1990: *Quebec Minister of Native Affairs Ciaccia negotiates a deal to end the standoff, but the Mohawks back out when the Sûreté du Québec refuses to withdraw. Jocelyn Turcotte, president of Sûreté du Québec union, says his officers do not know who issued the orders to attack the Mohawks. Negotiations break off.*

July 17, 1990: *More than 4,000 South Shore residents battle the police outside the Mohawk barricade on Highway 138 in Châteauguay. Angry over the prolonged commute to Montreal, the crowd demands that police attack the Mohawk fortifications.*

July 20, 1990: *More than 150 band council chiefs gather at Kahnawake to demand federal intervention.*

July 23, 1990: *Quebec Native Affairs Minister Ciaccia announces his intention to resume negotiations.*

July 26, 1990: *Federal Indian Affairs Minister Siddon steps into the negotiations for the first time, announcing that his government will buy the disputed land at Kanesatake and turn it over to the band council. A spokesman for the Quebec ministry of Public Safety says ballistics experts have test results showing that Mohawks killed Corporal Lemay.*

July 27, 1990: *Prime Minister Brian Mulroney urges Mohawks to settle the dispute, while Siddon says the federal government has already bought a portion of the disputed land.*

July 28, 1990: *Oka residents and town officials demonstrate against the federal decision.*

August 1–3, 1990: *South Shore residents continue their protests as Quebec Premier Bourassa meets with Kahnawake Grand Chief Norton and Konrad Sioui, provincial leader of the Assembly of First Nations. While Bourassa announces his agreement to Mohawks' preconditions, South Shore demonstrators disrupt traffic on the Champlain Bridge.*

August 5, 1990: *Quebec Premier Bourassa insists that the Mohawks have only 48 hours to settle the dispute or he will order a military attack.*

August 8, 1990: *Prime Minister Mulroney announces that more than 4,000 troops are on standby to replace the Sûreté du Québec. Former Quebec Superior Court chief justice Alan Gold is appointed mediator.*

August 9–12, 1990: *Gold negotiates a deal. Federal Indian Affairs Minister Siddon and Quebec Native Affairs Minister Ciaccia go behind Mohawk lines to sign the pre-conditions. More than 3,000 South Shore residents march on the Sûreté du Québec roadblock in Châteauguay.*

August 14–20, 1990: *Prime Minister Mulroney appoints Bernard Roy as chief negotiator, while Alex Paterson heads the provincial team. The Mohawks select 54 representatives to serve as negotiators, advisers, and observers. Each side presents proposals to end the standoff.*

August 20, 1990: *Mohawks boycott talks after armored personnel carriers and troops arrive in Kanesatake and Kahnawake.*

August 21, 1990: *LaSalle residents set up their own barricade on the northern end of the Mercier Bridge and harass Mohawks who agree to resume negotiations.*

August 23, 1990: *The troops move forward in Kanesatake.*

August 24–25, 1990: *Mohawks submit a draft agreement seeking recognition as an independent nation in exchange for removal of the barricades. Federal and provincial teams break off talks. Kahnawake band councilors establish a second channel for negotiations.*

August 27, 1990: *Quebec Premier Bourassa asks armed forces to remove barricades, while men on the Mercier Bridge make a separate proposal to the army: if troops allow small aircraft to land in Kahnawake, they will not resist an effort to recapture the bridge.*

August 28, 1990: *Federal Indian Affairs Minister Siddon and Quebec Native Affairs Minister Ciaccia negotiate with Kahnawake band councilors in Dorval. Prime Minister Mulroney urges the Mohawks to remove the barricades. Small airplanes land in Kahnawake and evacuate some Mohawks.*

August 29, 1990: *Kahnawake band councilors and moderates continue to meet with provincial officials in Dorval. When tanks and troops appear on the Mercier Bridge, the Mohawks agree to help troops dismantle barricades. At Kanesatake the Warriors feel betrayed.*

September 1, 1990: *After a dispute over tactics, Warriors attack Kanesatake band councilor Francis Jacobs and his son. The military ad-*

vances, sending troops through an abandoned barricade. The Warriors pull back into the treatment center.

September 3, 1990: *Soldiers and police raid the Kahnawake longhouse and seize weapons. The Warriors ask for Oneidas to represent them at negotiations.*

September 5, 1990: *Federal Indian Affairs Minister Siddon invites the Oneida representatives to Ottawa.*

September 6, 1990: *Quebec opens the Mercier Bridge to traffic, while the Canadian Forces offer to disarm Mohawks and escort them to a military location. The Warriors refuse.*

September 8, 1990: *Quebec Premier Bourassa dismisses any attempt to grant amnesty to the Warriors.*

September 9, 1990: *Four soldiers slip through the barricade and attack Spudwrench. After 10 hours of negotiations, the Mohawks are allowed to take him to a hospital.*

September 11, 1990: *Quebec Premier Bourassa rejects Mohawk proposal for an international tribunal to investigate alleged crimes. The Sûreté du Québec arrests Spudwrench.*

September 13–16, 1990: *The Canadian Forces announce that they are in control of the negotiations and reject all Warrior demands for amnesty and national recognition.*

September 18, 1990: *Kahnawake Mohawks battle troops and police on Tekakwitha Island.*

September 21, 1990: *Sûreté du Québec riot police disband a peace camp near Oka.*

September 22, 1990: *Kahnawake Grand Chief Norton convenes a meeting to discuss proposals submitted by Quebec Native Affairs Minister Ciaccia.*

September 24, 1990: *After days of disputes inside the treatment center, Stanley Cohen walks out and is arrested by the Sûreté du Québec.*

September 26, 1990: *Mohawks leave the treatment center. Their escape plan fails and troops herd them into buses for transport into Farnham military base.*

INDEX